A Girl In Trouble

She couldn't even glance back over her shoulder. Her footfalls thundered on the sidewalk, and the slaps of her soles made it worse, as though the sound of a girl fleeing would be enough to attract more creepy perverts over for a share. She ran until she was under the awning of Shinjuku Station, and then, once safely inside and hidden around a corner, she crumpled to the floor, trembling.

What a mistake it had been, coming here! It had all been for nothing. She had spent too much money, hadn't even come close to finding Kana, lied to her parents, and now this. Somehow, Grace still managed to feel small and ashamed as she heaved with the effort to catch her breath and keep in the tears. Her knees were too weak to stand on.

Right in front of her, the crowd continued to flow in and out of the station, without directing their attention to Grace for even a millisecond.

She was invisible.

D1563213

Coming soon from Loren Greene

SMALL BALL

EDOKKO

Meet You By Hachiko

Loren Greene

ISBN 978-1-7774352-0-2 (Paperback)
ISBN 978-1-7774352-2-6 (Hardcover)
MEET YOU BY HACHIKO

FIRST PAPERBACK EDITION
December 2020

www.lorengreene.com

For Zippo

I always intended the first book to be yours, however long it took!
I didn't really expect it to take nineteen years, but here we are.
Thanks for always being there for me.

Prologue

If you asked someone to describe Grace Ryan in a single word, they would probably reply with "average." That's if they didn't stop to ask, "Grace...who?"

Average height, average straight brown hair, average looks. Not particularly outgoing, studious or rebellious. Unremarkable in nearly every way. Grade school teachers recalled her as a girl with a plain face and a demeanour to match. A student who might fall through the cracks, not for failing, but for failing to stand out.

Looking back on class photos years later, teachers sometimes struggle to remember those students' names. They escape the notice of cliques and bullies, teachers and peers. If you think it's impossible to float through thirteen years of schooling without ever making a real impact on the world around you, you've never met anyone like Grace...or, more likely, you don't remember them.

She didn't mean to, but somewhere along the way, Grace had perfected the art of being invisible.

Chapter 1

Sometimes, Grace wished she could be like the smarter girls who were always complimented by the teachers, or the leader types who practically oozed charisma. Even the class clowns and the problem kids had it better than she did. At least they stood out for something.

Grace didn't have that advantage, but at least she was trying. Her face was currently under construction as she struggled to swipe liquid eyeliner in a way that sort-of matched the opposite eye. The look had been in-progress for ten minutes already as she squinted at *Hopteen* magazine, trying to get the same effect as the tutorial. Grace's eye barely resembled the one of the beautiful girl in the photo.

It's something, Grace told herself. It was different. It had the potential to make her noticeable.

Her boyfriend, Simon, was somewhere halfway between exasperation and acceptance. Thankfully, he wasn't there to see it as she struggled with brushes and pots like a kindergartner learning to finger paint. She could well imagine what he'd want to say, though. Something like, "Well, *I* notice you. Isn't that what's important?"

She could hardly blame him—Simon wasn't the self-defeating sort. He had a hard time understanding why, after a perfectly pleasant eighteen years flying under the radar, Grace would suddenly be obsessed with her looks.

It wasn't truly about looks, but that was hard for her to explain. If Grace herself wasn't quite sure, how was she supposed to convince him?

At least she *had* a boyfriend. That counted for something, seeing how Grace had never had even the barest interest in boys.

He was probably waiting for her by her locker, looking effortlessly unconcerned. Maybe thumbing through his agenda or texting one of his friends. Grace self-consciously rubbed away some of the powder on her cheeks. She didn't want to look like she was trying too hard. She might have to ease into this makeup stuff at a slower pace.

She didn't want to keep him waiting. Grace packed the cosmetics away with as much care as she could manage, unlocked the door, and peeked out into the hallway.

The coast seemed clear. She shut the door behind her and hurried upstairs, where Simon was approaching her locker from the opposite direction.

Trying to look as casual as possible, Grace fumbled her cell phone, barely catching it before it could clatter to the floor. "There you are!" she said, hoping he had missed her moment of clumsiness. "I didn't keep you waiting?"

If he noticed, he didn't let on. He slid black-rimmed eyeglasses onto his nose, his cheeks tinted. "Nah. I stuck around after gym to do some warm-ups with Kirk."

Simon's best friend played on the senior basketball team. The two were inseparable, with one exception: Simon, while athletic, didn't care for team sports. Kirk had long given up on recruiting him. "I haven't seen you the whole day. Been busy?"

"Not at all." Grace said, grateful that he hadn't been out looking for her while she secretly applied makeup in the faculty washroom.

A few seconds of silence betrayed Grace's nervousness. Simon looked her up and down, brow furrowed, obviously uncertain what had changed since that morning. As he studied her profile, Grace resisted the temptation to turn shyly away. "Hey, something's different. But you look great. As always! I mean, you always look great, but uh..."

Now that they were going out, he was, of course, obliged to say such things. It was part of the job.

Grace often imagined people staring when they saw her and Simon together, as though he were Beauty and she the Beast. He caught the eyes of other girls, with his smattering of freckles, easy smile and lanky, athletic build, but if he noticed, he never let on.

She loved how he turned that easy smile her way every day, until Grace wanted to hide her reddening cheeks. These days Simon even finished his morning jog by detouring down into the cul-de-sac where Grace lived with her mother. Grace ate her toast and drank her tea in the mornings on the front porch, where she could watch for him to run by. After school, they walked home together, except for days when Simon worked his part-time job at the grocery store.

They had been dating for just two months. The transition from friends to more-than-friends had been quick and anticlimactic; they had been so close over the last few years that Grace still occasionally forgot they were now *together*-together.

"Oh, that's a new necklace!" He beamed. "It's cute!"

"Thanks!" She put her hand on her neck to touch the plain black stone. All of a sudden, she found herself hoping he wouldn't notice the makeup after all. "But it's no big deal, it's really simple. I threw it together out of my craft box and the beads I got in town last weekend."

It had all started with necklaces in the first place. Back in the spring Grace had been surfing the Internet when she came across a tutorial for making jewellery out of pressed flowers and resin. The girl in the photos made it look so easy and fun that Grace wanted to try it for herself, but she couldn't read the text. The scan had come from a Japanese magazine called *Tamago*.

Before she knew it, Grace was obsessed. She downloaded thousands of scans from street fashion glossies, neatly ordered into folders on her laptop computer. The elderly shopkeepers at their local craft store were now on a first-name basis with Grace. She would stay awake well into the night, experimenting with beads and wires, ribbons, paint, varnish, clay, fabric and strings in every colour. She had been bitten by the accessory crafting bug.

Creating things with her hands, and holding those finished pieces, made Grace feel like she'd accomplished something.

5

Like she had license to call herself an *artist*, all of a sudden. Nobody, she thought, would ever have expected Grace Ryan (of all people!) to become a designer of fashion accessories. A cutting-edge craftswoman with daring taste.

That was, of course, why Grace couldn't bring herself to actually wear most of her creations. *Artist, cutting-edge* and especially *daring* were words way outside the scope of her image at school. It made her giddy, though, putting the final touches on a delicate resin necklace or hanging to dry a freshly hand-dyed scarf. For now, she kept the joy of making something new all for herself, and wore only her most subdued, *normal*-looking creations.

That didn't mean Grace was any less driven, the more her room filled with skeins of yarn and fabric scraps. The inspiration kept coming, every month, as scans popped up on the Internet of the newest looks in Tokyo. Grace couldn't believe the outfits she saw in those photos. *Art. Cutting-edge.*

Daring.

Simon leaned in close to look at the necklace, close enough that Grace felt her face start to burn. "Your design? Or from a tutorial?"

"Mine." She swallowed, hard. Was anyone watching them, with their cheeks almost touching? "Kind of on a whim."

"Oh, my bad. I thought it looked like something out of your magazine," Simon said with a knowing smile.

No amount of online scans could compare to the excitement Grace felt when a new issue of her *favourite* magazine, *SwEET*, arrived in the mailbox each month. *SwEET* was her penultimate; her fashion bible. It had everything from tutorials to street snaps. The cost of shipping the glossies and paying the proxy that sent them over from Japan was more than the monthly subscription price of the magazine, but, living in a town the size of theirs, Grace didn't have too many vices to spend her allowance on.

She dug the latest copy out of her bag, buoyed by Simon's

praise. "There's some good stuff this month that I want to try making. I might even try my hand at sewing some clothes, though it's still short sleeves and skirts weather in this issue. Must be nice to be in Tokyo, huh?"

Simon looked at the page Grace had opened. A teenager wearing a purple-and-black plaid skirt was on the open page, opposite a twentysomething woman in a frilly pink Alice in Wonderland-like dress, her bleached curls topped with a tiny silk hat. "It's something, all right. We'd never see anything like that around here."

In a bigger city you could get away with alternative fashion, but in their small town, wearing something different meant you were going to be stared at. Even though Grace was tired of blending in with the background, she wasn't sure she wanted *that* much attention.

Simon certainly wasn't the kind of boy who read fashion magazines, but that was all right with Grace, since he was the first boy who had ever noticed she existed. Putting aside the fact that he had been terrified of girls all through grade school, of course.

"Someday we'll go to Japan together, and you can take me to the places where they take all these photos." He grinned. "And you'll have to wear something eye-catching yourself, of course. I'll be your entourage."

"I guess so." She leaned against the lockers as they talked. "I mean, I'd *like* to go, but...it's a little scary to go to a place where you don't speak the language." Grace had been studying a few things on the Internet, but had never tried putting any of it into practice. She'd never met a real Japanese person in her life.

"I guess that's true."

"Plus, there are so many people." She took the magazine from his hand. "Nobody would notice someone like me. These girls have been putting together their wardrobes for years."

He laughed. "Wouldn't you like it better that way, though? If you want to try out these crazy fashions, I mean. You do hate being stared at..."

Grace frowned, unconsciously tucking a strand of brown hair behind her ear. "It might be nice to be noticed for once."

"Hey, now," Simon said, smiling that smile that caused girls' hearts to melt. Even Grace's skipped a beat when he turned it on her. "We don't want *too* many of those Tokyo guys to notice you!" He tipped his head in the direction of the emptying hallway. "Shall we go, Harajuku Girl?"

"Let's go," she replied, putting her hand in his.

Chapter 2

A typical day for Momokawa Kana was much like that of any other Japanese high school student: early morning, long classes, late night.

The call for breakfast came each morning at seven. Before going downstairs, she'd put on her school uniform, a powder-blue blouse and a skirt with a blue and green tartan pattern. She finished by pulling on knee-high navy socks trimmed with green, white, or blue ribbons, depending on her mood. It was as close as she ever came to testing the school's strict dress code.

It had been such a long week that Kana had already decided today would be a powder-blue day. With everything that was going on in her life, and no sign of any of it slowing down, she needed a reminder that good things were on the horizon.

It was Friday, and the heat and humidity that blanketed Tokyo throughout September had lifted to make way for more blustery weather.

Even better was the knowledge that a three-day weekend was coming up, meaning Kana would have all of Monday to do as she pleased. She desperately needed the break, though she knew she did so at the risk of her mother's ire. Even this early into the second term, her parents had been pushing her to add another day of supplementary classes to her already tight schedule.

Kana threaded a ribbon through the notch in her socks and tied it into a neat bow. A matching school-issue ribbon was fastened at her collar, tucked under a cream knit vest. She checked herself in the mirror, tried out a closed mouth smile. *Put on a happy face*, Kana told herself. At least until she got downstairs and out of sight.

"I'm off!" Kana shouted, to no one in particular.

"See you later," her mother answered from the kitchen. "Will you be home for dinner?"

"No, I have ESS club. I'll be late," Kana answered in a clipped tone, sliding into her black loafers.

Kana's younger brother, Shingo, waved at her on his way to the kitchen. He could afford a leisurely breakfast—he went to a local school, the same one Kana herself had attended until graduating junior high. Now her commute took her close to an hour, but it was worth it to attend one of the top-ranked private high schools in the city.

There was no easy solution for the lethargy she felt that morning. It was the culmination of four straight days of early mornings and late nights; her schedule this month was packed with cram school, regular school, preparing for the cultural festival, and pretending to go to club meetings.

Kana's brain and body were still waking up, so she took the time to enjoy the few moments of breathing space the quiet Noda Line afforded her before changing to the faster, fuller train that carried late morning workers and students from Saitama into metro Tokyo.

She usually studied on the second leg of the commute, where it was almost always standing-room-only, morning and night. It seemed wasteful not to use her commuting time for something productive. Some days, though, the crush of people was too much, and Kana could only stand there blank-faced, watching the fields and squat houses of Saitama be slowly overtaken by the boxy buildings of outer Tokyo.

Today, she hung onto a strap with one hand while clutching a book about English idioms in the other; one of those pocket-sized versions, neatly wrapped in brown paper by the cashier at a station bookstore. Idioms were more interesting than the grammatical points she had been going over all week, but it wasn't easy to concentrate without drifting too far into thoughts about what she wanted to do with the Monday of her long weekend. She would finally be able to do anything she liked. Maybe karaoke? A dessert buffet with Rumi? The girls from her class might even be planning something.

A whole day to do whatever she wanted. No school or

studying. Probably.

No matter how many times Kana's eyes scanned the page, the words seemed to flow right back out of her on the next breath. It was too warm, and she was sleepy. It had been a tough night. By the time she changed trains, Kana had given up on the book, turned back to the window and focused on the familiar platforms going by. A crowd left at Ikebukuro and another crowd replaced it. Kana shifted her position to let an elderly passenger sit down. Her body did everything on autopilot.

"Takadanobaba, this is Takadanobaba…the doors on the left side of the train will open. Please watch your step." Kana squeezed out of the train, idioms and satchel in hand.

She had stepped through the turnstile and out onto the concourse when she heard a familiar voice somewhere behind. "Kacchan! Wait!" A short-haired, pixie-faced girl came through the gates and grabbed her hand. "Morning! I saw you from the next car, but there wasn't room to move over."

"Good morning," Kana replied with a smile. Rumi was her closest friend at school. Shorter than most of the girls in class 3–7, including Kana, Rumi still had more than enough volume to drown out the rest of them combined.

"So, Shibuya today?" Her friend was already studying her own reflection in a hand mirror. "I don't have practice, so we could go shopping?"

Shibuya was one of the busiest spots in Tokyo on a Friday evening. Rumi loved going to the hip, youthful district after school, ducking into the lavatory to change clothes and apply her makeup. She would leave her schoolgirl persona stored in the coin lockers in Shibuya Station and emerge transformed, like a vivacious neon butterfly.

Kana longed to join in, but Fridays were packed enough as it was. "Sorry, I can't. I need to study today. And I have cram school tomorrow," she said, before Rumi could propose a reschedule.

"Not *all* day tomorrow."

"No." Kana kicked a pebble on the sidewalk. "But my mother wants to put me in some extra tutoring on top of cram school, after I messed up the last grammar test. I'm trying to talk her out of it."

"Aw, come on, it couldn't have been that bad..."

Kana bit her lip. "It wasn't awful. But it wasn't good enough. Nakagawa-sensei even called me to the staff room to talk about it."

"Ouch."

"I don't know why I'm not getting some of this stuff. I'm studying every day."

"Well, it's only English, no problem." Rumi shrugged as though she wasn't the student in Nakagawa's class most likely to fail to hand in English homework. If the topic wasn't volleyball, fashion or British rock music, Rumi couldn't be bothered. "If we go to Shibuya we can chat with some foreigners. It counts." She stretched and linked her hands behind her head, her satchel dangling from two fingers. As usual, Rumi had hiked her skirt up to show a bit more thigh than the school preferred—she thought it made her legs look longer.

Kana, by contrast, tugged her own skirt down to minimize her height. She gave her friend a chastising sideways glance. "Is that so?"

"I'm serious! All you have to do is find someone who looks lost and show them around. You can tell which ones are looking at the place for the first time. Or you could follow some English bands or celebs on social media, that'd be good practice."

"No," said Kana, "I do enough English *reading*. I think I need to interact with an actual person, have a conversation. Who knows, we may actually find someone to practice with in the city, right?"

"Yes!" Rumi enthused. "When are we going?"

"Well, not today or tomorrow, but how about we meet up Monday morning? The holiday?" The earlier she got out the door, Kana thought, the better her chances of actually enjoying a whole day off uninterrupted.

"I'm in. I've been waiting for a chance to wear my new hair extensions!"

Rumi was a fan of the visual kei style of fashion; a punkish look with wild hair and makeup made popular by rock bands in the nineties. It was rare to see v-kei fashion out on the streets these days, but fans of the style continued to show their support through their clothes, attitudes, creative flair, and of course pocket money.

Rumi had enough shoes for an army and her own sewing machine—her parents were both modern artists who encouraged their daughter's blossoming, if somewhat odd, creativity. The family lived in a suburb in the northwest of Tokyo. Since Rumi didn't need to hide her hobbies from her parents, the girls often used her apartment as their home base.

Kana smiled. "Sure. I'll do what I have to over the weekend, but on Monday, we'll have fun. I'll have to come up with something to wear."

"Speaking of that," Rumi said, fumbling to open her satchel, "have you seen the latest issue of *SwEET*...? You're in it!"

"Oh, I had forgotten I saw them. It feels like so long ago." Kana took the magazine from her friend's hand.

"I can't believe you ran into their street team without me, *again*," groaned Rumi, turning the pages for Kana. "Do they only ever come out on days when I have club practice? It's so annoying!"

Kana waved her off. "You've been in way more street snaps for magazines than I have. I've just had good luck lately." She'd been walking down Omotesando that day, on her way to buy a present for Shingo. The outfit she'd been wearing wasn't anything special, she thought, but a man with a camera had stopped and asked her for a photo.

It was the third time Kana had been approached to appear in that particular magazine. Once while decked out for a concert, during a brief period where her friends were crazy about visual kei bands, and twice more while wearing her handmade ribbon accessories. Visual kei had turned out not to be Kana's thing, and neither had Lolita, though she still loved admiring the cute, frilly dresses in the windows of shops on Cat Street. She had decided this year that she felt most at ease when she wasn't trying to fit perfectly into one style. When the *SwEET* photographer asked for her favourite brands and makeup, she'd smiled and replied, "All of them."

She had simple tastes, she thought, but unique. In Kana's opinion, that was what mattered.

Friday classes ran for seven periods. By the time students returned to their homerooms after cleaning up the classrooms, the sun had fallen behind ominous-looking clouds. What had been a pleasant day looked as though it was about to become stormy. Kana emptied textbooks out of her satchel and filled it with English notes, books and her electronic dictionary, intending to make good on her promise.

She glanced at the other side of the room with envy, where four girls were crowded around Rumi's desk, discussing after-school plans. Their other friends did not take fashion quite as seriously as Rumi did, but they could be counted on for company after school when their clubs weren't in session. Sae and Mina were members of the volleyball club, like Rumi, and Yuko and Yoko were part of the English club, the ESS.

The girls were chatting animatedly about a new movie they wanted to go to, deciding which theatre to see the evening show at. Kana frowned to herself—at a prestigious school like theirs, her classmates must truly be geniuses if they could get away with studying so little!

"Kacchan!" Yoko called when she caught her friend's eye. While Kana's other classmates usually called her *Kana-chan*, Rumi and the ESS club members often used a shorter form of the nickname. "Aren't you coming to the movie with us?"

"Sorry, not today," Kana replied with a shake of her head. "I have to study."

"Even though she did better on the test than me," Rumi told them, laughing. It was no secret that Rumi only bothered with English because it was a mandatory subject for all third-year students at Koen Academy. The sciences were her specialty. Some of the other girls enjoyed practising English, but between cram school and club meetings, they were getting much more speaking practice than Kana.

Yoko moved away from the group and returned to her desk to check her cell phone. "We'd better go if we want to be there on time."

"Yeah, you're right. Sorry, Kacchan, see you Monday?" Rumi offered her an apologetic wave.

"Sure. Monday." Kana waved them off in return with a forced smile. "Have fun!"

When she was certain her friends were well on their way to the foyer, Kana closed her own bag and slipped out of the half-empty room. The crowd outside began to thin out, all its students hurrying home or to cram school, so she didn't have to stop to talk to anyone else. Kana felt as though all she did these days was turn down invitations—not only from Rumi, but from Yoko and her English club friends, and her old junior high school classmates as well.

Focus. You've got to focus, she told herself. She was a few months away from the big exam, and it would do her no good to lose her drive now.

Maybe, Kana thought, she ought to start going to see Luke at lunchtime. The Australian assistant language teacher was exuberantly friendly, and never minded staying to chat with students in English after class. He spoke next to no Japanese, so any conversation with Luke was guaranteed to push a student's skills. But did she want to give up her lunch hours with her friends, on top of everything else?

It wasn't worth it, Kana decided. Maybe she could start coming in earlier to see him instead. There wasn't much difference between waking up at five-thirty and waking up at six, after all. If only school were closer to home!

By the time she reached Takadanobaba Station, Rumi and the others were long gone.

Kana didn't feel like going home yet, even though she had already turned down the movie invite. If she was *thinking* instead of socializing, at least, she felt more like the time had been used judiciously. After taking the train a few stops south, she walked the short distance to Jingu Bridge.

Their hangout spot wasn't busy that day. Aside from Kana, there was only a man waiting to peddle art to tourists, and a group of university boys passing around cigarettes. The artist smiled at her, giving Kana a glimpse of a glittering stone set in one of his front teeth.

Every so often, groups of people with cameras would wander through, hoping to spot "Harajuku girls" on their way to Meiji Shrine. They didn't seem to realize they had come at the wrong time, on the wrong day of the week—perhaps even the wrong decade. It had been a few years since the bridge was at peak popularity; back in the days when Harajuku closed the street to cars on Sundays. Jingu Bridge was no longer *the* prime spot to take fashion photos, but Kana still liked going there to people-watch, and Rumi treated the place as her own personal catwalk. She had posed for a hundred tourists' cameras since she had begun cultivating her style; she welcomed every photo, even the ones for which permission was not asked. Her striking face and elaborate handmade outfits had appeared in *Kira*, the most popular magazine for visual kei fans, more times than Kana could remember.

Standing up, Kana trailed along behind a large group of foreign tourists on the gravel path leading to the shrine. They were talking animatedly in a language she didn't recognize—something eastern European, she thought.

Though she went to temples and shrines from time to time, Kana rarely visited this particular one. The memory of standing in line for hours to make an offering during a long-ago New Year's visit with her parents was still fresh. The sight of thousands of people crowding into one courtyard wasn't something she'd soon forget.

Today was blissfully quiet, though. The sounds of cars on the freeway adjacent to the bridge were muffled, the thick treeline acting as a barrier. Kana smiled faintly as she paused on a small wooden bridge, realizing it must be a slow day for the shrine, as no one but the tourist group had passed her on the path. Perhaps she would go all the way inside and see the museum.

When she reached the cypress arches, the Europeans were already filing into the Empress' gardens. Kana crossed through the north gate and into the courtyard, where groups of tourists, both Japanese and foreign, took in the sights of the famous shrine honouring Emperor Meiji. Straight ahead she saw the main hall, a huge, copper-roofed building where she remembered throwing a five-yen coin to make a wish for the New Year, back in elementary school.

Before I had anything worth wishing for, Kana thought unhappily. What she wouldn't give to go back to those carefree days! She stepped up onto the wooden platform to peek at the cushions where the shrine keepers knelt to pray. No one was in the main hall but herself.

When she promised her parents she would take the School of International Liberal Studies entrance exams at Nishi Gaidai University, she hadn't quite imagined it would mean the end of high school as she'd known it. These were supposed to be some of the best years of her life! She wouldn't even be able to do anything fun in this year's school festival, because she didn't have time to attend rehearsals. What had happened to the carefree existence Kana had led the previous year, spending her nights watching television and sewing, and her weekends in Shibuya, singing karaoke?

It was a lot to give up, Kana thought. But she *did* want to get into Nishi Gaidai and study English, so she could go abroad someday. She wanted to work as an interpreter, maybe even for the government. That kind of skill took a lot more studying than Kana found she had time for, even with Koen's excellent International English program.

It couldn't hurt to say a prayer for her studies. Kana fished around in her frog-shaped purse for an offering. She didn't have a five-yen coin this time, so she withdrew a fifty-yen piece instead and tossed it into the wooden box. If five yen was a lucky coin to offer, Kana decided, then fifty yen must come with ten times the luck. She rang the bell and bowed, and even though no one was around to hear it, she kept her request to herself.

~*~*~

After supper, Grace went straight to her computer to do some research online. Her conversation with Simon had been on her mind since that afternoon. How would she ever visit Japan someday without learning at least a little Japanese? She needed to practice the few things she already knew, and pick up a *lot* more.

There was no way she would find any native speaker out here in the sticks. Instead, Grace had decided to put her energy into learning online.

Tutoring could be one idea. She had heard that there were tutors who could video call you, though that sounded intimidating. The idea of being on a video call with a stranger made her nervous.

Making a friend seemed like a safer bet. When she was small, Grace's class had written some letters to the students in a class in Hungary. They had exchanged cards and notes for a few months, and Grace had even picked up a few words in Magyar that she still remembered all these years later. With the Internet connecting the whole world, there had to be a resource out there for matching pen pals with each other.

At first, she had been positive that it couldn't be that hard, but after an hour or so of searching, the results were more disappointing than Grace expected. Sites that initially looked promising ended up seeming suspicious when she clicked on the profiles of pen pal candidates. Many were men in their thirties and forties, and their descriptions sounded more like dating advertisements. She also tried a Japanese language message board, a BBS, but the language barrier prevented her from even making it through the sign-up process.

Grace sighed. It seemed like these sites were the last place she'd find someone her own age, who liked the same things she did. She was savvy enough to know that giving too much information to the wrong person could land her in trouble. Who knew what these guys really wanted?

Maybe pen pal websites weren't the right place to start. *I could try looking at websites of things I like, instead, and try to contact someone there.* Much safer, Grace decided. At least she knew the territory when it came to her fashion sites.

With new resolve, she opened up her browser's bookmarks.

Her first visit was to StreetSwEETs, a blog for fans of *SwEET* magazine. The site had a gallery for users to post their own photos, as well as a social forum. Grace had an account, but had never posted anything in her gallery. It was embarrassing to put up a picture wearing boring clothes like hers.

When she clicked on the public gallery, though, a familiar image caught her eye: there, on the first page, was one of the pictures that had appeared in the new issue of *SwEET*—the elegant girl with the black and purple ribbons that had given Grace the idea to make bracelets out of ribbons. Someone had scanned the photo and uploaded it to the StreetSwEETs website.

Grace followed the picture to its owner's profile, delighted to see that the other photos were all of the same girl. Tall, with glossy, straight hair, shorter in the earliest image, and hip-length in the most recent. Unlike many of the other Japanese users on the site, her raven hair was undyed.

Grace felt a bit like a stalker going through this girl's profile so meticulously, but she couldn't help herself, reading through the model's personal profile with growing excitement. "Makhanikana" was an eighteen-year-old high school student living in Saitama, Japan. Her hobbies were crafting, clothing design, travelling, reading, shopping, and "English."

Grace almost leapt right through her computer. The StreetSwEETs website *was* operated by overseas fans, and required at least some English to navigate around. It made sense that Japanese users of the site would have some interest in English. Then again, Grace thought, she herself had been studying French since Grade Four, and she couldn't carry on anything resembling a conversation.

Maybe this "makhanikana" wouldn't be the best choice for a pen pal, but that didn't mean that Grace couldn't send her a private message complimenting the magazine photo. She logged into her account and, jaw set with anticipation, clicked on the messaging system. There, though, Grace stopped. What could she say? Talking to strangers wasn't her strong point. What if this girl didn't understand her message, or worse, took offence?

She had watched some subtitled videos on the Internet, trying to pick up some of the language, but hadn't gotten beyond *konnichiwa* and *kawaii* yet. Somehow, she didn't think she could form any sort of coherent message out of the words *hello* and *cute*.

But this might be your big chance, Grace told herself. She swallowed her fears long enough to write her opening:

| megumi_709 | Hi there, |
| | I wanted to send you a message after I saw |

No, that wasn't right. Better to keep it simple, in case a lot of text would overwhelm a non-native speaker. Grace erased the line.

megumi_709	Hi there, I saw your profile and photo in SwEET magazine this month. I'm a big fan! I love your outfits so much. They're *kawaii*. I wanted to say hello

"That sounds totally stupid!" she groaned. Even if makhanikana didn't reply; even if she deleted the message right after reading it, that was better than making her think Grace was some kind of weirdo. One more try, she decided, typing a third version of the letter, trying to be honest without coming off as creepy, flattering without falling all over herself. When she had finished, she sat at her computer for a long time, reading and rereading the message. But would her English be too difficult for a high school student? Was it too desperate-sounding?

Grace wasn't really sure.

What did she have to lose, though? She would never *really* meet this girl. If it didn't work out, she could always make a new profile with a new name. Grace was already on guard at school every day. Why bring her anxieties into the digital world, when she could be whoever she wanted online?

Your private message to makhanikana has been sent.

Chapter 3

Home > Settings > Private Messages > Sent Items	
Hi from Canada	
megumi_709	Hello, I found your profile, so I hope it's OK to send you a message out of the blue like this. I'm a big fan of *SwEET* magazine from Canada and I saw your picture there. I really love the outfit you're wearing, especially the ribbon necklace and bracelets. Did you make them yourself? I love Asian fashion, especially Tokyo street fashion! Please send me a message sometime if you'd like to talk. :) Warm regards, ~ Grace

Grace awoke to the smell of bacon wafting into her room. It had been a long time since she'd had company on a weekday morning. Pulling on a bathrobe, she stumbled downstairs, rubbing sleep from her eyes.

She found her mother in the kitchen, standing over the stove. "Hi honey, good morning."

"Morning." Grace yawned, shivered. The smell of sausages made her queasy. "What's going on?"

"Breakfast," her mother replied, tapping the outside of the frying pan with her spatula. "I'm going to the optometrist, so I took the morning off work."

"Oh. Fun, I think." Grace's perfect eyesight must have come from her father. Even after twenty years as a tenured professor, he didn't even need reading glasses.

Camilla turned an egg over in the pan. "I'll be home before dinner, though. How about you? Doing anything exciting at school today?"

"Like what?" Grace smiled faintly. "The daily drudgery. Very exciting."

Her mother ignored the jibe, flicking open the breadbox with one hand. "By the way, you need to remind your father to book your plane ticket for Christmas break—and when you do, also remind him that you will *not* be going up there for Easter."

"Yeah. Sure." Grace's good mood soured in an instant. It was her father's turn to have Grace for Christmas, and Camilla had become irritable the moment the weather started to turn, even though they spent the entire summer together. "I'll let him know."

"Good. How's Simon doing? I haven't seen him go by in a while. Is he still running every morning? I hope he's treating my daughter right!"

She groaned. "Mom. We're just dating." Somehow, whenever anyone brought up the fact that she and Simon were a couple now, Grace felt her cheeks heating up. Nobody else she could think of had been single for their entire high school career.

"Every date counts!" her mother admonished, shaking the skillet. "At least wear something nice when you're going to town. Wear that nice yellow top I bought you for your birthday." Grace's eighteenth birthday had been in August, and once again her mother bought her an assortment of hideous clothes. The shirt in question was a flowing, bell-sleeved monstrosity Grace had no intention of looking at ever again, let alone wearing.

"I can just wear whatever I'm wearing to school. You know? I don't think I really like the colour of that top so much, anyway."

Camilla looked her daughter over with a critical eye. "Bright colours look lovely on you, Gracie, don't be silly. You have warm skin tones. Yellow goes beautifully with brown hair and eyes."

"If you say so." Grace rose from the table and padded to the door, running fingers through her hair. "I'm getting a shower."

"Don't you want breakfast first?"

"No thanks." Grace wrinkled her nose in distaste. She wrapped her bathrobe tighter around herself and climbed the stairs to the bathroom, flicking on the lights.

As she rinsed her hair and towelled off, Grace paused in front of the bathroom mirror to look at her reflection.

Boring, she thought. *Nothing to see here.*

Her minuscule makeup collection sat in a wicker basket by the sink, but after yesterday's experiment with the eyeliner tutorial, Grace wasn't sure she felt ready yet to try anything else that looked like an attention grab.

But baby steps, she told herself. When her classmates had been buying drugstore teen magazines and talking about who was hot and who wasn't, Grace hadn't been ready to join in. She knew she was a few years behind when it came to this stuff. Books and art and music were still more appealing than flirting with boys.

The other girls in Grace's year had graduated to the world of bush parties, steady dating and smoking out in the woods behind the school. Grace had been left behind, but hadn't much cared. She already had two close friends who trusted her and loved her. She had hobbies. What was she supposed to do, out in the woods with the cool kids and their two-fours?

There *were* other students like her at St. Clare, girls who didn't drink or smoke, girls who also liked painting and crafting and listened to piano arrangements of pop songs. Those girls had never adopted Grace into their circles, though, and it was too late for her to try to fit in with a new crowd.

She wanted to be someone a bit more remarkable than the girl whose name nobody remembered. More than "Jean's friend," or "Simon Summers' girlfriend."

Simon turned heads everywhere he went. Even though he was a year younger than Grace, his circle extended to students in every grade at St. Clare. He was athletic, book-smart, funny. People *liked* him, They said hello to him in the hallway. Had he attracted this much attention before they started going out, Grace wondered? Or was it *because* they were going out that she began to notice?

It made her uncomfortable. Like people thought maybe she didn't deserve to be with him.

Grace wanted to become someone who could look natural by his side. Did she need makeup and an image change to make it happen? She wasn't sure. But maybe, she thought, those things could make it easier. Give her some confidence.

She wished the daring styles she saw in *SwEET* and the other magazines she collected could be the answer. Grace had been following Tokyo street fashion for over a year. It astonished her that such bright, bold, colourful styles could co-exist with the navy-suited salarymen and office ladies mincing down the streets in their uniforms. In Tokyo, Grace thought, you could wear whatever you wanted. Any style you liked could be yours.

She knew how it worked here as well as anyone, and the cardinal rules: Don't attract attention. Don't be flashy. Don't be dowdy. And of course, don't be outdated. Fashion, here on the outskirts of Conception Bay, was about what was available. Kids whose parents worked in town had an advantage; they had easier access to new clothes. They could make a subtle statement by standing out just a little. Of course, nobody wanted to stand out *too* much.

Especially not Grace.

Some students had to drive twenty minutes from the outer communities to reach St. Clare Regional High School, but the Ryan family lived on a cul-de-sac off the community's main road. The students in her neighbourhood could walk to school every day, rain or shine. They had to—they were too close to qualify for a ride.

Grace had never minded being ineligible for the bus service. In elementary school, she and her best girl friend Jean had ridden the bus together every day, but after Jean moved to a new house, Grace had needed to get used to sitting alone. Aging out of bus privileges had seemed more of a relief than an inconvenience.

Grace slung her bag over the back of her chair. Mr. Gates had them sit alphabetically in homeroom, as in many other classes, which meant she never ended up sitting near Jean, whose last name was Yetman. Her best friend waved a greeting from her seat in the back corner of the room, then rose, glancing at the clock. Grace had barely enough time to plant her backside in the plastic chair before Jean was standing over her.

Grace looked up. "Hey, morning."

"Morning," Jean replied with a serious expression, which wasn't unusual for her. "You're late."

"Really?" The clock read eight-fifty. True, she usually arrived at school by half past the hour, but it wasn't as though the bell had rung. "Sorry, Mom was dishing out a lecture-plus-guilt trip. Were you looking for me?"

"Yeah, kind of." Jean looked uncomfortable, adjusting her

cat's-eye glasses with one finger. "I've got to cancel on tonight. Sorry it's so last minute."

It was unlike her friend, who kept a meticulously organized schedule, to back out without notice. They were only going to grab pizza and hang around the shopping plaza, but Jean had been the one to suggest the idea in the first place. "Sure, no problem. What's up?"

"Well, my friends from the drama club are getting together, and I got invited. I only found out about it yesterday."

"The drama club?" Grace echoed. Jean had always been involved in more extracurriculars than she had time for; the band and debate club among others, but this year marked the first time she'd shown any interest in theatre arts. Grace had trouble imagining straight-laced Jean, with her long brown hair, glasses and perpetually tidy style of dress, playing any personality but the one she'd been born with.

"Yeah. It's going to be at Christian's house." Jean managed a small smile.

"Ah," replied Grace uncertainly. So this was about *him*.

Her best friend's current crush was a boy with height to rival Jean's own, who let his untidy blond hair hang past his ears. He also played percussion in the school concert band—in other words, not only creative, but the highest level of cool, according to Jean. From the moment she'd seen Christian Barber, banging out a wild solo at the concert band's first practice of the year, Jean had not-so-secretly adored him.

He was a much more unpredictable type than Jean usually preferred. Grace couldn't quite decide if that was a good or a bad thing.

"Well...it's too bad, maybe we can go another day. I was planning to buy some sewing supplies. I wanted to try making some of my own clothes."

"Oh. Well, that'll be interesting, I guess." Like Simon, Jean took care to dress smartly every day. She considered street fashion tacky and loud, and wasn't afraid to say so. Of course, some of the styles Grace was currently enamoured with *were* over-the-top, but it bothered her that Jean would be so vehemently against them.

Still, Grace planned to convince her best friend that some of the more subdued Tokyo fashions were interesting and fun. She held out her left wrist. "Check out what I made a couple of days ago, looking at a picture from a magazine. Not bad, hey?"

Jean glanced at the bracelets and nodded. "Yeah, that's not too bad, I guess. As long as you don't start on the frilly dress stuff next."

Grace frowned. Even if she enjoyed the Lolita look, she was far too shy to wear anything like that to school. "I don't think that's for me. But I was thinking about an image change."

"I was afraid of that. Tell me more."

"Well, I haven't totally decided. But I kind of want to create a *style* for myself. Something that's unique, but also subtle so that I don't have to buy a lot of new clothes and things. I thought it would be cool to make some more accessories that can complement the stuff I already have."

When Jean remained silent, Grace pressed on. "I did some research on resin casting for making homemade jewellery. I even ordered earring posts and things to help get started. And in my magazines I've seen a few cool ideas using bows and ribbons, that you can use on the spot to accessorize without having to *make* anything. Picture something like a black outfit, skirt and turtleneck or a tank top, maybe winding the ribbons up the arms for a pop of colour. It would look chic." When Jean still didn't say anything, Grace started to lose some of her momentum. "I mean, I'm not sure if that would work for me, but it looked cool in the picture. Accent colours, that is."

"Grace, I don't mean to criticize, but you can't tie ribbons around your arms and wear them to school. It's too..." Jean looked at a loss for words. "Too *weird*. Like you're going to a ballet recital."

In the time they had been friends, Grace had almost never

been hurt by Jean's opinions, only by her straightforward manner. Jean's unrestrained attitude toward Grace's fashion sense, however, had started to get on her nerves. "Wow. Harsh."

Jean looked uncomfortable. "Like I said, I'm not trying to criticize. I'm *worried* for you. I know you've been thinking about your..." She paused. "Your image."

Grace rolled her water bottle between her hands, frowning. "It's not like I'm wearing anything wild. Anyway, people aren't exactly lining up to associate with me in the first place."

"Look, it doesn't matter, I only thought you might want to be careful. It's still early in the semester, so if you want to join any teams or clubs or anything this year, you want to be able to make a good impression, right?"

"I'm not interested in that stuff," Grace said with a dismissive wave. "It's your thing, not mine. Anyway..." She trailed off. "It's not like I can discover some rare musical or athletic talent at this point. I guess I could form a handicrafts club?"

Jean didn't seem like she was in any mood for jokes. "I don't know, I thought you might...I mean, I hoped that now that I was in drama, you might get interested in it too, you know?"

"Drama?" Grace repeated, slowly. "Wait a minute, this is about the *drama club*?"

"Technically, yes."

"Have they been saying something about me?"

"No, no," Jean reassured her. "Nothing. I've never even mentioned you to them."

"Okay. So what is it, then?" Grace tried to keep a tremble out of her voice. "You don't want me to make a bad impression in case you *do* ever mention me?"

The late bell cut off Jean's response before it left her mouth. Mr. Gates rose from his seat to restore order to the classroom. "Never mind. Listen, we'll talk later, okay?"

"If you're sure," Grace murmured, "that your other friends

won't disapprove."

Jean stopped mid-turn. "*What* did you say?"

Grace froze. Why had she said that out loud?

"I don't know what your problem is, but you've been acting different lately, and it's starting to get on my nerves." Jean whispered acidly, aware that the classroom had grown quiet. She was so close Grace could feel the irritation radiating from her friend. "Maybe you shouldn't be criticizing who *I* hang out with, when all you do lately is sit around imagining your fantasy life in Japan."

Jean pulled away and, without waiting for a reply, returned to her desk. Their homeroom teacher shushed the class one last time before the PA system crackled to life.

Grace did not so much as glance at the back corner of the classroom. It had been a long time since the two of them had fought, and she felt guilty, but she had no intention of taking back the comment. Or the changes she'd been making to her life, for that matter. *If she'd been more supportive of my interests and less focused on making me look good to her other friends, this wouldn't have happened,* she thought.

Grace's conscience was quick to cool her anger, though, and she soon began to regret her words. *I'm making things hard on her, I guess. She's the one who got stuck with a wallflower for a best friend, after all.*

It hurt that Jean could so rarely make time for them to hang out, and now the drama club appeared to have bumped Grace even further down the priority ladder. Worse, there was the sinking feeling in the pit of her stomach, that if she did not run back there to apologize, she might lose her oldest and dearest friend. *I'm a coward,* Grace thought bitterly. *Every time I say what I think, I end up covering it with a lie.*

She would apologize as soon as homeroom let out. Jean was the logical type; she would forgive and forget, as she always did. As the first period bell rang, Grace stood up right away and made a grab for her backpack. "Jeannie—"

But Jean swept right past her, not even glancing sideways. Grace hesitated, watching her best friend's long brown hair disappear into the sea of students in the hallway, and sat heavily back down. *I really am a coward.*

Fourth period should have been English, a class shared with Jean. Instead, Grace spent the hour hiding in the Annex wing, a section of the school that had once housed live-in teachers. She wasn't ready to face her best friend; not yet. If she gave Jean space, surely the next time they saw each other, Jean would want to make up.

A moment before the lunch bell rang, Grace slipped out to beat the crowd, heading straight to the library. She almost never ate with Jean, who had band practice at lunchtime more often than not, but she didn't want to take the chance that they might meet by accident.

Here, students were still packing up their books. Grace headed for an empty computer workstation and sat down, anxious to take her mind off the fight. It wasn't as though they had never argued before, but since the new year began, it felt more and more like Jean was pulling away from her. Maybe, Grace thought, she was just being paranoid, but she couldn't shake that sense that something was wrong.

Online life, at least, offered a brief distraction from what was going on in the real world. Grace brought up StreetSwEETs, where there were new photos in the gallery to look at, and someone had posted about a community meet-up in Los Angeles. New patterns for dresses Grace would love to make but would never wear were available in the DIY section. What caught her eye, however, was a pop-up window that appeared when she logged into her account.

You have 1 new Private Message. Click here to be taken to your inbox.

makhanikana	Hello, Grace-san. I was surprised to get your mail. It is okay to send it. I didn't think SwEET was sold overseas too, I have been to Australia but only once. Where do you live in Canada? Are you near Vancouver?
	Thank you for your compliment. I too like Tokyo street fashion, especially in Shibuya.
	If you like you can send me a mail anytime. I am studying English for entrance exams right now. It's good practice. I like to meet people from various countries, so, it's very nice to meet you. If you don't mind, please tell me about you.
	From, Kana

Grace skimmed the message, barely containing her excitement, and read it again slowly, twice. It was strange and kind of thrilling; she had never before made the first step to contact someone she didn't know.

She knew embarrassingly few Japanese words, but her phrasebook taught the suffix -*san* in the first chapter as an honorific that denoted respect for someone you didn't know well. So, to her new friend, she was Grace-*san*—Miss Grace. The idea made her smile. She was in, she had made contact—and she, Grace, had done so first! *Take that, Jean!*

~*~*~

The unexpected message had come at the perfect time, Kana thought. Here she had been, wishing for a solution, and then one appeared out of the blue! The gods who watched over Meiji Shrine seemed to have been looking out for her.

Kana had read through her new friend's profile twice since receiving the private message. It might be fun to have a friend overseas, she decided. This girl, Grace, was a fashion fan, and her written English was so easy to understand. It was almost too good to be true.

She'd been working for the past few hours. Glancing at the clock, Kana decided it was time for a bath and bed. Tomorrow would be a long day with cram school first thing in the morning. She slid open her closet and took out her *futon* and powder-blue bedding, balancing them on one arm with practised ease. Kana laid the *futon* out on the floor near the sliding balcony door.

The bathwater had already grown more tepid than she preferred, even though her mother laid a cover over the bath to keep it warm. She couldn't truly relax, anyway; even the pleasant surprise of the message from Canada wasn't enough to help her forget that she would need to set an alarm for seven o'clock if she wanted to finish the work that would be due at cram school the next day. The assignments for Luke and Nakagawa would have to wait until evening. Then, if she had any time left, Kana thought, she would have to work on a nice outfit to wear on Monday. Something cool, even though summer had officially ended, she thought drowsily. Was it time to bring out her good fall boots yet? She'd noticed girls wearing thin over-the-knee socks with their pumps on the train. It was almost time to rearrange her own wardrobe for the season.

Kana drained the bathwater and brushed her teeth at the sink. She checked under her eyes in the mirror, up close, for signs of bags. Could it be her imagination, or were they looking particularly puffy tonight? Maybe it was time to buy some of those caffeine facial kits the girls had been talking about.

In her room, she towel-dried her hair, side-stepping the *futon*. Her bedroom exhibited a mix of Western and traditional styles. Above her computer desk, under the lengths of purple organza she had strung around the perimeter of the room, Kana proudly displayed her academic achievement awards and her collection of watercolour prints. She loved to look at the landscapes when she sat at the desk, daydreaming.

Slinging the towel around her neck, she sat down under the watercolours to turn off her computer. A prompt about a new message appeared at the top of her StreetSwEETs inbox.

Kana clicked it, even though she knew she should already be in bed.

| megumi_709 | Hi Kana-san,

I'm really glad to hear back from you! Your English is great. Do you learn English in school over there?

I'm in high school too. You said to tell you about myself, so I'll try, even though I'm not so interesting...

Well, I turned 18 last month, in August. I live in a small town in Newfoundland, about 20 minutes from the capital city, St. John's. That's on the east coast of Canada. It's a quiet place, and there's nowhere to buy the clothes I see in Japanese magazines. I've been trying to make things by myself, but I'm not very good!

I haven't been able to wear much of what I've made, not yet, anyway. So I guess you could say my hobbies are crafting and reading. How about you?

Hope to hear from you again,

~ Grace |

She frowned. This new message was a little harder to understand than the first one, and longer, but she *had* asked. Her hair needed a few more minutes to dry, so Kana decided to write a reply right away. She reached for her electronic dictionary to parse out unfamiliar words.

When she was satisfied that she understood the message, she began to write a response.

makhanikana	Hello Grace-san, you are the one who is replying fast! What time is it where you live? Here, I am about to sleep. For your question, English is taught in school here in Japan. We learn it from junior high school. Right now, I am in the third grade of high school and I wish I will go to Nishi Gaidai University (called Nishidai) next year, maybe, if my test is good enough.
	I have never been to Canada, but I want to go, someday. I don't know about Newfoundland. But you are near Prince Edward Island which I heard about. Do you know about 赤毛のアン (red-haired Ann)? She is a famous character, so I think most Japanese know her well.
	Sewing as a hobby is great! I don't have a machine at my house. I can sew handmade a little. Also, I do like to make accessories.
	I'll go to bed now, but it's nice to talk to you so please send me another mail if you can. Next time please tell me more about your school life! Is school very different between Japan and Canada? Do you wear a uniform? Are you in a club?
	Would you rather to talk by mail? I can't use this BBS from my mobile phone, but I have a mobile phone mail. I will give you my mail address.
	It's thehealinglight@saftbank.ne.jp.
	♡ Kana

Kana set her alarm for ten minutes earlier than usual, hoping there would be a new message to read in the morning.

Chapter 4

Hi Kana,

Here's my email address! Though text messaging would be fine with me, honestly. I can send email from my phone (though it took a while to figure out since I NEVER use it for that, lol) but I'm writing this one from my computer because I thought I might have a lot to say!

It's so funny that you know about "red-haired Ann" as you call her—that's Anne of Green Gables! It's a very famous Canadian book. I never expected to hear it's popular in Japan.

School here is pretty different from where you are. (Yeah, I've looked up some stuff online about Japanese schools!) My school is super close, called St. Clare's. It used to be a Catholic school with the elementary school next door. I've been with most of my classmates pretty much since kindergarten. We start at 8:50 and end at 3 pm, and there are seven periods every day. Most of the schools here don't wear uniforms anymore, though a bunch of them used to. I kind of always wanted to try one, to be honest. >_>

I have SO many questions to ask you about Tokyo, too! I've been doing a lot of research online to learn about fashion. There's a lot of information out there about Lolita, visual kei, *mori-kei, decora, gyaru* (Gal) and some other styles...some of those haven't really been popular in a while, though. It's kind of hard to know what's trendy and what's passé, since I have to depend on what's been translated into English and shared on the Internet.

In my town, though, almost nobody dresses in a fashion style that actually has a name and rules. Not like Japan at all, I guess. Is there a name for your style?

~ Grace

From: thehealinglight@saftbank.ne.jp

Wed, Sept 24, 8:09 AM

Hello Grace-san!

Thanks for your email!!

I don't think I can easily send an overseas text (SMS) message. We would need to use an application for it. But if email is fine, please don't mind! In Japan an email is just like SMS message. Everyone uses email here for short messages. It's so convenient.

I want to know more and more about school life in Canada! I can't think about going to school with the same classmates since kindergarten. You didn't go to any junior high school? It's so different from here. But, I'm envious of your short days. We start school at 8:30, and two times in one week there is a 7th class. It takes until about 16:05. If I could go home as soon as you, I'd be very happy!

My school is about 50 minutes from my home. I should take three trains to reach it every day. My home is a small town in Saitama prefecture. Saitama has good schools too of course, but I chose my school for its very good English reputation. It was very hard to get in, but I love my school and my classmates!

The styles you talked about are very popular, I think. Lolita is more common in Harajuku than Shibuya. Visual kei and decora girls also go to there. Sometimes they still go to the bridge, Jingubashi, on weekends to show off their clothes. Rumi likes Harajuku, so sometimes I go together with her.

There is no word for my style. I think of it as just "my style." (This is common in Japan, too.) It means to wear what one likes, though most of the time people like to trend. I don't have money, so "my style" is somehow cheap.

♡ Kana

It was rare for her to be home before dark on weekdays, even on days without cram school, in part because her mother believed Kana attended club meetings. That two-hour slice of unaccounted time was something Kana kept entirely for herself.

When she first quit the English Club, Kana had tried to study on those days. The problem was that she never seemed to be able to concentrate. She felt burnt-out by the time she had gotten someplace quiet and opened her texts. She'd stare into space, daydreaming about what university life was going to be like. Hum along to her mini-disc player, mouthing the lyrics. English music helped her feel like she put in more effort, so she listened to American or British classic rock: Blondie, the Stones, Pink Floyd. Most of the lyrics she couldn't follow, but it still felt like any little bit could help.

Kana knew she was squandering time, but being at cram school until eight and for another five hours on Saturdays pushed her to her limits. She rarely even managed to turn in homework for her actual classes these days. It was tedious and exhausting, but she endured it, living for her "days off."

When Kana came home one Tuesday, though, after lingering too long in Yoyogi Park on her way back, she found her mother standing in the hall wearing a sour expression. "It's late."

"It's not even seven yet."

"You're never home for dinner anymore."

Momokawa Himeko herself wasn't usually home in time for dinner. Kana couldn't remember the last time she'd eaten with more than one family member at a time.

"I'm sorry." Kana didn't have a rebuttal prepared. "There was an ESS meeting, so..." No way could she admit that she had spent two hours watching a group of junior high students practising softball in the park.

Her mother shook her head. "If it wasn't an *English* club, Kana, I'd say you were wasting your time. You should be trying harder to get home right after it ends. Your entrance exam is going to be here before you know it."

"I know."

Himeko continued to fuss even as Kana removed her shoes, sounding more like she was talking to herself than to her daughter. "I wonder if we can put those extra lessons in on Sundays. Or maybe cut down the club attendance to once a week. Why do they have it twice a week, knowing that entrance exams are coming up? When I was in school, third-years weren't even allowed to attend club meetings!"

"Not all the members are graduating this year, you know." Kana said dully. In reality, all of the clubs at her school would soon be restricted to first and second-year students, but she could hardly reveal *that*. There would be no excuse for after-school escapes without using the English Club as a shield.

Her mother wasn't listening. "Not that I don't think you can do it. Of course you can, if you're prepared. Ah, if only we had put you in cram school in junior high, it would have been better. If only I'd been home, making sure you were ready for all this."

Kana's mother was a rare breed for her age, raised during a time when most women still quit their jobs right after getting married. When Kana was younger, she had found it difficult and embarrassing to have a working mother.

Mother and daughter quarrelled often lately, and almost always over one of two things—school, and the time Kana was or wasn't spending there. Himeko had pushed her daughter even harder when it became clear Kana had a natural aptitude for languages. For Kana, who had enjoyed learning as a child, her mother never seemed quite as overbearing as when the time came to choose a prospective university. As soon as she selected Nishi Gaidai, the amount of pressure increased tenfold.

She knew her mother wanted to secure a good future for her, so when Himeko pushed her to study more, Kana obliged. It wasn't worth the energy to fight it. Besides, she didn't have to look too deep to know she had inherited plenty of ambition from her parents. Kana wanted to succeed, and she knew *how* to do it; she just had to keep it up until she had that acceptance letter in her hand.

On days like this, though, Kana wanted to crawl into her *futon* and forget about English and Nishidai, possibly forever. She thought about those kids and their carefree softball game, wondering how long it'd be before she wouldn't feel guilty about having fun.

~*~*~

Now that they were communicating away from StreetSwEETs, Grace couldn't stop herself from checking her messages again and again. Peeking at her phone under her desk during class, turning the sound up when she had to put it away. She didn't want to miss a chance to respond in real time.

Jean hadn't said a single word to her since they'd had their argument, either. It didn't bother Grace now as much as it did then, but she still felt uneasy every day, especially during homeroom. She was used to chatting with Jean while they waited for class to start; now she had taken to hiding in one of the first-floor booths that had once housed pay phones, writing messages to Kana on her cell.

The last bell of the day rang, startling Grace out of her reverie. She pushed aside the notebook she'd been doodling outfits in and hurriedly jotted down the last few notes on the board.

"Hey, that's not bad." A shadow fell over her desk as Grace scribbled the final line. She looked up with a hint of trepidation. Jean's grip tightened around the spine of *Death on the Ice*.

"Thank you," Grace replied. Was the fight over? She desperately hoped so.

Jean peered at the drawing. "I didn't know you had gotten into sketching. Are you going to, uh, make this? This outfit."

"Maybe." Grace tried to keep her tone as neutral as possible. "What do you think? I still need to settle on colours."

"Good. I think it's good." A hint of a smile sneaked onto her lips. "As long as you stay away from neon and electric blues."

"I was thinking something in dark grey or blue. Maybe green."

"I think that'd be...nice."

"Sorry about the other day." Grace looked down at her desk, fingers curling around her pencil.

"No big deal. You were kind of right, anyway. Christian barely talked to me." Jean looked irritated. "I didn't mean to blow you off. Accept my apology?"

"Sure." She tried to sound as casual as her friend. "Same here?"

"Should we make up for it tonight and go to the plaza? I'm free."

Even though it was a weekday, Grace couldn't say no. Her homework, and her messages, too, could wait.

"A Japanese pen pal? How did that happen?" Jean opened the floodgates for the topic Grace had been dying to talk about. They were trying on sample makeup at the drugstore, and she thought about maybe spending some of her allowance money. Grace had been saving up to start buying a newer, bolder wardrobe, but more makeup would go a long way toward an image overhaul too, she thought.

"It was an awesome coincidence! We met on a fashion blog. This girl, Kana, she had her photo published in this month's *SwEET* magazine. You know, that one with the street snaps that I started ordering."

"Hmm."

"She's the same age as me, since she's had her birthday already. And she goes to school in Tokyo, but she lives out in the sticks like us. How cool is that? Getting to commute by train all the way to Tokyo?" Grace smiled as she applied foundation to the back of her hand. "Hey, do you think this colour is too light?"

"Do you wear concealer now, too? What are *you* trying to cover up?" Jean sniffed, but Grace knew she was kidding. Both of them were lucky enough to have fairly clear skin.

"I thought I might at least buy some, even if I don't use it often." Grace held her hand out to look at it from a distance. "I saw this makeup tutorial in a scan from *RunRun* magazine and it calls for both concealer and foundation. To even out the skin, I guess, rather than cover something specific." She decided not to include too much detail. The distinctive Gal subculture that *RunRun* championed was a bit much, with outlandish colours and thick makeup. That hadn't stopped Grace from saving dozens of scans from *RunRun* and *Tamago* magazines onto her computer. Even though the style didn't seem to be as popular anymore, Gal magazines knew their makeup techniques.

"I think your makeup has been getting better." Jean studied the foundation Grace held. "But maybe you should go a little lighter on it, and use more earthy colours. Less of the purples and blues."

"But will it even be noticeable if I use something like brown?"

"Absolutely." Jean took the bottle out of Grace's hand and replaced it with another, two shades lighter. "You want to enhance what you've got. Not everybody has those nice big chocolate-brown eyes of yours."

Grace put the bottle in her basket. She wanted to direct the conversation away from her cosmetic colour choices and back to the real source of excitement, her new friend. "So Kana is super smart," she said, "and her English is amazing. No way would I ever be able to speak Japanese like that! And she makes her own jewellery too, like I want to do, and she's into fashion, so we have a lot in common."

"Ah." Jean made another noncommittal noise as they moved to the cash register. "That's cool, I guess. As long as she doesn't turn out to be some kind of crazy stalker type."

"No way," Grace replied, irritated at the suggestion.

"Sometimes you know when you can trust people."

"Well, be careful, that's all. Sometimes people aren't what they claim to be. Especially on the Internet. Not saying that your friend's like that, but you shouldn't trust anybody online too fast, you know?" Jean's voice softened. "Anyway, it's getting late, I'm going to call my mom. Want a ride?"

"No, my mom is on her way already," Grace lied, turning her head. "I'll head out in a bit."

She waited as Jean called home. Then Jean looked expectantly back at Grace. "Hey, that party might not have turned out like I planned, but the club is getting together for pizza Friday night to welcome the new members. Do you want to come?"

Grace frowned. "But I'm not a member."

Jean punched her lightly on the arm. "But you've been my friend forever, you doof. I want to introduce you to everybody. Christian will be there, too."

"I guess," Grace mumbled. She had three classes with Christian, and didn't find him particularly charming, but it was her duty as Best Friend to appraise the guy. "Friday, you said?"

"Friday at seven. Pizza Expertise. Need a ride?"

"No thanks. I'll find my own."

Jean gathered her bags and gave Grace a wave as she left the drugstore. "See you tomorrow, then!"

When she was certain she was alone, Grace returned to the makeup counter and continued to look at the samples.

She felt happy to have made Friday plans, even if she had to share Jean with the drama club, but also a little annoyed at how Jean had implied Kana and Grace were too close. As if *her* new pals could be trusted, but Grace's friends needed a background check!

Grace opened her backpack to grab her phone, but there were no new messages. It was early morning over in Japan. She pocketed it, still annoyed with Jean's mistrust and obvious disinterest. Right now, Grace thought, she might have preferred to talk to Kana rather than Jean.

Kana's descriptions of life in Tokyo sounded so glamorous—that morning, she'd casually talked about spending her day in the trendy district of Shibuya, wearing fashionable clothes and window-shopping in upscale boutiques.

She'd snapped photographs with her cell phone to send Grace, who inspected each as if she were judging a fashion show. Kana's phone took such nice pictures. Grace felt a little envious.

One of the photos showed a display of chic, expensive-looking designer handbags. The price tags were five digits long. Grace didn't have any concept of how Japanese yen converted into Canadian dollars, but that many zeros seemed astronomical for a purse. "Your family must be rich," she commented.

"No," the answer came back. *"I can't buy. I just like to window-shop. As long as I'm together with Rumi, we can look anywhere, because she is friends with shop employees."*

Kana sounded wistful when she compared it to her own situation, where her parents had money, but poured it into tutoring and something called cram school. Rumi's parents seemed progressive in comparison, letting her socialize and dress as she liked—in electric, eye-catching colours with over-the-top makeup to match. Grace had never met a person like Rumi in her entire life.

Taking her basket to the counter, Grace paid for the makeup before walking out into the dusky evening. There was no sign of Jean; her ride had already come and gone.

Instead of calling home, she wandered over to the mom and pop bookstore, a local shop she'd been coming to since she was young. The sleepy-looking clerk, a woman close to Grace's grandmother's age, manned the counter. A movie played on a television mounted in the corner of the store.

In the travel section, Grace plucked a copy of *Friendly Planet: Tokyo* from its place between *Beijing* and *Singapore*. It had a tiny map on the back page, all jumbled up like coloured spaghetti. She studied the words, searching for the dot that represented Shibuya on the circular Yamanote train line. The name of the station was even printed in a bigger font than its neighbours, as if to say, *"Look! This is where it's all happening!"*

Grace bought the book. She wanted to know *all* about where it was happening.

Chapter 5

Let's try!	
From: thehealinglight@saftbank.ne.jp	Fri, Sept 26, 9:18 PM

Grace-san

It's very fun to talk with you everyday. If it's OK, I want to be less formal with you. Please listen to my request.

I thought I would give you a nickname, as my friends and I do. I hope you'll like it. Your handle on StreetSwEETs is Megumi, so may I call you Megu-cchi? It's cute, don't you think so?

Megumi-chan and Megu-rin are also so cute. You can tell me if you like it better. Sorry, Grace-chan is hard to say. 。：˚˚('∀`)・。

♡ Kana

Re: Let's try!	
From: megumi_709@geemail.com	9月27日 (土) 10:57
	詳細を表示

Hi Kana-san,

Yes, of course!! It's SO cute, I love it!

Do you think it would be OK if I'm casual with you, too? Ever since I started doing research about Japan, I've wanted to call someone "-chan!"

~ Megucchi (!)

The bathroom counter had been gradually overtaken by pots and brushes, bracelets and rings, but Grace still hadn't quite worked up the nerve to try more than one new thing at a time. Instead she experimented with new looks in the privacy of her bedroom, and tried to incorporate them with baby steps at school. She felt sometimes like everyone was staring. The magazines offered lots of tips, but she was still afraid of doing it wrong.

Grace put great effort into finding something to wear to the pizza party that would suit her new style. It seemed impossible to keep track of what Jean considered "eccentric," so she decided to play it safe, settling on acid-washed denim and a pink top with elbow-length sleeves. She tied a sparkly white silk sash around her waist as a belt and finished the outfit with chunky bracelets on each arm. Not bad, Grace thought, admiring her reflection. Retro, but cute. Retro was perennially in, anyway, wasn't it?

The pizzeria, in the same plaza as the bookstore, was an easy walk from the Ryan house. She left the house full of confidence, hoping this would be the perfect first impression.

She was irritated with Jean's lack of devotion, but Grace still wanted her approval. If they weren't going back to the way things were, she reasoned, these new friends might be permanent fixtures in Jean's life. It was important to work her way in with them now, rather than later.

The weather was typical Newfoundland fall, and Grace had to zip her puffy jacket up all the way to keep out the damp chill, but she felt exhilarated to be out in it. Fall was her favourite time of year, and the view over Manuals River looked better than ever in late September with the leaves gathering on the paths. She took the stairs behind the school and cut across the river, not to save time, but for the scenery. A longer walk, Grace hoped, would calm some of the butterflies in her stomach.

When she arrived at the plaza, still out of breath from hiking back up the other side of the river, Grace found she felt more anxious, not less. She wished she had asked Jean for a ride, if only so they could arrive together.

It was too late to back out. She took a deep breath and pushed the door open.

She spotted the drama club, occupying a big corner booth. Even though Grace had come right on time, Jean was nowhere in sight.

Grace stood frozen in the lobby, not sure she was up to facing this table of strangers alone. Christian Barber, the legend himself, was the only person she could be certain she recognized.

The girls were dressed for a night out on the town, not a pizza party. They wore spaghetti-strap tank tops despite the cold weather and party makeup. Grace started to suspect the club might have other plans for after dinner that Jean hadn't mentioned. She stood against the wall, hoping no one saw her.

It wasn't like Jean to be late. Other club members arrived one after another, and were directed to the table without taking notice of Grace. She shifted awkwardly as the hostess welcomed guest after guest, hoping that Jean would appear and rescue her any minute. Barring that, Grace would settle for a sinkhole opening up directly below the Pizza Expertise lobby.

When Grace's irritation started to reach its boiling point, Jean swept in at that moment with two girls beside her, laughing at some unheard joke. She offered a tiny wave when they faced each other. "Hey! You made it!"

"Yep. Perfect timing," Grace lied.

"Great, come on in, I see everybody over in the corner there." Jean led the way, plopping into the seat opposite Christian. Grace had no choice but to take the spot next to her, nearest the wall. "Hey, guys."

"Hey, Jean," offered one of the boys, a tousle-haired brunette sitting to her left. The girls Jean arrived with sat down on his other side.

"This is my friend Grace," Jean announced, patting her

shoulder. Grace offered up what she hoped looked like a friendly smile, and a few others looked up to nod briefly, then went back to being absorbed in the menu. Grace snatched hers up and pretended to look equally interested.

Someone had already called for a pizza and drinks, as the last guests trickled in, too far from Grace's vantage point for her to get a clear look at. She thought she knew a few, but she couldn't put faces to names. One sat across the table from Grace and did a double take. She covered a smile and whispered something to her friend, who also glanced over. Grace clutched the menu, her cheeks burning.

She'd expected Jean to say something, to get her involved somehow, but nothing happened. It wasn't until Jean left to go to the washroom that the boy sitting on her other side looked at Grace and smiled. "I know you."

"Yeah. You're in my chemistry class. Brian?"

"Right, that's it. You're going out with Simon Summers, right?"

Swallowing hard, Grace could only nod.

"Good for you. Simon is a nice guy."

"Thanks." She wasn't sure what to say to that.

"I didn't realize you and Jean knew each other, though."

"She's been my best friend since pretty much forever." Grace tried to relax. Brian didn't seem like a bad guy, and she had come here to socialize, so why not? "We were even desk partners in Grade One. I never imagined she'd ever try out for the school play, though."

"Why not?"

"Well...she was never into performing before," Grace muttered, aware how hollow her words sounded. "But anyway, she seems to like it. Maybe I should give it a try sometime."

The two girls across the table tittered.

Reddening even more, Grace stopped talking. A moment later, Jean returned and plopped back into her seat, ending further conversation with Brian. Mercifully, dinner arrived at the same time, and she didn't need to explain what had happened.

As they ate, though, things got worse instead of better. One of the seniors who had been smirking at her pushed aside the pizza and addressed Grace directly. "Interesting makeup. It's very...striking."

"Thank you," she replied with caution, sensing the compliment might be insincere.

"There was a big eighties boom a few years ago, right?" the girl continued, speaking more to her friend than to Grace.

"Sure," the other girl replied. "Bright colours for eye shadow were really in, then. It would be nice if that came back into style—I bet you think so too, Grace."

She wasn't sure how to respond. "I guess so."

Jean intervened, sensing Grace's discomfort at long last. "Why bother waiting until things are 'in' or 'out' of style? If it makes you feel good, there shouldn't be a time limit on it."

The two girls exchanged dubious looks. Obviously, they weren't too fond of Jean, either, but she wasn't as easy a target. Both excused themselves, and Grace couldn't help but wonder whether they were off to snark somewhere more private.

That thought, and the sinking feeling in her gut, were her cue to leave, Grace thought. Gathering her coat, she mumbled a goodbye to the table, not too surprised when no one but Brian even offered her a nod.

Jean followed her to the door. "Listen, about those two morons..."

"Don't worry." Grace waved her off. "I'm used to it."

"You shouldn't have to be."

"But I am." She smiled wearily. "People don't notice me when I blend in, and they don't like me when I stand out."

"I know." Jean gave her a hug. "I'm sorry. The outfit is cute."

"You think so?"

Her friend raised one eyebrow. "Well...it's *unique*, but yes, it's cute, too. I promise."

It felt good to have Jean's approval on something at last. Maybe, Grace thought, that was enough of a step in the right direction.

~*~*~

Without the regular conversation practice at English Speaking Society, Kana started to feel more and more like she wasn't doing enough to prepare for her entrance exam. On school grounds, at least she *felt* like she was studying, even when it was more like socializing. And, she had to admit, with Kurokawa Shiori in charge, club meetings were more like studying than ever.

They were halfway through the school year, and it had been almost that long since Kana had quit the ESS. It was a shame, since she had been a proud member since her first week at Koenkou. They were a friendly club, always poised to recruit newcomers. Girls like Yoko, who were part of another time-intensive team, appreciated that the ESS would welcome them whenever they chose to show up.

Kana had originally intended to drop down to "sometimes" attendance when she became a third-year, but by the end of May, she'd stopped coming to meetings at all. She'd told the others that she'd become too busy (not *entirely* a lie) to attend, but in truth, it had stopped being fun after the former leader graduated. It was awkward, because Kana and the new leader Kurokawa had never had any problems with each other before. Under Kurokawa's leadership, though, the club was more than ever about *practising*, and less about *enjoying* English, and Kana's parents were paying her cram school more than enough for *that*.

So she had backed away, without the usual fanfare for a retiring member. The younger students, her *kouhai*, were sad to see Kana go, but not as sad as they might have been had they known the reason for her departure.

Sometimes, though, she found it hard to stay away. Kana thought she might drop in and visit the club; see what they were doing. Maybe they would even have a small task she could help out with for the upcoming culture festival. Just a chat in real time in casual English might be enough to help her feel like she wasn't about to tip into the bog of grammatical rules and drown.

Today, though, didn't seem to be the day. When she peeked into the space the ESS shared with the Literature Club, the members were all chatting in Japanese, not English. Yuko and Yoko were there, along with Michiko and Hatsue, two second-year girls. Two boys, Kazuki and Mitsuki, were drawing on the chalkboard. The turnout looked decidedly small.

Kana edged the door open. "Sorry to interrupt."

"Senpai!" Michiko stood to greet her. *Senpai*, upperclassman, was the term the younger students all used for third-years.

Kana entered and set her bag on the table. "It's been a while. I thought I'd come say hello—where is everyone?"

Yoko, also in Kana's class, made a face. "Culture festival preparations."

The annual festival had been on almost everyone's minds, but not Kana's. She had chosen the most noncommittal task available for her own class's project. The rest of 3–7 was staging a musical, and Kana was only part of the crew. She would be handling a spotlight during the half-hour show—no preparation, no mess, no fuss.

"The ESS isn't in the festival this year," Hatsue said, indignant.

"What? Why not?"

The second-year student put her hands on her hips. "Waste of time, Kurokawa-senpai says. Everyone's too busy with exams or with their own class's productions for the festival. Even though we *always* do something for the festival."

"That's too bad." Kana wasn't surprised, but she tried to look sympathetic. So much for the hope that she would be able to help out.

"It's so good to see you here. Were you thinking of coming back?" Yoko asked hopefully. Along with Yuko, she and Kana had always been in the same class and the same club, back as far as junior high school. "Everyone's missed you, you know."

"I don't think so," Kana replied, dubious. She couldn't commit to anything when she hadn't yet seen their leader. "I was only stopping by today. Sorry."

"Senpai is a third-year, so of course she's busy," Kazuki pointed out. As usual, he was all business. "She needs to study."

Yoko made a face at him. "Well, *we're* third-years, too, you know."

"But you're applying for Nishidai, right, senpai?" Hatsue used the abbreviated name for Nishi Gaidai. "You must have to study a lot to get in there."

"I do. I mean, I am," Kana hastily corrected. "But I might come again to the club meetings sometimes. I mean, speaking English is good practice."

Yoko patted her shoulder. "Don't worry, the ESS is great practice nowadays. It's like having one extra class after school."

Everybody laughed, but Kana sensed the tension in the air, especially among the senior students. It seemed she hadn't been the only one unhappy with the direction the club had taken —but nothing at all had changed since she left.

"Stay for today, Kacchan," Yuko pressed, pulling out a chair for her. "It'll be just like before, you'll see. We're going to have free talk."

Free talk! Kana smiled. It would be nice to talk in English for a while. Email exchanges with her pen pal were fun, but it was so much easier and less embarrassing to practice with other non-native speakers. She hoped she could teach them a few new phrases, too. Gratefully, Kana joined the circle and tried to put Kurokawa Shiori out of her mind.

Chapter 6

Hi, Megucchi

I wanted to tell you about the end of bunkasai (cultural festival). Our musical show was a big success. This is the last high school cultural festival for my class, so it had to be the best. Everyone was so happy yesterday when we celebrated.

I'm a little sad that I didn't join in a role. But even the stage crew is very important for a musical. I hope next year, I can have a lot more fun at the university's cultural festival instead.

♡ Kana

Kana-chan,

Thanks for telling me about your festival. It sounds so cool, I'm super jealous we don't have anything quite like that. The closest we get would be sports events maybe? We have a basketball team that's really popular so if they're doing well there's a lot of school spirit going on. Or sometimes there's a fundraiser for something, like last year we had a wake-a-thon where you stayed at school all night and tried to stay awake.

Different topic: You surprised me the other day when you said you wanted a straight perm. Your hair is so straight already! Is straight hair in style in Japan now? It seems like in the magazines, girls are going for big hair with huge curls. I think they must be getting extensions too—some of that hair is CRAZY long.

I've been thinking about hair a lot lately. I hate my hair! It's so plain and boring. I don't know what to do with it, though. It's super thick and it doesn't curl well. I'd like to wear it like they do in the magazines, the "older sister" look. Would that make me look goody-goody, I wonder?

I'm trying to change my image, but it seems like people don't really like my ideas. I wonder what I'm doing wrong.

~ Megucchi

Re: Hair	
From: thehealinglight@saftbank.ne.jp	Sat, Oct 4, 12:45 AM

Actually the big style right now is curl hair. I think it's not for me. Maybe for some special event, but in my daily life, straight hair suits me. If I can get a straight perm, the hair will be very very flat, perfectly flat. It can be smooth.

The "older sister" look is so cute for you. Do you like to have fringe? I think that would be cute, too. Please send me a photo if you cut your hair. ♡♡♡

I also got a very good mock test score this morning at cram school. I can use it to send my pre-application form to the university. It's thanks to you! You always answer my questions without ever becoming annoyed. You should tell me if it's too much, OK?

♡ Kana

Kana cleared off her low table as soon as she'd written the reply. She hadn't expected it to take quite so long to answer her messages—the afternoon had started to slip away, and she found it easier to concentrate when the sun shone into her room. At least it would soon be time to get out the blankets and convert her table into winter mode. Sitting under a *kotatsu* with the heater turned on underneath, Kana thought, had to be the best thing about cold weather.

Setting aside the pile of notes, Kana withdrew a study guide from the stack on the floor. The mock exam scores had lifted her spirits considerably. It seemed to Kana as though she was on the right track at last.

Before she had a chance to turn to the page she'd marked, her cell phone made another noise, and she reached over to pull it over by its purple strap.

"What if I cut it very short?" read the message.

She was talking about her hair, Kana realized. This kind of question was new. Megucchi usually preferred to talk about Kana's life and Kana's friends rather than her own. Kana thought she seemed lonely. Megucchi often talked about her best friend spending too much time with other people.

"Maybe." Kana changed her character input to English with practised ease and tapped out a reply. "But maybe not too short? I used to cut my hair short, and I missed it."

The chime came again a few seconds later, as Kana was positioning a red check sheet over the first page of the chapter. *"I was thinking just past the shoulders."*

"I think that would be cute!" She added a *kaomoji* for good measure.

"And you think bangs would be good? Fringe?"

Kana didn't reply; she had started in on the exercises. *After I'm done with this, I'll answer,* she told herself. *Megucchi knows I had cram school today. She'll understand that I'm busy.*

But the sound came again before Kana reached the end of the assignment. She tried to ignore it, but the temptation was too great. Within a minute, she reached for the phone. *"Sorry if I'm bothering you. I've bought all these clothes and makeup and stuff, but I can't deal with wearing them. I feel like everyone's going to laugh at me. Hopeless, right?"*

The wording puzzled Kana for a while, to the point where she checked her dictionary to make sure there weren't other meanings she might have missed. *What a strange thing for Megucchi to say.* Kana didn't see any reason why her friend would be "hopeless" over clothes or a haircut.

"I think if you want to do it, other people will just get used to it, right?"

Kana waited a while, until the assignment was long complete, but no reply came.

~*~*~

The bell above the shop door tinkled, attracting the attention of a tall girl standing at the counter inside. She had dark brown hair styled in a messy updo and a friendly smile. She couldn't have been more than a few years older than Grace herself. "Hi love, do you have an appointment today?"

"No, I'm sorry. Is it a problem?" Grace clutched her backpack to her chest. Maybe today wasn't the day, after all.

"Not at all! I'm free." The girl pointed at the coat rack. "Hang up your jacket there and have a seat. What's your name, my love?"

"Grace. Grace Ryan."

"Grace." The hairstylist scribbled something down in her book. "Okay, Grace, I'm Maisy. What can I do for you?"

"Well," Grace said shyly, opening her bag to withdraw the latest issue of *SwEET*, "I think I need a new look."

~*~*~

Shibuya seemed extra busy, teeming with people, but that was fine with Kana. She had come to take pictures of her favourite places to send to Megucchi, and the livelier the better, she thought.

Her friend seemed fascinated by everything Kana said about Tokyo, even the most mundane things about day-to-day life, and Kana felt guilty sometimes that she might be boring her friend by rambling on about English grammar. She had sent Megucchi pictures of her school and her friends, but knowing Megucchi wanted to visit Shibuya someday, Kana thought it would be good to get a few more photos there.

People-watching was what she liked most about Shibuya, because the things you could see in the run of a day there ranged from the mundane to the outrageous. Kana often came to sit and study while waiting for Rumi to finish club activities on Tuesdays, sometimes even to this very cafe. She loved to sit here on rainy days, watching hundreds of brightly-coloured umbrellas bob across the intersection at a time.

Sitting at the counter facing the train station, Kana snapped a few photos of the crosswalk, then began to write a message to Megucchi. She flipped open her dictionary to look up how to write *pedestrian* in English.

"It's a good view, isn't it?"

At first Kana assumed this question wasn't addressed to her, but when she glanced up, she saw that the young man seated to her right was looking in her direction. "Oh? Yes, it is, isn't it..."

He pointed at the dictionary in her hand. "That's a fancy electronic dictionary. Are you studying English, or something else?"

"Ah, well, yes," she replied, embarrassed. The young man—more like a boy, she thought, now that she could see his face—looked about her age. He wore a solid black *gakuran* jacket, like the boys at Koen Academy, but his untidy tinted hair and unbuttoned uniform implied a school much more lax about rules than her own. A silver pin with the Roman numeral III was turned askew on his collar.

"*Oh,*" he continued, this time speaking English. "*I think maybe you study hard. Sorry. I...*"

Kana smiled encouragingly, unsure what he wanted to say.

"Sorry," he said again, switching back to Japanese, "I don't mean to bother you. But when I saw you take out your dictionary, I wanted to ask for some help. With English."

"Really?" she replied, dubious. Of course, it was impossible to tell from his uniform whether he attended a high-academic school, but this boy didn't *look* like the type. "Do you have a question? I'm not sure I'll know the answer, but I can try."

His response surprised her. "Actually, I'm looking for a study partner. I don't go to a cram school, so I've been trying to find a tutor to work with before my entrance exam."

Uneasily, Kana glanced down at the dictionary in her hands. Could this be a misguided attempt at flirting? "I don't know. It would be better to ask a native speaker for help. I'm just a student, like you."

"*Foreigners are full in Shibuya,*" he said in heavily-accented English, "*but not all are cute girls.*"

"You mean to say, *Shibuya is full of foreigners,*" she corrected, avoiding his gaze.

"See? You're very good. And I'm willing to pay you, like a tutor. Kind of like a part-time job, right?"

"I'm serious. My English isn't good at all," she protested. "Even going to cram school, I make a lot of mistakes. And I don't have time to tutor someone else. I need to study." She wanted to say something else about the "cute" comment, but she didn't want to offend the boy, even if he had made a pass at her.

"You're upset." He kept looking Kana in the eye in a way that made her feel off-kilter. "I'm sorry if I offended you. Can we start over?"

"I...uh..." Kana frowned. How she wished Rumi were here! Her friend always knew exactly how to deal with these situations.

"My name is Otsuka. Otsuka Daisuke," he continued, reclining in his seat as he introduced himself. "It's nice to meet you."

"Momokawa Kana...nice to meet you."

"Then, *Miss* Momokawa, will you meet me?" He delicately pronounced *Miss* in English, with just a hint of a *-su* sound at the end of the word. "Maybe tomorrow?"

"What?"

"Tomorrow. Let me show you that I'm serious." He smiled. "Then you can decide if you'll tutor me or not. So let's meet back here, okay?"

Kana exhaled with a long, slow breath. This guy was clearly set on trying to prove himself. Why should she care about whether this strange boy passed or failed his exam? It had nothing to do with Kana.

She thought back to something Rumi had said weeks ago. Hadn't she suggested Kana find a conversation partner, and that was how Megucchi had ended up coming into her life? That had turned out for the best, she had to admit. With Megucchi's help, Kana's English had improved by leaps and bounds, even in the span of a month.

She didn't owe this stranger anything. *But we might be able to help each other,* Kana thought. An extra couple of hours of conversation practice would be a great replacement for ESS, even if it meant giving up her remaining free afternoons. What was the harm in giving it a try? "Fine. I'll meet you just one time, to see how things go. Not tomorrow, though."

"How about Thursday? Four-thirty?"

"That's fine," Kana agreed, then switched to English. "*See you Thursday. And for study, not for play!*" Hoping he wouldn't see how flustered she had become, she gathered her things and left.

Determined not to look back, Kana strode to the stairs, still shocked by how easily he had flirted with her, and even more shocked that she had given in. Better to aim straight for the exit, and not give Otsuka Daisuke the slightest inclination that she felt anything but indifferent about their next meeting.

Even if he *did* have a cute smile.

~*~*~

Grace felt like an entirely new person. Maisy had taken her boring hairdo and utterly transformed her, using a razor to thin it out at the bottom and sides, causing it to fall around her face in a wispy, layered cut that reached past her shoulders. She had also brought back bangs Grace hadn't seen since age eleven, parting them neatly in the centre to frame her face. Maisy, thrilled with the results, gave her a discount as she rang up the sale, telling Grace that she looked "adorable."

In Grace's memory, no one had called her *adorable* since preschool. As easy to fire up as ever, she blushed a bright red, and Maisy called all her co-workers over to see. For some reason, though, this time Grace felt flattered rather than embarrassed at their attention. As she left she wrapped her scarf closer around her neck and hid her nose and mouth under the folds of cloth, grinning to herself. Who knew that something like a haircut could have that kind of effect?

It had been a good time for a change after all, Grace decided.

She hurried home, still in high spirits. Tomorrow would be different, she thought. *Tomorrow, I will be different!*

Her closet was packed with clothes. Most of this would have to go, Grace thought, or at least be creatively recycled. She picked out two favourite tops, one black with cap sleeves, and one dark blue sleeveless, holding them next to each other. The two were a good match, she thought, so she changed out of her school clothes into both shirts, along with a pleated black skirt. On went a brand-new pair of electric-blue tights and her mother's knee-high boots. Grace finished the look with a handful of bracelets made from leather thongs.

She stood in front of the mirror. This was it! On their own, the makeup and accessories hadn't done anything but make her look like she was trying too hard. Paired with the haircut, though, she felt good. Like this could be something she could wear without judgment. Grace snapped a photo to send to Kana, then sat down to remove the borrowed boots, in time to hear the front door open and shut.

Grace did feel nervous about what her mother would say. She was sure to make some embarrassing remark about how her daughter was growing up into a proper young lady at last, and how she'd better be home by curfew if she was going out with Simon. Her mother would be ecstatic to see Grace getting dressed up as if she were going on a date.

She went downstairs to get it over with, still dressed in the blue and black outfit. Camilla straightened items on the coffee table.

"Hi sweetie." Her mother looked up and her eyes widened. "Wow, what's this? New hair?"

"Well, you're always saying I should do something different," Grace replied, suddenly feeling smug.

Camilla smiled. "I guess I do say that, don't I? It looks great. It suits you."

"I saw it in a magazine."

She stepped closer and lifted the ends of Grace's hair, where Maisy had layered and thinned the surface. "Well. Your dad won't even know you, the next time he sees you! Assuming he even notices, that is."

"Ha ha. Very funny."

"By the way, you need to tell your father to email me your plane ticket—knowing him, he's put you on a daytime flight *again*. That's a vacation day I would rather save for when you're actually around." She sighed heavily. "Did you talk to him about it?"

Grace had little patience for her parents' dramatics. "I don't think he's bought the ticket yet. I told him I wanted it to be after the second week of December, since the dance is that week, though you're going to have to clear it for me at school if I have to leave before the actual semester end date."

"I don't see why he thinks *that's* necessary. You shouldn't be missing any school at all."

Surprisingly, her mother had turned the conversation to trip logistics rather than the event. She'd expected the mere mention of her going to a formal dance at school would be the perfect distraction to end a potentially uncomfortable conversation. When it came to what Camilla's ex-husband was or wasn't doing right, though, she always had an opinion. "Mom..."

"What?" Camilla gave her the side-eye, as though the whole thing was somehow Grace's fault.

Grace swallowed. Why did she always have to deal with defending one parent to the other? "I know you'd rather I not, but school isn't out until a couple of days before Christmas. I *always* go up there right after my last exam. What do you want me to do, here?"

Her mother seemed to soften a bit, and she turned away. "That man has the money to book you on a flight close to Christmas, God knows. But I get it. It's his last *official* turn, after all. Well, when he sends you the ticket, you can forward it to me. Or print it and put it on the fridge. I'd rather not have to deal with it."

"Okay." Grace sighed.

Camilla, her ex-husband already forgotten, obviously wanted to return to the previous topic. "Well, anyway, I love it. The haircut, I mean. This outfit is nice too; you look sophisticated. Grown up! Ah, Gracie, I never thought I'd see the day when I didn't have to drag you to the salon, or worse, trim your hair while you slept—"

"—Okay, Mom. I get it." Irritated, Grace backed out of the kitchen and fled to her room, ignoring her mother's cackle as she climbed the stairs in as dignified a manner as possible. At least the topic hadn't gone back to the formal dance!

Once the door was firmly shut, she flopped into her armchair. Her parents had to be *so* predictable, not to mention galling! They both seemed to think they were funny, but Grace hadn't inherited one iota of their outdated senses of humour.

Her phone trilled, distracting Grace from her ire. She opened her inbox and saw Kana's name.

"Wow! Thank you for sending me your picture. So cute! You are so lucky to have brown hair. Is it natural?

I wish I could dye my hair, but my school has strict rules. If we come with dye hair we must go home until it is black again. This happened to Rumi twice before. The discipline teacher says we should wear plain black socks, too, but I have been all right until now. Hehe~ Lucky!"

Brown hair, exotic? That was a new one. "It's natural!" she replied. "But trust me, B-O-R-I-N-G."

A moment later, Kana's response came. *"My classmates would be envious of your hair colour. Your clothes are very nice too. It looks comfortable."*

"Thanks."

"It's cold in Canada now, right? Must you wear a coat?"

"Well, Canada's pretty big, there's a huge range of weather, but in NL it's not too cold yet. Only a light jacket right now. The temperature's been OK so far. I just love fall, so it's perfect for me."

October was Grace's favourite month, and walking on the forest path behind the school that afternoon had been exhilarating with the autumn leaves falling all around. She loved the smell of burnt leaves in the air at this time of year. Grace wondered if autumn smelled the same in Japan as it did here.

"Here, it's OK to go without a coat, but lately I have worn long sleeves every day. Many girls from my school look cold, but they don't wear a cardigan. I envy girls who can wear short sleeves and skirts all year long."

Grace could relate to that. She wasn't the biggest fan of cold, and she hated snow and everything that came with it. "Not me!" she wrote in reply. "Wrap me up in a scarf and some good solid boots."

She twisted the leather bracelet on her wrist. It was nice to be told she looked cute every once in a while. Kana's compliment had hit exactly the right note. And it hadn't been so hard to put herself together, had it?

She stood and went back to her closet. Some items were worn to the point of fraying, and others were brand-new, gifts she hadn't cared for from Christmases past. Grace gathered as much as she could carry, threw the heap onto the bedspread and began to sort them into piles. If she was going to do this, she thought, she wasn't going to leave herself any room to chicken out.

Chapter 7

♡ Hachi	
From: thehealinglight@saftbank.ne.jp	Thu, Oct 9, 3:02 AM

Hi, Megucchi!

I'm waiting for the train now, I'll leave Omiya soon. Then I'll meet Rumi at Shibuya like always. She's going to there for shopping.

Of course this place is my favourite place in Tokyo! By the way, this place is also somehow famous. A long time ago there was a dog named Hachiko who waited outside of Shibuya Station every day for his master to come home on the train. But one day his master became sick and suddenly died. Still Hachiko comes every day to wait. He came for more than ten years, so we call him "Loyal Dog Hachiko" in Japanese.

Now a statue of this dog is there outside of Shibuya Station and it is a meeting place. If a person meets someone in Shibuya or becomes lost, they always find each other at Hachiko. Rumi and I do this, too.

♡ Kana

Re: ♡ Hachi	10 月 9 日 (木) 21:18
From: メグッチ	詳細を表示

Ahhh, he sounds so cute!! I've seen pictures of the dog statue but I didn't know about the history. Thanks for telling me. Even though I've never been there, I think Shibuya might be my favourite place in Tokyo, too!

I still want to hear the whole story of the Mystery Guy?!? I'm dying to find out. I can't imagine what I would say if someone came up to me like that and strong-armed me into English lessons! Keep me posted!

~ Megucchi

Kana was just about ready to meet her new "student" in the cafe above the scramble crossing, while Rumi was planning to look at clothes.

The 109 building, or Maru-Kyu as it was nicknamed among young Tokyoites, didn't carry much selection in visual kei styles anymore, but every once in a while Rumi came up with something amazing. It helped that she knew many of the shopkeepers (one was even an upperclassman from the volleyball club the previous year) and kept up with the latest trends.

"Are you *sure* you don't want me to come with you?" Rumi glared in the general direction of the crossing, as though daring Otsuka Daisuke to come out and face her.

Kana could only manage a weak smile. "I should be all right...he could be a perfectly nice guy. I *did* say I'd do this, after all."

"Under pressure," Rumi emphasized.

"Under pressure," Kana agreed. "But I'm not too worried about it. We're in a public place, and it's not like I'm going to give him my address. I won't even tell him what school I go to."

"Okay. But if you need me, you'd better call for me right away, got it? I'll be waiting in Maru-Kyu for as long as you need me to."

Kana preferred to avoid the busy shopping centre. It was exclusive and expensive, and the hordes of teens and twentysomethings that crowded Maru-Kyu after school made fighting the mob a daunting task. "I'll be fine, but thanks."

She pulled at the sleeves of her powder-blue blouse, wishing she had thought to wear a cardigan. The weather was chilly, and *koromogae*, the day on which schools changed to the winter uniform, was about to arrive. Most of the Koen Academy population would go right on wearing their cream sweater-vests anyway, instead of their blazers, only switching short-sleeved blouses out for long ones. Rumi, to her credit, never looked cold in her blouse and vest, with her skirt barely reaching halfway to her knees.

The five-way-stop of the scramble crossing brought traffic to a halt. "There's the light. I guess I'll see you later?"

"Yeah. See you!" Rumi waved and bounded toward the west side of the scramble, while Kana headed northwest.

The Hoshibacks cafe was filled with people, not uncommon for that time in the afternoon, but Kana wanted to secure a spot at the upstairs counter again. She climbed the stairs to the second floor and claimed the remaining set of two stools, right in the middle of the long counter.

With ten minutes to go before her pupil was scheduled to arrive, Kana pulled out her phone, but there were no new messages waiting. It was, she remembered, around four in the morning in Canada.

"Hi Megucchi. I hope my message doesn't wake you!" she wrote.

"I'm in Shibuya right now waiting to meet someone. A guy asked me to tutor him in English, so I thought I would try it once. He's a high school boy though and somewhat cheeky. He wants to learn better English...is this familiar to you?? I wonder if I can really do that? I think it would be better for him to go to a cram school."

When she laid down the phone, it was exactly half past four. Kana put on her reading glasses and began unpacking her notebooks, pens and electronic dictionary. If he wanted to impress her with his drive to learn, Kana thought, he would have done better to arrive early.

Half an hour later she was still watching the intersection, tapping her foot under the counter. It was getting late enough that dusk was falling. She couldn't believe after the hard bargain he'd driven to get her to agree to this meeting, Otsuka Daisuke would be a no-show!

Kana put away her book, checked her watch one last time, and decided to cut her losses. She fired off an annoyed message to Rumi and set about packing everything back in her satchel to leave.

Now that it was after five, there were heads and shoulders as far as the eye could see. Frustrated, Kana tried not to be annoyed that she would have to take the train with the rush hour crowds all the way to Omiya. Was it too late to eat with Rumi? Ducking her head, Kana hurried to bring up the rear of the group crossing the street, only to find herself caught by the elbow and whirled back to the corner.

"Momokawa-san," Otsuka Daisuke gasped, seemingly having appeared from nowhere. "I'm really sorry–"

"Oh, so *now* we're being polite, are we?" Kana asked testily, noting the pedestrian lights flash, then turn red. The timer had run down with her on the wrong side.

"I'm telling you, I'm sorry!" He let go of her sleeve. "I came from my part-time job. I got kept late. Can't I make it up to you?"

"I live pretty far away, so I need to get home," she replied, stone-faced.

"Me too, but the trains are packed right now. Why don't we wait until after rush hour?"

There was no arguing that it would be an uncomfortable ride home if she left now. Kana frowned.

"Come on, no tutoring session would last half an hour," he pressed, with the barest hint of a smile. "Surely you don't have to go yet? We could go get some cake at a cafe, my treat."

Her resolve faltered. She did indeed have a fondness for cake, and her packed lunch from that afternoon seemed like an eternity ago. Plus, the boy's unwavering persistence in making it up to her was kind of sweet. "All right...but just until it's less busy."

"Of course, *Miss* Momokawa." The smile became a grin. "Follow me, I know a great place."

He led her up Center Street to a small side road, and from there, into a cafe with plastic recreations of sweets, cakes and parfaits displayed in the window. An older girl in a frilly white apron and a black skirt waited tables. Her eyes lit up when the pair entered. "Dai-chan! Hi!"

"Yo." He grinned at the waitress and held up two fingers. "Two, please."

"Right over here." She brought them to a corner table and laid down two menus and two glasses of ice water. Kana sat, feeling for a moment as though she were under a microscope as the pretty waitress's dark, kohl-rimmed eyes surveyed her from top to bottom. "Take your time."

"Sure thing," Daisuke replied.

Kana could not help stealing another glance as the girl turned away, the round tray against her chest. She also could not have helped noticing that the waitress had spoken to Daisuke in a very familiar way. "A friend of yours?"

"My sister, actually," he said, to Kana's surprise.

"Seriously?" Kana couldn't see any resemblance, but it was hard to tell under the expertly-applied makeup. She suspected a hint of Gal style in the techniques, as well as the sparkles and streaks in her long, bleached hair. This was the kind of girl who, after work, would undoubtedly be found over in Maru-Kyu.

Daisuke leaned his chin on one hand, following her gaze to the counter. "Yeah. We're close, I guess. She took care of me a lot when I was young."

"Is she much older than you?"

"Twenty-three," he confirmed. "Six years older. Her name is Miki."

Though she was curious about this sister of his, Kana covered her interest and turned her attention to the menu, instead.

A moment later Miki returned to take their orders—as well as another opportunity to scrutinize Kana's face and uniform. "So, Dai-chan, are you going to introduce me to your friend?"

"Oh yeah, of course. This is *Miss* Momokawa," he explained, again inserting English into the introduction.

"It's nice to meet you." Kana wondered if he intended at all to mention that they were not friends, but near-strangers who might shortly be study partners.

"I'm Otsuka Miki," the waitress replied with a quick bow and a dazzling smile. "Nice to meet you." She glanced at her brother, who looked utterly nonchalant. "Rare to see you around these parts. What brings you out?"

Kana quirked an eyebrow at her companion. She had assumed he was a regular Shibuyaite, or at least went to a nearby school. She realized that Daisuke really hadn't told her *anything* about himself yet.

If he was trying to impress her, though, he was doing better than before. "I'm here to study. *Miss* Momokawa will hopefully be helping me with my English before entrance exams."

"Is that so?" Miki looked at Kana with renewed interest. "That's great, I thought you had given up on that. I'm so sorry if my brother causes you trouble, Momokawa-san."

"Oh, no, I'm sure it'll be fine. He knows that if he wants my help he has to work hard at it. Very hard."

"That's the spirit!" Miki told her, nodding her head emphatically. "I used to help him with homework, but English is way out of my league. Definitely not good enough for an international school. But if you ever need me for anything, ask, okay? I'm always somewhere around here, even when I'm not working."

Kana returned the smile. "Sure."

The bell over the shop door sounded, and Miki inclined her head to invite in the new customer. "Welcome!" Glancing back at Daisuke, she gave him another nod. "I'll talk to you later. Be right back with your cakes!"

"Thanks."

When she had gone, Kana looked over her pupil with a critical eye. "An international school? What high school do you go to?"

"That's the thing," he said with a sigh, but still managing a charismatic smile. "I go to East Shinagawa High School. If you've heard of it, that's probably because it's full of punks."

"No, I've never heard of it. I know where Shinagawa is, but I'm from Saitama, not Tokyo."

"Trust me, you're better off that way." Daisuke rolled his eyes.

"So, you're *not* a punk, then?"

He laughed, but didn't seem certain whether or not she was kidding. Kana wasn't too sure, herself. "Come on, what do you take me for?"

She frowned and raised an eyebrow. "Please. You have bleached hair, baggy pants with the legs rolled up, and your *gakuran* jacket is wide open. In my school, that kind of thing would get you sent home. And called a punk."

From Daisuke's expression, she had either nailed it or mortally wounded him. "What? No! This is *fashionable.*"

"I'll let you decide that, but you can see why I'd have cause to wonder. *Mister* Otsuka." This last, she said with a slight smile.

He returned it, apparently having decided she was kidding. A moment later Miki reappeared with their drinks and cakes, set them down on the table, and left again to welcome more customers.

"To each their own," Kana concluded, adding syrup to her milk tea. "So, you're not from around here either, then?"

"No. We live in Kamata."

"*Kamata?*" In the south end of Tokyo, Kamata was far enough that it was almost part of the next prefecture. Like Kana, this boy had a long commute to make it to Shibuya. "What are you doing lurking around here? Your part-time job?"

"Yeah. Last time, I was in Harajuku with friends who are starting a band. They asked me to work up some lyrics for a song, so I came up to check out their practice spot, walked down this way, stopped to have a coffee and found you as I was about to leave. That's where I came from, today."

"A band? Do you play an instrument?"

"I do play the piano," Daisuke replied, looking away bashfully. Kana felt her heart skip a beat. "But for this band I'm a lyricist. They want to do some covers, but with English words to make it more cool and fresh."

"You're writing the lyrics for them?"

"Sort of. I'm translating them from Japanese to English, and fixing them up. I do occasionally write music, though."

"Wow, you can write music? That's fantastic." She wasn't a big fan of any particular bands, preferring talk radio to any other type, but Kana did enjoy American rock and some pop music. She had a mini-disc player that she sometimes carried when she came to the city alone. It was outdated compared to the digital music players hanging from the bags of the other girls in school, but it did its job.

Daisuke leaned over, having polished off his slice of cake in record time. "I've written a few songs before for the piano, both the composition and the lyrics. I'm studying to get into an international music school."

"Really?"

"Really." He smiled, but a completely different smile from the ones she'd seen before. Daisuke wasn't trying to win her over anymore. He seemed so much more sanguine. "I want to play on a world stage. And if I manage to start writing my own songs, someday you're going to hear my lyrics sung by the best of them, all over the world."

Though she wasn't quite willing to say it, this earnest boy had charmed her more in three sentences with this admission than he had in all his previous efforts. "Impressive."

He nodded. "Japan, China, Europe, America too. Once I conquer English, I'll move on to the next language."

Kana raised her eyebrows. "That's...a very ambitious goal."

Shrugging, he swirled his coffee in its cup. "Sure. But it's good to have lots of goals, even if you only ever manage to accomplish a few of them."

She regarded him with renewed interest, looking for a sign

that he might be anything but serious. Despite Daisuke's swagger, though, he seemed to be genuine. "Okay...I may be able to help you after all."

"Were you testing me?" Daisuke raised his eyebrows in surprise.

"Well, maybe. If I wasn't, I am now." Kana scooped the last bite of her Mont Blanc into her mouth. "Here's your test. If you can talk to me for five minutes in English, you've got yourself a partner."

"*Let's get it started.*"

~*~*~

Wracked with anticipation, Grace tried to prepare Simon for her haircut before they actually saw each other, but her worrying had been for nothing. Simon had plenty of nice things to say about her new look.

"I don't mean to be insulting or say you didn't look good before, but this is *nice,*" he told her, squeezing her hand. Grace could only offer an embarrassed smile in return. "That haircut really suits you."

"Thanks," she managed, staring down at her sandwich. "I thought it would be a good change."

"I think so too," replied Simon. He had bought the school lunch and a cafeteria poutine, wolfing it down before Grace had eaten half her sandwich. The two of them were having lunch in her hiding spot in the Annex.

It was Grace's go-to for when she didn't feel like facing a crowd. The classroom they sat in, formerly a home economics room, was well-kept but hadn't been used for its original purpose in some time. The few teachers who had their offices in this wing of the building would enter to use the fridge and the sink, but never shooed Grace away. She had a feeling quite a few loner-type kids had used this wing as a hideout over the years.

Having such a small student population in a school building

of this size—St. Clare's was originally designed for Christian Brothers to live as well as work in—made it easy to find privacy, and that put her at ease. Now that Jean was suddenly playing the other side, Grace preferred to retreat with Simon back into the quiet space of the Annex. Here, she was safe from having to face anyone but him.

Her new canvas backpack made a chiming sound. Grace had covered it with pins, fabric paint and squares of black and green flannel, and hung charms from an old charm bracelet on every zipper. She had even sewn a pocket on the inside for her cell phone. Grace tried to look casual as she opened the bag to silence the phone. "I'd better check that. It must be Kana-chan."

"Looks like a success! I now have a student. Wanted to tell you before anyone else. Good night! (´▽`)ノ"

"Hmm." Grace smiled to herself as she typed out a reply.

Simon was watching. "Was it her?"

"Yeah!" Grace held the phone to her chest. "She says she's started tutoring someone in English. This guy came up to her in a cafe and talked her into it."

Simon grinned. "It sounds like you guys are getting to be good friends. I hope you're telling her nice things about me."

"Maybe." She smiled shyly.

"Even if you *do* seem to be spending quite a lot of time locked up in your room." Simon put his hand over hers. "We haven't gone out as just the two of us, in like a month, you know?"

Grace lowered her eyes, her free hand twisting around the phone strap. "Yeah, I guess you're right. Sorry."

"Well, I mean, it's not like we need to spend every waking moment together." He glanced away. Grace thought he might be embarrassed. "But my friends have been busy with the season starting up."

"Oh, yeah." Simon wasn't a member of the basketball team, though he sometimes joined them for scrimmage games when they were short. "And Kirk is probably going to be team captain next year, right? I guess he isn't going to have much time for a while."

"Probably not. But it's going to be a good year, I think," Simon replied. "They have a shot at the provincials. This team is solid."

Grace put her hand on his. "Well, if you have the time, I have the time. I don't want you to think I'm ignoring you or anything."

"No, of course not, but with Kirk out and Jean in that play, I thought maybe you and I would get to see more of each other."

Grace blinked, confused. "Play? What play?"

Simon's eyebrows rose a fraction, but as usual, his expression revealed nothing about what he was actually thinking. "I figured you knew. She tried out for that musical the drama club is putting off at Christmas."

"Right, I remember hearing about a musical at some point." Grace thought back to the last few times she had seen Jean. They had been in two classes together the day before, and another the day before that.

"Wow. Well, I'm surprised you didn't hear *more* about it. Jean's got a lead part, opposite that drummer from the jazz band, the one with the crazy hair."

"Christian?"

"That's the guy." Simon looked pained.

"The lead." Grace shook her head. "I didn't even know she tried out for the musical! Why didn't she bother to mention it to me?"

"I don't know."

Grace could feel irritation bubbling up. Again. "She used to have a report ready for me whenever Christian Barber changed his *socks*. What happened? And I thought we were good. After the pizza party, she seemed totally back to normal. Mostly."

Simon shrugged. Grace noticed he was avoiding meeting her gaze. "Can't say I know. Jean is nice and all, but she's your friend, not mine. *She* didn't tell me about getting the part...I heard it going around in homeroom. I guess she could have forgotten to mention it."

"How would she forget it? She would have been over the moon." Grace paused as a thought struck her. "Maybe she's mad at me again."

"Gracie." Simon sighed deeply and put his hands on her shoulders. "You have to stop being so paranoid. Since when has Jean ever *not* let you know right away when she was mad?"

"Well, that's true, I guess...but..."

"No 'buts.' If you want to know why, then you should ask her."

Grace shook her head. "I can't *accuse* her."

"You aren't accusing her if you don't suspect her of anything." Simon's voice held a hint of exasperation, so Grace looked away, focusing on the table. She hated when he got impatient with her anxieties, even though deep in her heart she thought he was right. She knew she jumped to conclusions and assumed the worst too quickly, but it still hurt to be reprimanded for it.

His expression softened a bit. "Hey, but I wonder if maybe she wanted to tell you at a special time and surprise you?"

"Oh, yeah. That could be it," Grace agreed, not truly believing it. It seemed much easier to wish that was the case, though, and hope that she would be pleasantly surprised to discover it was true.

When Grace next saw Jean, it had been almost three days since she found out about the musical. Her friend had missed two full days of classes in a row. When she finally managed to catch up to Jean, it was after school, outside the drama room, where Grace had been waiting since final bell. She wasn't surprised to see Jean rush up moments later with her arms full of manila envelopes and file folders. "Hi, Jeannie."

"Hey!" Jean shuffled her burden into a more balanced pile. "Long time no see! Wow, I love the hair."

"Thanks." Grace shifted from one foot to the other, feeling extremely awkward. She wasn't great with starting these kinds of discussions, so she hoped Jean would come right out and tell her about the musical. "It's been a couple of days, but I haven't seen you in homeroom or anything. I wanted to make sure everything was all right..."

"Oh, sure, everything's cool," Jean replied with a flippant wave. "I've been super busy, that's all. A couple of teachers let me off their classes while we're prepping for the musical, as long as I turn in homework. And of course there's lots going on after school."

"Right," Grace said, pointedly keeping a smile on her face. There was the mention of the musical, but where was the big news?

Jean paused, glanced over her shoulder, then held up her index finger. "Wait here for one sec." Grace nodded. Her friend peeked through the window of the drama room and, apparently finding it empty, twisted the handle and nudged the heavy yellow door open with her foot. "Come in for a bit. These things are heavy."

"What have you got there?"

"Oh, it's all the scores. I'm going to be handing them out to the orchestra today." Jean dropped the stack of folders on an armchair and tossed her knapsack down beside them. "It's going to be a great show!"

Grace bit her lip, her smile faltering. "I honestly didn't even know we were having a musical until a few days ago. You never mentioned it until now."

Turning to rearrange the top items in the stack, Jean almost seemed to be hiding her face. "Oh, really? But we have one every year, you know? Obviously the club is always involved."

"Do we? I never noticed."

"Seriously?"

"Seriously." Grace paused. "So you're going to do the music? Playing your clarinet?"

"Er, no." Jean's movements slowed down a fraction. "I'm *helping* a little with the music, but I'm not going to play in the orchestra. I managed to get a stage part."

Grace tried to put some energy into her voice. "Wow, great! Congratulations! Is it a big part?"

A hint of embarrassment had crept onto Jean's pale cheeks. "I guess it is, though there are a lot of big roles in the story."

"You...didn't tell me that you had—that is, I didn't know you were trying out or anything." Flustered, Grace tried to cover her reaction.

Jean straightened and looked her in the face. "Sorry about that. I didn't want to say anything until I knew I'd gotten it."

And then what happened? Grace wondered, but she didn't speak. Instead, she nodded, slowly. "That makes sense."

Even without saying it, Jean seemed to know what was bothering her friend, and gave her a hesitant smile. "Seriously, I am sorry. I should have told you, but I haven't seen you lately. Didn't even get the chance to say anything about your haircut when I saw you in the hall. It suits you, by the way. The outfit is cute too."

"Thanks," Grace replied, mollified at the compliment. "I've been...trying to change my attitude."

"That's awesome, I'm super happy for you. And listen...I know you've been caught up with your pen pal and your crafting and all, but I've been busy too, so it's half my fault we haven't seen each other." Jean perched on the arm of the chair, glancing at the clock. "If you want, you can come to this little end-of-the-year party we're going to be having after the first dress rehearsal. I mean, it's a long way out, it's in December, but I'm going to be crazy-busy until then. It's at Christian's house."

"You want me to come?" Grace was ashamed to admit she had never been to a high school house party. Her own birthdays were always low-key, and Jean's parents never let her host.

Simon often received invites to parties, but Grace had never gone along to one. "That would be nice. I'll go."

Hopping off the chair, Jean gathered some of the folders into her arms. "Great. Invite Simon, too, if you want. I'll give you the details later, when we have everything set, but for now I've got to get going. I have to meet with the orchestra at three-fifteen."

"Sure."

"And if I'm not around much, or don't come to homeroom, no need to panic." Jean winked. "I'll take any excuse to spend more time rehearsing with Christian."

"Getting away with murder, as usual." Grace managed a strained-sounding laugh.

"It's a talent, I know."

"Oh yes, there's no doubt about that." Grace allowed herself to be ushered out into the hallway. "Remember last year when you talked us into that concert I wanted to see on campus?"

"Do I ever!" Jean's poise and mature beauty had gotten them into the eighteen-plus venue, but Grace's youthful face had gotten them kicked right back out. "And that guy who wanted to call the cops because he thought you were like, fourteen?"

"They shouldn't have age-blocked it in the first place," Grace said sourly. "It's not like they were serving drinks. We have as much right to like the band as anyone else."

"That was my finest moment." Jean looked starry-eyed remembering it. "I could have won a debate competition with that kind of conviction. Mind you, *you* were closer to eighteen than *I* was!"

"Well," Grace laughed, "now I *am*, so the next time we go somewhere where there's an age limit, I'll have my real ID in hand, and you'll only have to talk yourself in."

"Where's the fun in that?" Jean grinned. "I think it was perfect. I don't think I've ever been so proud as I was when he gave up and let you come back."

Grace could only laugh. This was the best friend she

remembered; irrepressible, funny, dramatic. It hurt that things hadn't quite been the same between them since school started. Grace wished she knew why.

"Listen, I really have to go." To Grace's surprise, Jean shifted the armload of folders and gave her a hug. "I'll see you sometime later in the week, okay?"

"Okay."

Jean hurried off to the music room. When Grace was alone, she sat down slowly against the white concrete wall.

Maybe Jean really *had* simply forgotten to tell Grace about the auditions, those few times they had seen each other. It wasn't as though there had been much opportunity to talk.

She still felt uneasy about the whole thing, but not as much as before. Simon could have been right after all—maybe she was being paranoid.

She sighed and pulled her bag into her lap. The alert light on her phone blinked: Kana was still awake, Grace realized. It was another message about her student.

"He's also a little bit cool and handsome. But just a little bit!" read one line.

Grace wasn't sure she had ever seen Kana use that much punctuation before, or the word *cool*. She knew from the Internet that it was common in Japanese to describe a boy you liked as *cool* rather than *cute*. The sudden appearance of the word was a yellow flag for Grace.

Could Kana be developing a crush?

Grace wanted to ask outright. Real friends would be able to talk about these things, wouldn't they? Jean and Simon kept referring to Kana as her *pen pal*, but that word seemed so impersonal. Grace wanted to think of Kana as a real friend, but one who she didn't see in school every day.

She typed out a quick reply, hoping for more details.

Communicating through text was so much easier than talking in real life—it made her a little braver, made her words closer to her real feelings. She could be more familiar, to show her friend that she valued their exchanges.

And if Kana didn't think of her the same way, well, that would sting a little, but it wasn't as though Grace intended to ask her straight out how she felt about their friendship. She liked to imagine that if she were truly tested, Kana would come through.

Chapter 8

Hi, Megucchi...

I woke up! And now I'm thinking about what happened yesterday again. I must be losing my mind????

((((; ﾟДﾟ)))

At the beginning I thought I needed to tell him "Stop. I don't want to see your face anymore."

This boy, Otsuka-kun, is just so interesting. He writes words for songs, but in English, not Japanese. He can play the piano and wants to go to a music school. He wants to study abroad in Italy or Estonia. But looking at him, I definitely thought he was a punk!!

He's also a little bit cool and handsome. But just a little bit! (・_・)♥(-_-)

I'll try to sleep again. I wanted to tell someone. I can't say anything to Rumi about this, or she will never stop!!

♡ Kana

Re: COOL AND HANDSOME!!!!	10 月 25 日 (金) 4:46
From: メグッチ	詳細を表示

Wow!! That was not at all what I was expecting you to say!?

That's amazing that he can sing and write (and in more than one language!)! It's too bad all the famous music universities are super far away from where I am, because I'd love to meet him someday.

Do you like him? Hehe~~ (It's fine if you're not sure yet!)

~ Megucchi

The weekend had arrived at last. Time to get serious.

Kana woke up at eight in the morning, cooked her own breakfast, and sat down with her books and a pillow tucked under her legs. She set a timer on the table with a two-hour limit, and, opening one of the practice tests, patiently began to circle each multiple choice answer.

She had reached question 60 when her phone buzzed. Kana tried to ignore it, but she could see the activity light glowing on the display from where she sat.

Sighing, she paused the clock and got up to look. The message was from Rumi, and the entire screen was an animated template of a girl walking with shopping bags hanging from her arms. The caption read, *"I'm about to head to the station. Should I meet you there? What time?"*

Kana stared at the image for a moment, watching the cartoon character's arms swing back and forth as she walked. Meet her where? Had she made plans with Rumi today? Since her mother hadn't pressed the issue of extra tutoring on Sundays, Kana might well have mentioned she had no plans. She *had* intended to spend it doing mock tests, though. Maybe Rumi had gotten the wrong idea?

Sighing, Kana wrote a clipped reply. "Sorry, I completely forgot about it. How about next week?"

"Can't. Tournaments over the next four weekends. Last activity before third-years get the boot for exam time. Come on, you said you weren't busy!"

Rumi might have invited Yuko or Sae instead if she'd known Kana would cancel at the last moment. She hated inconveniencing people almost more than anything else. Glancing at the clock, Kana opened her closet.

Her friend waited by the statue of the loyal dog. Rumi stood out from the crowd, wearing the kind of maximum-impact outfit that was rare even in Harajuku these days—platform boots, tight black pants and a striped tank top under a wild blue jacket festooned with studs and loops. She looked like a rock star en route to a show; her makeup was dark and striking, and her short hair streaked through with colourful clip-in extensions. Seeing Kana approaching, Rumi waved and motioned her over. "Finally!"

"Sorry to keep you waiting. I wasn't dressed for going out." Her lounge pants and brown cardigan, while nice and warm on lazy mornings, weren't exactly Tokyo wear. She hadn't wasted much time getting ready, though; Kana's lacy ribbon-adorned black and red skirt was a favourite and a staple of her closet. Since the weather was cool, but not cold, she had chosen simple black over-the-knee socks, patent shoes with low heels, and kept her hairstyle simple by pulling it back into a low ponytail. Kana hadn't worn this combination before, but it looked like a cross between just-woke-up and going-to-a-dance-party, so she thought it appropriate. She had finished the outfit with a necklace and a red hair clip. Rumi ought to consider herself lucky that Kana had made it all the way here in under an hour and a half!

Rumi shrugged. "Don't mind, don't mind!"

Kana adjusted her hair and smoothed her skirt. "Well, I'm glad I made it, anyway. Where is it you want to go?"

"Maru-Kyu, of course!"

"Of course." Kana's smile never wavered.

"And maybe after that, somewhere for lunch, then Cat Street? Winter's coming up fast. I need another cool pair of boots."

In Rumi's case, it went without saying that *cool* meant *edgy*. As they set off, Kana checked her watch, noting it was almost eleven. She wondered how much it would take to convince her friend to let her go home before five.

Shopping with Rumi, however, was never a quick affair, and it was one Kana usually took pleasure in, so she soon forgot herself and began to enjoy the brisk autumn day. After browsing

Maru-Kyu and having a cheap lunch in a family restaurant, they walked up Cat Street, trying on clothes in tiny secondhand stores. They stopped to rest on a bench halfway between Shibuya and Harajuku, warming their fingers on bottles of milk tea. Finally, at the end of the walk, they made their way to a department store. Rumi, all business, picked out a dozen pairs of boots to try on.

Relieved to be resting her aching feet at last, Kana took her cell phone out of her purse and found two messages waiting. The first was from Megucchi, wishing her good night and good luck with her study. A pang of guilt struck Kana briefly. Then she saw the second message, from Daisuke.

"Do you have time today? I wrote something. I wanted you to check the English. I'm in Harajuku right now and the band's practising—you could come see, if you want to."

Kana's heart beat a little quicker when she saw that the message had come just moments before. Daisuke, in Harajuku right now? It would be easy to turn him down saying she wouldn't be in Tokyo today, and she was the slightest bit tempted, especially as the afternoon was waning. But...

"What's wrong?" Rumi had noticed her reaction and set aside the boots. "You got a message?"

"Er, yeah, it's my study partner, Otsuka-kun...he's nearby now, and wants my help with something in English."

Immediately suspicious, Rumi bounded over to read the message for herself. Kana held her phone out.

"Band practice? That's right, you said he was into music. That's great." Rumi looked impressed. "I'd like a boyfriend in a band. Maybe you should meet this guy?" She looked at Kana slyly. "Maybe *we* should meet this guy?"

"You'll come with me? But do you think we should go?" Kana clutched the phone tightly, hoping she didn't look as nervous as she felt.

"Let's do it," Rumi decided, putting the boots back on the shelf. "I wonder what kind of band he's in?"

Thirty minutes later, Rumi and Kana were in the "practice hall." It turned out to be a tiny apartment. "The place belongs to one of the university guys in the band," Daisuke explained as he ushered them in. "He lives in one room and we practice in the other. Sorry about the size of the place." It felt cramped, but clean. Kana could only nod as she looked around the tiny entryway.

"Nice to meet you! I'm Ohara Rumi!" Her friend introduced herself with a quick head bow.

"Otsuka Daisuke." The boy returned the gesture with a big grin. "O!"

"O!" Rumi echoed, grinning back. Kana hadn't noticed until that moment that their last names started with the same character and sound. Both of her friends seemed to be quite pleased with themselves.

"Come on in. The other guys are having practice, so I'm in the kitchen working on lyrics." Daisuke led them the few steps from the entryway to a tiny kitchenette, its counter thick with paper. The girls took one stool each while he stood, plucking a pencil from somewhere in the mess. "Sorry for the short notice, *Miss* Momokawa. I finished these lyrics today, so I wanted to make sure they were right before I gave them to the band."

"Right, of course." Kana read over the words in Daisuke's neat penmanship. She couldn't help but notice what nice handwriting he had.

The grammar sounded strange in places and the vocabulary a little unrefined for a romantic song, but overall it was well written. She realized it *was* a love song—even though the chords coming from the next room sounded like hard rock.

"I know this song." Rumi sounded surprised as well. "This is Banana Archery."

"Yeah. I'm working on making English lyrics for this one. It's going to sound amazing...I hope."

"Hey, good choice." Rumi gave him the *OK* sign. "I love Banana Archery."

"This is...not bad," Kana concluded, while her companions looked on. "Your wording is a little off here and there, but not so far off that I can't understand it. Even though I don't know the original song. But it seems to fit into a rhythm."

"I hate English, so I don't really understand," Rumi told him matter-of-factly. "But even if Kacchan says it's good, you'll still need a second opinion. She's not very musical."

"Rumi!" Kana hissed.

"What? I'm only trying to help. So, Otsuka-kun, won't you sing the song for us?"

"*Rumi!* I'm sorry, you don't have to do that."

Daisuke's easy grin charmed them both. "I'm no vocalist, Ohara-san."

"No need to be formal with me. You can call me Rumi; everybody does."

"Thanks. How about I tap out a melody for you, and you see if you can match it to the words?" He seated himself at the tiny electric keyboard crammed in beside the fridge. "As long as you don't complain about my making it up as I go along."

"Of course not!"

He cleared his throat and laid long, dark fingers on the keys. From the cheap keyboard came a song that Kana thought she knew from somewhere, a radio hit her classmates sang at karaoke. Daisuke had a low, husky voice. He carefully enunciated each word, playing and singing at half-speed. "*If you need to run, need to hide, just remember I'm behind, come to me, when you need a friend...*"

When he finished, Kana couldn't stop smiling.

"That was good," Rumi admitted, her musical ear undoubtedly putting his voice under severe scrutiny. "I'm not sure about the way the words go at the end, though."

"Well, there are fewer syllables when you translate it to English. I can rework it. Our vocalist would sing it better than I could, anyway."

Rumi shook her head. "I wouldn't say that at all. And you are about to become my new favourite karaoke partner. You know this band? Are you a fan?"

"Yeah, I love them!"

"Then it's settled. Karaoke tonight? How's eight o'clock for you?"

"Only if the lovely *Miss* Momokawa will be joining us?" Daisuke glanced at Kana, who still held the lyrics in her hand.

"What?" Kana felt she had missed something crucial in the last ten seconds of the conversation, but wasn't entirely sure what it was.

Rumi stifled a laugh. "You're in for karaoke tonight, right?"

"I...don't know," Kana said slowly. "I should get home...it's so late and I haven't gotten any work done today."

Frowning, her friend crossed her arms over her chest. Rumi was exceptionally good at looking incredulous, and she did so now. "Homework? Didn't you stay in yesterday for that?"

"Yes, I know *you* never would, but I had cram school yesterday, and my entrance exam to think about." She rolled her eyes.

"What is there to think about!? You only have to do one English exam to get in!"

Kana stood her ground. "And because we *only* need to do that, it's very high-level! I need to be studying every chance I get!"

Daisuke, seeing Kana's temper flare, stepped in. "No, she's right, we do need to be studying, not playing around. I should have thought about it. I need to go home and study, too."

"You can't be serious!" Rumi groaned, looking from one to the other. "Otsuka-kun already agreed! And I thought you were staying out all day!"

Frowning, Kana didn't want to respond. She couldn't help but be annoyed at how flippant her best friend's attitude was. Kana wasn't athletic or musical, but she always conceded to

Rumi when the volleyball club took first priority, or she was dragged to some live concert by a band she'd never heard of. "Rumi..."

She sighed. "Fine. I thought that we'd get a full day together today, that's all. Maybe you could sing English songs?"

Kana sighed, too. "Okay, okay. I'll go to karaoke for a *little* while. One hour, then I have to get home."

Seeing her victory, Rumi grabbed Kana's hands. "All right! That's perfect. Why don't we grab dinner and then head there? Otsuka-kun?"

"Since I think the lyrics passed inspection, I'll go over them with the band first, and then I'll catch up with you. See you at eight in front of KaraBan?"

"We'll be there!"

Kana allowed Rumi to drag her out the door before opening her mouth to protest more at being deprived of yet another study day, but Rumi spoke first and rapidly as soon as they were out of Daisuke's earshot. "*Kana!* That guy is really cool!"

"What?"

"Otsuka-kun! I can't believe he turned out to be the real thing! So I'm going to tell you now, go for it!"

"...What, exactly, am I going for?" They stopped in front of Laforet and stood among the rush of early-evening patrons. "He *is* pretty cool and a nice guy, but I haven't got time for—"

"Oh, come on," Rumi groused. "After exams, then. I know. But I think he likes you. And I love how he calls you *Miss*! Isn't that romantic? Well, for someone who likes English, I guess."

"I guess so." Kana wasn't so sure. She *did* find Daisuke attractive, and even if she couldn't appreciate his music like Rumi could, she liked the sound of his voice. He seemed like a genuinely nice guy, and smart, too. She supposed it hadn't been fair to judge his academic ability based on his clothes. And he *had* been gentlemanly in taking her out to make up for being late, even if he had admitted at the end of the evening that he could get a discount from Miki. To a girl better versed in romance, that might have been a turn-off, but Kana thought it was cute that he wasn't too cool to introduce her to his sister.

He also had beautiful handwriting. Maybe not the first thing most girls looked for, but to Kana, it was kind of a nice touch.

The problem was the timing. Even if she was interested, Kana hadn't planned to date anyone until after graduation. Another distraction would be the last thing she could afford right now.

She and Rumi kept talking about Daisuke over dinner, and changed the topic only when they were standing outside KaraBan, waiting for the boy himself to show up. Kana pulled out her phone to write a quick message.

"Hi, Megucchi. Tonight we will go to karaoke. I'm not good at it, but Rumi is a nice singer so I don't mind just to listen. Mister Otsuka will come too. It seems he is talented. I'm outnumbered!" She completed the text with a winking *kaomoji* emoticon.

"Is that Otsuka-kun?" Rumi asked with a grin.

"No, it's my friend in Canada." Kana had told Rumi about Megucchi, back when they had first started exchanging messages. She traded emails so frequently with her classmates that Rumi had never really asked who Kana was writing to. "You remember her, right?"

"Oh yeah, you told me before. She had a pretty name."

"Yeah, I call her Megucchi. Or Megumi," Kana replied. "It means *yasasugata,* and that's her name in English. *Grace.*"

"Cute!" Rumi leaned over to look at the screen. "How old is she? Do you have a picture?"

"She's the same age as us, now that we've both had our birthdays." Kana opened the newest picture Grace had sent her. "I think you'd like her, too, she's into Harajuku street fashion. She imports all the magazines."

"All of them? Even *Kira?*" *Kira* was a popular visual kei magazine that Rumi bought without fail every month.

"Well, maybe not *Kira.*" Kana conceded. "She seems more

into stuff like *Hopteen* and *SwEET*. She found me after I was in last month's issue."

"Oh, right." Rumi was still looking at Kana's screen when the reply popped up.

"*Sounds fun! But isn't it kind of strange to call him* Mister *Otsuka?*"

Kana tapped out a quick answer, conscious that Daisuke could appear at any moment. "Well, we only just met. Japanese people don't use given names unless they know each other well. And he calls me *Miss* Momokawa, so *Mister* Otsuka is natural, isn't it? His first name is Daisuke."

As if summoned, Daisuke himself turned the corner, his arms bare despite the cold, hands stuck in the pockets of his frayed jeans. Kana snapped her phone closed. "Hey! Hope you weren't here long."

"We just got here," Kana said as they followed him into the lobby. Rumi went ahead of them to make a reservation at the front desk, leaving Daisuke and Kana together by the elevator. Kana wasn't sure what to say to her study partner now that they were *hanging out,* so she pretended to be interested in a poster on the wall.

When Rumi came back, she held a basket with two microphones and a clipboard. "I got us the two-hour deal, since it came with all-you-can-drink soda."

"Two hours?" Kana repeated, dismayed. It was already eight-fifteen, and the trip back to Saitama would take an hour. She would be lucky to be home by midnight.

Rumi shrugged. "Sorry. It was cheaper that way. You can go early if you want, I'll stay alone or with Otsuka-kun for the other hour."

Kana sighed and followed her friend into the elevator. It was fine, she told herself, she could always look over her grammar book between songs. Sing in English and work on her pronunciation; yes, that would be fine. The homework, she supposed, would have to wait a little longer.

Chapter 9

Happy Halloween!	11 月 1 日 (日) 12:16
From: メグッチ	詳細を表示

Hi Kana-chan,

Sorry I didn't talk to you all day! It's Halloween and I've gone and turned out the lights at our house. We had SO MANY trick-or-treaters. A lot of kids were dressed up in costumes from Japanese anime shows (!!!). I did my best to look impressed every time I answered the door. ;)

Now that I have some time to write about it, I was actually really interested when you said a couple days ago that Mister Otsuka's sister looks like a *gyaru*.

(I know I know! The English word is "Gal." Either is okay, really, I think.)

Gyaru/Gal is probably the best-known Japanese street style online, even though I read that it's not as popular anymore. There's even a manga comic book coming out here that's all about high school gals, Kogals. I think the Japanese version is over, but the English one is still coming out very slowly. (I MAY have gone on and read ahead online.)

I don't know if the real *gyaru-kei* is really anything like the comics, but it looks so cool. The super-tall platform boots, or wearing the big white scrunchy socks with a school uniform. So awesome! It looks fun to totally go wild with your clothes. I read online that there are *gyaru* circles even now, even in the West, in places like Los Angeles. In the big cities. (But not HERE, of course.)

I'd love to give it a try, but I don't have the nerve!

~ Megucchi

Hi, Megucchi

Halloween sounds so fun! Cosplay is great isn't it? Here, nobody can do trick-or-treat, but last year I went to a parade with my friends from school. We dressed up and stayed out so late. This year of course, everybody is so busy.

Kogal is a little outdated these days. You still see girls who like it, but not so often. A lot of Kogal wear another Gal style after school. My class wore Kogal cosplay with the super long~est white socks for last year's school festival, though it didn't suit me! LOL!

Gal styles seemed not so popular anymore during my junior high school days. Recently though, this style came back more and more. The style changed a little bit. A lot more *kirakira* (sparkling) and there are more older Gals like Otsuka-san.

Something like, Hime-gal or Mode-gal, is more popular now. Or Onee-gal (older sister look). Before's Kogals mostly became some other type. Sometimes Mote-kei but they often come back to calling themselves Gals.

I'm surprised you know about Gal circles (*gyarusa*) and there are *gyarusa* all over the world! It's amazing. Rumi is part of a *gyarusa* for Rock Gals. All her friends in the circle are very cool, but just like you, I don't have the nerve! Ha ha!

You're going on a date tomorrow (today??), right? I'm interested in hearing about going on a date in Canada! Don't forget to tell me about it, when you get home. (≧∇≦)/

♡ Kana

Now that Grace's wardrobe had been cut apart, sewn up and generally overhauled—though she hadn't had the nerve to wear more than the most conservative of her new outfits to school—she began Phase Two of her makeover plan.

The strange tension between Grace and Jean over the past weeks had driven her to do it. Grace made a checklist, with Simon's begrudging help, of all her personality traits, good and bad. He found it difficult to participate, complaining that as her boyfriend he felt bad about criticizing her. Grateful but somewhat annoyed, Grace insisted that she would much rather hear the bad points from him than from Jean. At least Simon would pull a few punches.

Together they wrote everything down; every adjective Grace could think of to describe herself, and a few contributions Simon insisted on adding. ("A Lawful Good girl like you can't have a character sheet that's eighty percent negatives," he admonished.) When they finished the list, Grace broke out a pack of highlighters to outline the things she wanted to work on.

In yellow, she started with *self-critical*.

"Hey, not saying that one's easy, but you can get started by toning down the self-deprecation." Simon set two mugs down on the table and slid one across to her.

"Wow. Have you considered becoming a therapist?" Grace ran the highlighter over the words a second time. "But I'll give it a try." Then she wordlessly highlighted *forgets promises*.

After they had worked through the negatives (*Moody. Pessimistic. Silly. Goody-goody. Indecisive. Gutless. Spoilsport.* And the list went on), Grace indulged Simon by letting him talk about the positive aspects. She had to admit, it did make her feel a little better. She folded the paper into a tidy square before turning her attention to her date. He reclined in the plush chair, sipping hot chocolate from the tall glass mug.

Grace sighed into her own cream-and-cocoa-topped drink. "Now all that's left is to actually stick with this." *This*, meaning her image improvement project.

"Listen, I absolutely want to support you, you know that, right?"

"Mm-hmm?" Grace was still thinking about the list.

Simon laid down his coffee mug and leaned closer to the table, inserting himself in Grace's field of vision. "This wasn't quite what I had imagined for our five-month anniversary date, though."

"Oh." Grace's grip tensed around her mug. "Sorry. I was excited to talk it over with you someplace quiet."

"I know, but it's the first time we've made it out to town in months. I wanted you to have a little more fun, you know? Not be thinking about all this stuff going on with Jean and focusing on all these negative things."

"But it's for a positive reason," she protested. "It's good for both of us. Right?"

"You...well, I like you any which way, you know." He looked a bit embarrassed and sat back up. "But it's up to you in the end."

"I'm...tired of being a background character in my own life." Grace directed her gaze at the table.

A long stretch of silence came between them, as both parties seemed to pause and think about which direction the discussion should go next. Those moments happened much more frequently since they started dating, Grace noticed, so she usually tried extra hard to restart the conversation. Simon was a talker where she was usually a listener; as such, the tactic of asking him a leading question rarely failed. "So, played any good—"

"So, about the winter—"

They both stopped and laughed, and Simon put his hand on his chest. "I *could* tell you about what's going on in my WoW guild, but what I really wanted was to ask you about the winter formal."

"Are you asking me if I'm going, or are you asking me to

go?"

"Either. Both."

"I want to go," Grace replied, genuinely apologetic. "But I can't. Dad's booked my tickets for me to go up to Toronto over Christmas. You know what he's like."

Grace's father wasn't negligent *per se*, but he did have a tendency to do things without consulting others. He hadn't even asked her when school would be letting out. She was scheduled to leave for Toronto on the evening of her physics exam—a full week before the winter formal. She didn't have anything ready to *wear* to the dance, but since was the first time Grace had actually been asked to go, she was annoyed with her father for quashing her plans.

Disappointment darkened Simon's face. "Oh...well, I knew you wouldn't be here for Christmas, of course, but..."

"I know. I'm sorry," she said meekly. "I was...kind of looking forward to the dance, myself. Jean's been talking about it nonstop for months."

"She has? About the winter formal?"

"Yeah. Of course, she wants to go with Christian." Grace couldn't stop herself from letting her eyes roll. Jean went to all the school dances, rarely without a date. She'd stopped trying to convince Grace to join her years ago. "She doesn't expect him to ask her, but you know how she is. I'm sure she's going to come right out and ask him instead, soon enough."

"That's Jean for you. Falling for her leading man, but taking the lead."

Grace sighed. "Between practice for the musical and then making up everything she's missing at concert band, I hardly see her."

"Sounds busy."

"Very. Kana's busy too; her entrance exam is coming up in like, less than a month. I'm lucky if I hear from her once a day now. Except for grammar questions." She frowned at her hot chocolate, feeling uncharacteristically irritated. "Those keep coming. I'm trying not to text her so much, though. I don't want to intrude on her study time."

"You're so sweet." Simon grinned, making her think he was being sarcastic.

"What?"

"Only you would ever be concerned about talking to a friend because you don't want to intrude on *study time*."

When he said it, it did sound kind of ludicrous, she thought, so they laughed together, and then laughed at each other for finding it so funny. The awkwardness between them seemed to have abated a bit. "But seriously, she's busy, you know?"

"It's okay, it'll be over with, soon enough. In the meantime, with both your girlfriends so busy, it's not so bad to have you all to myself until Christmas."

Her heart swelled. Simon was just so *nice*.

~*~*~

Almost without even noticing, Kana had fallen into the same habits that had gotten her through her high school entrance exams three years before. A quick nap between study and breakfast, one on the Noda Line when she could get a seat, and another in math class, where her teacher marked her name down in the register without a word and allowed her to sleep. Neither math nor science would be part of the Nishidai entrance exam, so she put them on the back burner. Those subjects that Kana would not need for the exam, she would use to get a little extra rest in—or a little extra reading.

She felt confident about the test now, though she wouldn't have dared admit it to anyone else. As the weeks had passed, alarmingly fast, she began to feel even more confident, though she wouldn't allow her schedule to let up even one bit. Concessions of time to her friends and family were paid back in full from her sleep schedule instead—nights after going to karaoke or out for crêpes, she would stay up and study until dawn.

Cutting back on sleep had a negative impact, though, as Rumi, Daisuke and even Luke had pointed out that she looked unwell. The dark circles under Kana's eyes hadn't faded for weeks.

"Hey, are you all right?" Daisuke abruptly switched back to Japanese from the conversation they had been having in English.

Kana shook her head, trying to clear another long day's worth of cobwebs. "Sorry. I'm just tired."

He looked concerned. "If you're not feeling well, you should go home."

She wasn't sure she could. The evening rush had already started, and the trains were certain to be standing room only for the next few hours. "No, I'm fine. Let's go back to what we were doing."

She picked up the textbook and flipped to the spot where they had left off, but she could see that Daisuke remained unconvinced. "You're sure?"

"I'm sure." She wasn't, really; but she couldn't face an hour on her feet. Maybe after the study session she would go to an Internet cafe and relax in one of their chairs for a little while. She thought she remembered there being a cheap one up Koen Street, by the police box shaped like a face. "Why don't we go over this reading passage? I'll read it out loud in English, and you give me the translation at the end. Sound fair?"

"I don't mind reading it out if you want."

"No," she replied, a little more firmly than she meant to. "I could use the speaking practice. Okay, let's start. *The first day was uneventful. Moving in their classes, they got set up at the inn and settled in rooms of six. Each class visited a temple they had chosen beforehand, then they...*" she blinked and trailed off, losing her spot on the page. It was harder to focus than usual. "*Then, they returned to the inn for dinner. Many of the girls were... were already...*"

"Momokawa!"

She looked up, startled. Daisuke always spoke informally, but he had never called her by her family name without *some* sort of honorific. After all, it wasn't like they were...

"*Momokawa!* Hey! Hang on!"

Kana had tilted her head so far to follow his voice that she hadn't realized her body had gone along with it. She slid off the stool. She angled her legs down, but the moment she touched the floor, her knees buckled, knocking her off-balance. She crashed into the square beam that separated the bar tables and felt cool concrete against her back.

Cold, Kana thought, and that was the last she remembered.

When she came to, Kana thought she was at home in bed. The moon peeked through her curtains into the darkened room, as it always did, and the covers were pulled up to her chin. The only thing out of place was the veranda door, somehow having moved to the opposite wall. When she sat up to look closer, a wet cloth fell from her forehead onto her lap, and Kana realized she was not in her own futon.

In the dark, the room seemed unfamiliar, and a jolt of fear ran through her. How had she gotten here? Hadn't she been in Shibuya? She threw aside the covers and tried to get up out of the western-style bed, but the same wooziness she'd felt in the cafe overtook her again. She stumbled and dropped to the floor on all fours.

For a few seconds she was sure she was about to pass out.

Pausing to catch her breath and clear her head, Kana crawled over to the curtains and opened the door to the veranda, shivering in the cold night air. When she thought the strange feeling had mostly passed, she stood up again and inched her way forward to lean against the railing. The concrete was ice-cold on her bare feet.

She knew this place now—the balcony looked down ten

stories onto Hikarigaoka's main thoroughfare. She was at the Ohara house—but how? Kana felt a bit fuzzy on everything since meeting Daisuke after school. It was obviously very late in the evening. She put her hand in her skirt pocket, looking for her cell phone, but came up empty.

"Hello? Rumi?" she called, stepping back into the room. Her legs still felt like jelly.

A moment later there were footsteps in the hall, and Rumi opened the bedroom door. Kana was surprised to see Daisuke close behind. "Kacchan!"

"Rumi," she repeated, dazed. "What happened?"

"Sit," Daisuke instructed, and Kana immediately obeyed. "How do you feel?"

"A little dizzy."

"You passed out," he continued. "Do you remember?"

She didn't, but she thought she had some fading impression of it. Coffee. And then, cold. He'd looked afraid, back then. "A little. But how did I get here?"

Rumi sat down beside her on the bed, picked up the washcloth. "Otsuka-kun called me and my parents came. My mother wanted to take you to the hospital here in Tokyo, but we told her that we were tired, but if you didn't wake up soon we would take you back to Saitama. Otsuka-kun came with us and carried you to the car, then to the house."

"Thank you," she said, feeling a rush of gratitude mixed with shame.

"Don't worry about it," he replied, looking embarrassed.

"I called your mom, too," Rumi continued uncertainly. "But she said 'Oh, okay, let her rest.'"

"Of course," said Kana, frowning. "I fainted while *studying*, so I guess that means she doesn't mind."

Both of her friends looked uncomfortable, so Kana glanced away, clenching her skirt with both hands. Eventually Daisuke broke the uneasy silence. "Do you think you're okay?"

"Yes. I'm fine."

"Is that the truth this time?"

"Yes." Her cheeks burned with shame. "I'm just exhausted. I've had some trouble sleeping lately." She didn't dare tell him that she'd been staying up until two, and even later on weekends.

"Oh, that's a problem." Daisuke furrowed his brow. "Do you drink a lot of tea before bed?"

She did. It was unavoidable, on her schedule. "You're right. That might be it."

"Or maybe you're overworking yourself? We could always have fewer sessions. I'm doing better now, I think."

"Oh, no." How to tell him, without telling him, that she looked forward to their study sessions much more than sitting at home by herself? "I'm fine. Your exam is coming up soon too, so we can't slack off now." She covered a yawn, resolving to apply a bit of concealer the next time she had a tutoring session. Her school prohibited makeup, but Kana doubted anyone would notice a dab of cover-up and a little liner to brighten her eyes. "Sorry."

He yawned too, and seemed to be holding back a laugh. "But no, really, do you want to take a few days off?"

"No, no! I'll be fine, I promise." She felt better already. She must have been sleeping for hours, Kana realized.

"Then I'll see you on Wednesday. But leave your books at home." He winked playfully.

"What? No, of course not. We can't afford to lose time," she protested.

"Ah ah ah!" Daisuke grinned at her. "No protests. It'll be educational—I promise!"

"Okay." Kana wasn't quite certain what she was agreeing to, but she owed Daisuke now. "Sorry I made you worry. And you came all the way out here, too. It's a long trip back."

"It's fine, but I need to go really soon."

Rumi pointed at the clock on her bedside table. "Are you going to be okay? It's past eleven. How far is Kamata from here?"

"I'm not too sure. Where are we, Nerima? But I have to go, or I won't make it to school on time tomorrow." He wound a muffler around his neck. Daisuke never wore a coat, or even buttoned his uniform, for that matter.

"Nerima, yeah. We're around the corner from Hikarigaoka Station. Maybe it'll be about an hour or so from here?" Rumi backed up toward the door. "I'll let my mom know you're awake." She might have imagined it, but Kana thought her friend flashed her a thumbs-up as she shut the door.

"You didn't have to come all the way here with me," she told Daisuke, wishing she could muster up the courage to put her hand on his. "Thank you."

"Of course I did." He looked embarrassed, tugging on the ends of his muffler. "What kind of gentleman would abandon a girl who had fainted? Come on, *Miss* Momokawa. Aren't we... friends?"

Friends. She wondered about that pause. Why did it take him so long to choose which word to use?

"Then, you didn't have to stay so late," Kana whispered, aware that the room seemed much smaller than before with the two of them standing so close.

"Of course I did," Daisuke whispered back.

She shook her head, but secretly, butterflies filled her stomach.

~*~*~

Hours later, long after her mother had dropped Simon off and warmed up some leftovers for dinner, Grace lay on her bed with her hands folded over her stomach. A text from Simon had made her uneasy all over again.

"I had a great time tonight. I hope we can go out more often —I've missed you a lot lately. Love ya!"

Love ya.

Probably innocent, she knew. Probably wasn't meant to be so serious. Was that why he'd softened it with an exclamation point?

Yet it had been the first time either of them said the word *love*. *It's normal,* Grace told herself. *It's been five months, after all. You're behind the times.*

Still...

Did she love him? Grace certainly enjoyed being around Simon. She could tell him anything; she could expect him to be honest in return. She liked his jokes and his scent, and the feeling of being held, and even kissing him.

But did she *love* him...?

Grace wasn't quite sure.

~*~*~

When they next saw each other, Kana tried to forget about the disastrous end to their previous study session, but Daisuke wouldn't have it. "Today's lesson is a field trip," he insisted.

"Oh, did you want cake or something?" Kana teased. Daisuke was one of the few boys she knew that had as much of a sweet tooth as she did. She had never before met a cool-guy type that liked strawberry shortcake so much.

"Nope, something different." Without even sitting down, he began putting Kana's belongings back in her satchel. "I thought I told you to leave your books at home?"

"Just something to do while I waited for you," In truth, she had been too curious for anything to stick. The twenty minutes she had spent alone had ended up wasted. Wrapping up in her muffler, she followed Daisuke down the stairs and outside to the scramble crossing.

When they were out on the street, however, he led her to the station, rather than to the cake shop. He didn't glance at his phone or at a map, but confidently navigated their way across the city by subway, changing trains once, onto the driverless train that crossed Tokyo Bay. They disembarked near a shopping centre in Odaiba.

This was a part of the city Kana did not visit often; in truth, she had only come to Odaiba once when she was in junior high school, in the summertime, to the swimming pool. From the station she spotted the boat-shaped museum that stood beside the pool—the man-made island was small enough that you could see most of the way across it.

He led her into the shopping centre and up several sets of escalators. Kana was starting to feel more confused than curious now; what on earth could Daisuke have possibly wanted to bring her all the way to Odaiba to shop for? She was about to start questioning him, when the bottom of the escalator came into view, framed by a huge red *torii* gate, its shape resembling a π symbol.

"What on earth...?" *Torii*, the gates found at Shinto shrines, were most definitely out of place on escalators in malls. At the top of the escalator, Daisuke led her out the exit doors onto the roof.

Kana turned in a slow circle. She had seen plenty of odd things in Tokyo, even *torii* on top of buildings before, but this was a new one. A Shinto shrine sat squarely between the two entrances, one to the parking lot, the other to the shops. Looming in the background she saw Odaiba's huge television station, its enormous spherical observatory rising up over the shrine.

"Unbelievable," was all she could manage, inspecting the statues placed on either side of the offering box.

"This is the only shrine on the island." Daisuke told her matter-of-factly. "Ridiculously busy on New Year's, let me tell you. Its specialty is supposed to be business, but I always come up and ask for whatever I need, because the placement is amazingly cool."

"Right." Indeed, even the tiny shrines she had spotted among the graffiti-streaked buildings in Shibuya couldn't compare to this.

"And then there's the view." He turned and gestured out at the sun setting over Tokyo.

Kana had caught a glimpse as they had come out onto the roof, but the shrine had immediately captivated her attention. Now she looked more carefully and recognized the familiar skyline from this new angle. Tokyo Tower, across the water, was clear as day. Its spotlights were already lit for the evening. Water buses and cruise boats were scattered around the bay, colourful beacons made warmer by the setting sun.

As Kana looked at the scenery, Daisuke came up beside her. He was a little shorter than she—standing beside him like this made her self-conscious of her height, but he didn't seem to notice or care. "Nice spot, don't you think? As good a view as the TV observatory, but it's free." He paused and gestured at the statue. "Okay, the regular floors of the TV station are free too, but they can't compete with Oise-sama here."

"You always look for the cheapest way out."

"That's not true. We could have saved sixty yen by walking across the bridge."

Kana couldn't help but laugh. This boy was frugal to the point of rivalling her mother. She thought it was a good trait, though; even if he came off as a little stingy, he seemed like a responsible guy. He never failed to treat her when he convinced her to take a break from their work and go to the cake shop, and he paid her for her tutoring, every Thursday without fail, with money neatly tucked in a plain brown envelope. Even when he showed up late for a session, the missed time was always accounted for in the payment.

When it came right down to it, Kana thought, she enjoyed tutoring him, and even more so, she enjoyed his company. She supposed, though, that he truly did consider their relationship a business agreement. Aside from the subtle flirting that had gone on literally since the moment they met (did he do this with *every* girl he met?), he was always a gentleman, and put their work first. For Kana, who felt like the serious one among her friends, finding someone else who was even more focused (and one who wore his hair longish and wild and his *gakuran* wide open, at that!) was a shock.

As they stood on the roof with the skyline on one side and the shrine on the other, she couldn't help but think that whether he meant to or not, he had created quite the romantic atmosphere. And to be truthful, she didn't mind all that much.

"This place isn't too far from school, so sometimes I like to come up here and listen to music," he said seriously, breaking into Kana's train of thought. "I like heights. I've pretty much got all the best views in Tokyo on a mental list." He tapped the side of his head. "Tokyo Tower is great, but it's always crowded. The Ferris wheels are over way too quickly. But here's a good tip; the government building is the best spot on the west side of the city. The other high-rises in Shinjuku are okay, but it's hard to explain a lowly high school student hanging out on the top floor of the swankiest hotels in the city. I love them, but I avoid them unless I really need the inspiration."

"And this?"

"Maybe not the best view of the city, compared to the other places in Tokyo Bay," he told her, "but it's got the shrine, right?" With that, he went over to it, and took a five-yen coin out of the pocket of his school uniform.

Kana did the same. Standing side by side, they tossed the coins into the offering box, clapped their hands twice and closed their eyes, silently making requests. *I had a lucky break last time I made a wish,* Kana thought to herself, remembering Meiji Shrine in Harajuku. This time, though, she didn't pray for success in school or entrance exams, good friendships or health as she had before; for the first time ever, Momokawa Kana made a selfish wish and hoped that the boy beside her felt the same.

~*~*~

Simon's message stayed on Grace's mind for days after their date. Her first instinct was to ask Jean for a girl talk session—after all, Grace and Simon would never have gotten together if Jean hadn't convinced her to accept that first date. Jean's preoccupation with everything else going on, though, made Grace hesitant to request even a sliver of her time.

She thought she might try Kana instead, but every time Grace started to write her friend a message she stopped, ashamed. She hated spoiling their fun talk about fashion and culture with a silly thing like this. Besides, Kana had more than enough to deal with—her entrance exam was a few days away.

With her list of exactly three friends to lean on, that didn't leave Grace with many options.

She couldn't ask her mother. Camilla would make a big deal of it, because she adored Simon. Her mother was sure to say Grace was only nervous because Simon happened to be her first boyfriend.

No one else at school was close enough to be a *friend*. Erin who sat in front of Grace in English had always been nice, and Nancy, the captain of the girls' basketball team, sometimes asked her to partner in the math class they shared, but she couldn't imagine asking either one for love advice. She certainly couldn't ask any of her teachers—Grace wasn't sure some of them even knew her name.

That was about it for the people she interacted with on a daily basis. For the most part, she always kept to herself, unless someone else noticed her first. She wanted to stay out of the reach of school bullies who preyed on people like her, girls who preferred books to gossip and computers to sports.

Sometimes Grace wondered if the reason she had gotten through her school years unscathed so far was *truly* because she hung out with Jean, who was well-liked, or whether she, Grace, was too boring for anyone to notice.

And so in the end, she turned to Jean, as she always did. With exams on, most of the musical rehearsals had been put on hold. There wasn't going to be a better time than this to talk it over.

"'Boy troubles'? *What* 'boy troubles'?" Jean asked incredulously when Grace broached the subject. They sat in the local Tims, a much more casual affair than the place Simon had taken Grace on their date. Instead of foamed milk in glass mugs, they drank double-doubles out of brown paper cups.

Cheeks burning, Grace stared down at the table. "Well, last weekend Simon and I went out for our five-month anniversary. And at the end of the date he...he said he loved me."

"Okay," Jean said, waiting for her to continue.

"That's it. He said...that."

Her friend looked as though she couldn't believe her ears. "Yes. And what did *you* say?"

Grace honestly couldn't remember. "Well, it was a text message, I can't remember if I actually replied."

Jean wordlessly put her head in her hands.

"I didn't know what to do!" Grace tried to defend herself. "He never said that before! I was caught off-guard, you know?"

"That's so you," Jean replied with a tiny smirk. "Ah, young love."

Grace winced. Her friend was hardly a serial dater, but did have a half-dozen boyfriends under her belt so far. Grace wanted to reply back with a snarky comment of her own, but she couldn't think of a single thing to say.

"I bet you put that boy through hell this week," Jean continued. "Poor Simon!"

"That's, ah, that's exactly why I wanted to talk it out." Grace stared at the table, trying to control her expression. "I'm not sure exactly...how I feel about him."

Now Jean looked confused. "What? But I thought you guys were doing great."

"We were! I mean, we *are*. But I thought that love was supposed to be different from this. We have fun out on dates and stuff, and I love him, but I don't know if I *love* him."

"Well, okay. Maybe he wants to move a little more quickly than you. How are you guys doing with intimacy?"

"With what!?" Grace jumped, burning her fingers with coffee. "We're not...I mean..."

"Okay, okay, I get you. Right, you haven't even said *I love you* yet." She shook her head. "Come on, he's your very first boyfriend. These things take time."

Grace wasn't sure which of the *things* her friend was referring to.

"It's okay if you don't know if you're in love yet," she continued. "It's hard to switch someone from being a best friend into being a boyfriend, right? You have to change your whole way of looking at the person. That's fine. You guys can just keep having fun, and the right time for you to say it back will come along. You'll *know*."

"You really think so?" Grace asked dubiously. "But what if it doesn't? What if I'm not into him like that? What if I can't...feel like that about guys?"

"Of course you can!" Jean covered an incredulous laugh. "You're not suddenly into girls or anything, right?"

"No."

"Then you'll eventually feel more confident and it'll come out naturally. Don't stress over it! And if it doesn't work out with Simon, there are other fish in the sea. You guys have been close for a long time, after all. Maybe you can't un-friend-zone him, in your head."

"I don't think that's it." Grace couldn't explain how she felt, because she wasn't sure what exactly it was she was feeling, but that didn't sound quite right.

"Give it *time*." Jean smiled, the picture of confidence.

Maybe her friend was right, Grace thought. After all, Jean had so much more experience than she did at these things. And Jean had been the one to break up with every boyfriend she ever had, so she *knew* how to tell if you were really in love with someone. Right?

Chapter 10

EVEN MORE COOL AND HANDSOME!!!!

From: Kana-chan	Sun, Nov 29, 9:35 PM

Hi, Megucchi

I've got a question. Please don't answer if it's embarrassing! When you said you had your boyfriend, I was surprised. You seem like a shy girl. How do you manage, when you are so busy?

I never had a boyfriend before. Rumi has lots of course. When you have to go to cram school and live far away, it's difficult. So some girls wait and never date in high school.

I thought it would be easy. I didn't even like any boy! (´△\`) How did this happen to me???

♡ Kana

Re: EVEN MORE COOL AND HANDSOME!!!!	11 月 30 日 (月) 10:45
From: メグッチ	詳細を表示

It's funny that topic came up...I don't know if I'm the right person to ask about love advice, though. (Simon is my first boyfriend, too.) I didn't think I'd ever *have* a boyfriend and didn't care too much. It happened very suddenly. We were always hanging out doing friend stuff, and he liked me.

It's harder than I expected. I feel like he wants more from our relationship (!! still a weird word to say for me) than I am giving him. I feel bad, honestly.

But that doesn't mean you shouldn't take a chance on Otsuka-kun! After all, he's in the same situation with university, right? So I'm sure he'll understand when you're too busy to see each other, especially now. And when the tests and stuff are all over, you can celebrate together!

~ Megucchi

"This is it," Kana told Daisuke with a nervous smile. "I'm ready for Nishidai."

"You can do it!" he replied. "You'll do better than me, anyway."

"Oh, don't say that," she pleaded. Daisuke had worked so hard these past months to prepare for his exam that she couldn't bear the thought of him failing.

Kana could tell he wasn't as confident about how things were going, but there wasn't anything more she could do for him. They were long past the point where Daisuke could keep up with her level, as well, so they hadn't had a proper tutoring session since. Instead, Daisuke had taken to meeting her at Takadanobaba Station after school, an act that was extremely exhilarating and embarrassing for Kana at the same time. What if someone *saw* her, talking so casually with a boy from another school? A boy with blonde streaks in his hair, at that?

She felt just a *little* bit pleased with herself.

"You should...probably go," he said. Did she detect the slightest hint of disappointment? "But we should go out somewhere and celebrate, you know, after the test. Maybe on Sunday?"

"Are you kidding!? You should get *your* exam over with, first!"

"Oh. Yeah! I guess that's true." He rapped his knuckles on the side of his head. "For some reason I felt like today was the real deadline, but that's only for *you*. I still have a week to go. But maybe after that...?"

"Where would we go?" Kana asked.

"Anywhere but my sister's place," he told her, deadpan.

Kana laughed, but her stomach was in knots. Could this be a request for a date? After all, with the end of the entrance exams, she and Daisuke had no real reason to see each other again as teacher and student. What were they supposed to be now? Friends? Or something else?

"How about we go for a walk around town? Ginza? I'm sure

they have some sort of illumination going for the holidays. I can look it up."

"That would be fun," she agreed.

They stared at each other for a moment, neither quite sure what to say. "I...I'd better go," Kana reluctantly said, clutching her satchel. "I have a lot of reviewing to do tonight."

"Of course," said Daisuke. "I'll take the Yamanote today too. Let me get my pass."

She waited for him, and the two of them climbed the stairs and stood on the clockwise platform. Kana looked sideways at her companion, still unsure. "So...where are *you* going? Kamata is the other way."

"Oh, I thought I'd go to...Omiya Station. That's a great name for a station."

She laughed. "Is that so? And what's there, at Omiya Station?"

"*Taiyaki*," he said with a serious expression. The fish-shaped custard-filled cakes were one of his favourite sweets, as Kana well knew. "I'm going there to buy *puchi-taiyaki*."

If he thought he was being smooth, he was wrong—there were any number of shops between here and Kamata that sold *taiyaki*. Still, Kana, let it slide. She didn't mind the company.

At Omiya Station, Daisuke accompanied her to the turnstiles, where they finally parted. As he had promised, there was actually a *taiyaki* shop, though Kana didn't believe for a second that it was the real reason he had come all this way. "So I'll see you on Friday?"

"Definitely," she promised. He waved goodbye and turned back.

She rode the Noda Line back home, still a little dazed. So Daisuke *did* want to keep seeing her after her exam? What would they *do*, now that they weren't studying? The thought intimidated Kana. She couldn't afford to stay hung up on it any more tonight, though. Tomorrow was the big day—and she had dozens of pages of notes to review before she could close her books.

The evening did not go as smoothly as Kana planned, however. Her father had come home, on a rare long weekend off, and dinner turned out to be a longer affair than usual with all four of them home. She had to wait for her parents to bathe before she had access to the bathroom. Warm and sleepy from her bath, Kana hit the books with a vengeance. All those English grammatical quirks would have to be fresh in her mind for her to use them correctly.

She didn't even notice when her parents, and then Shingo, went to bed. She continued on, methodically moving her notes and books from one pile to the next as she finished them. Her stomach growled, but the hunger would keep her alert.

At three in the morning she laid her pencils aside, finally ready for a break. Kana knew it was long past time to finish, but there was so little left to review now. She didn't want to just *pass*—she had to *ace* this test. Everything she needed was right here in the final two chapters of her study booklet.

Setting a ten-minute timer, she lay flat on the floor, her legs warmed by the heater under the table. *Another hour of review should do it,* Kana told herself. One more hour and she could sleep. She felt so very tired.

~*~*~

The Barbers lived in a new subdivision, at the top of an enormous hill with St. Clare at its base and cul-de-sacs of upper-middle-class homes dotting the slope. The place was huge—Christian's parents clearly had money. When they pulled into the driveway, Simon's father whistled. "Wow. Nice."

Simon nodded appreciatively. "Looks like it. Dad, can you come back for us at ten?"

"Ten?" his father questioned, glancing at them in the rearview mirror. Maybe, Grace thought, ten was early for a high school party. She wanted to have an escape route ready, though, just in case she wasn't having a good time.

"Grace might turn into a pumpkin, you know?" Simon covered for her with a casual grin.

"Okay. I'll be here, then." Mr. Summers chuckled.

Simon helped her out of the car and waved his father off before they walked up to the front step together. Grace slid her phone into her skirt pocket and put what she hoped was a friendly, casual smile on her face. In reality, she felt sick, almost trembling from nervousness.

It had taken her over a week to decide on an outfit to wear tonight. Grace viewed it almost as a debut: the old her would retire permanently, and the new, confident, capable Grace would impress not only Jean, but all of her friends as well. Grace didn't have much interest in spending time with the drama club, but she felt obliged to prove to Jean that she could co-exist with these newcomers in her life. She thought her clothing selection was a little bolder than she felt like being, but maybe it would help make the sense of confidence stick.

The outfit, she had mostly made herself out of old clothes, and the rest pieced together with items from the craft store. What had been a plain black skirt was now festooned with cloth belts, and she wore black over-the-knee stockings and ankle boots borrowed from her mother's closet. A pink-and-black plaid shirt had been cut down and transformed into a corset that peeked out from under her sleeveless white blouse. The arms of the shirt had become arm warmers tied shut with black ribbons. She used the last few scraps of the shirt to put together a short tie decorated with silver pins. The outfit had been inspired by a picture she saw in *Kira* magazine, and not the kind of thing she would have ever imagined herself wearing even a year ago. As she looked in the mirror, though, she felt thrilled with what she saw—cool and different, without being too far from the clothes one might see in the shops at the mall. No one would ever have to know that in Harajuku she would have paid ten times the cost for something like this.

Christian himself answered the door and let them in, introducing himself to them both, though Grace wanted to remind him that they had several classes together. She decided it was better not to say anything.

He heaped their coats in a pile on a bench and showed Grace and Simon to the living room. Club music was pumping through the house—Grace winced at the volume. Loud bass made her stomach feel funny.

She found Jean in the kitchen, chatting animatedly with a few girls Grace recognized from the pizza night. When Jean saw the pair enter, she waved them over, but her eyes travelled up and down Grace's clothes uneasily. "Grace, Simon, you made it."

"Yeah, the place was a bit hard to find," Simon laughed.

"How was the dress rehearsal? You guys all ready for opening night?" Grace tried to stand in a relaxed pose, cradling her arms in front of her. The cold air coming through the open kitchen window cut through her light blouse.

"Oh, it went great," Jean said happily. "By the way, this is Chloe and Darcy, they're both members of the crew. I think you met Grace already, and this here is Simon."

"Nice to meet you."

"Nice to meet you, too." Chloe seemed to be sizing Simon up, her eyes lingering. Grace couldn't help but notice, but didn't say anything.

"Thanks for the invite," Simon offered, politely directing his gaze at the other girls. "I heard the orchestra practising for the musical earlier today and they sound fantastic. Can't wait to see the show. Can we get the tickets at the door?"

"You can buy your tickets at the door, or from any drama club member, namely me." Jean winked. "I've been holding a pair for you guys."

"Hey, great! Thanks." Simon started to help himself to the soda on the table, prompting one of the two girls Jean had been chatting with (Grace didn't remember who was who) to hurry over and find him a cup.

"Let me get you a beer," she offered, working a can out of the box on the table.

Grace's temper flared, but she tried to stamp it out. *New Grace does not get angry needlessly. New Grace is not possessive and has no reason to be jealous. New Grace does not tell her boyfriend what to do.* Not that she needed to; Simon was extra serious about his diet when he was in running training mode. He wouldn't even have a glass of wine at her mom's Thanksgiving dinner.

Grace didn't drink at all. Fortunately, Chloe (or Darcy, whichever one she was) didn't seem interested in offering *her* anything. Simon declined with that devil-may-care grin and poured himself a cola before leaving Grace with Jean.

"Your outfit is so...interesting." Jean commented, leaning close to Grace's ear. Grace detected a hint of alcohol on her breath.

Not quite certain if that was supposed to be a compliment or a reprieve, Grace smiled wanly. "Thanks." She decided not to push the issue further. "So Christian has a pretty nice place, eh?"

"Yeah, I guess so," Jean replied. She seemed distracted by something.

"Have you, uh, talked to him?"

Now Jean gave her a funny look. "What? I talk to him like, every day."

"No, I mean..." Grace lowered her voice, conscious of the two strangers in the kitchen. "You know, weren't you going to ask him something...?"

Jean inhaled sharply. "Oh, that. We shouldn't talk about that here."

"Okay." She looked sideways, where Chloe-or-Darcy mixed a drink. Both girls had been Grade Ten or possibly even younger; did Christian's parents actually let their son share free access to the liquor cabinet? Grace frowned, but Jean didn't look concerned in the least. New Grace accepted other people's decisions even if she didn't agree with them, she told herself. Instead of saying anything, she helped herself to a root beer.

Simon hadn't said the word *love* again since that night. Her silence had made their next meeting a little awkward, but in the time since their date, her worry had slowly faded. Now she felt happy to be around him again, and—dare she admit it?—excited to be going with him to this house party.

He ambled to her side with his hands in his pockets when Grace came out of the kitchen, looking largely disinterested. She poked him lightly on the arm. "What are you thinking about?"

"Wondering how long it will take for someone to wreck something in this house." He nodded in the direction of a coffee table with a lace doily, topped by a delicate-looking statue of an angel. "Christian's parents have way too much nice stuff left out. I'm guessing *they* didn't know there was about to be a party here."

"Half an hour," Grace replied.

"I'll take that bet, give it fifteen minutes. Some of these guys are loaded."

The party had obviously been in full swing long before they arrived. The Barbers' living room was filled to capacity, plus a few extra. Grace had gone through thirteen years of education with some of these people, but she found she couldn't remember many of their names. Instead, she hung back as far from the pounding music as she could get, watching the groups mill about, hips and heads nodding along to the music.

Simon's best friend Kirk eventually showed up with his girlfriend. To Grace's dismay, the boys wandered off together. She looked around, but Jean was nowhere to be seen, aside from the occasional glimpse of her long, dark hair sailing along in the crowd.

This wasn't what Grace had expected at all. When she'd been invited to this party, she'd imagined Jean would take some time out of the socializing to chat with her or at least introduce her to people she didn't know. So far, aside from the few words they exchanged in the kitchen, Jean had been ignoring her.

Worse, Simon had been constantly followed by the two girls from earlier, and now they stood nearby in a group, watching, as he played darts with Kirk Small and a few other guys from the basketball team. Grace knew they'd immediately marked her a non-threat. Perhaps she should have done something like slip her arm into Simon's, but when it came down to it, she wasn't sure she wanted "clingy" to be among her improved personality traits. So she stood back, waited, and edged over to the window to try and catch a snatch or two of their conversation. To her surprise, though, they weren't talking about Simon at all.

"...Have a chance," the dark-haired one was saying as she nursed a cup of something orange. This was the girl Jean had pointed to first, so probably Chloe.

"Then somebody should tell her," Darcy replied, picking at her manicured nails. "Christian's a nice guy, but if the other girls find out, she'll be hearing about it for*ever*."

"Do you think she pretends it's for real? When they're doing their scenes?" A tall, blond cast member giggled, puckering her lips. Grace's heart seemed to stop, but she stayed where she was, listening carefully.

"Better hope not. If she does, she's in for a surprise." The last girl, who Grace recognized from her own homeroom class, laughed harshly. "I didn't think there was *anybody* in school who didn't know Christian was taken. I mean, come on, he's really cute. Not *my* type, but cute."

"I hope tall, slim and amazing at darts isn't your type either," Chloe said enviously, her eyes devouring Simon as his third shot landed squarely on the bullseye. One of the guys offered him a high-five. "*That* is the type of guy I'd like to be seen with at the dance."

"Didn't he come in with some girl, though?" Darcy pointed out. "You were there."

Chloe scoffed. "Some nobody Grade Eleven, I think. I didn't know her at all. Jean's friend, right?"

"I think so. Jean's nice, though. I feel bad for her. Don't you think we should say something?"

"*I* think it'd be funnier to watch and see what happens."

Heart in her throat, Grace drew away from the group and backed up until felt the bookshelf press against her back. This was, she was almost certain, a disaster waiting to happen. Jean's crush was the talk of the party. There might even be the possibility that Grace herself had started the rumour by bringing it up in front of those two gossips.

Deciding to come back for Simon later, Grace hurried to the kitchen, but Jean was no longer there. Nor was she in the living room or the porch, so Grace climbed the stairs to the second floor, wondering if there were partygoers up there, too. She glanced inside a bedroom, and listened for movement in the bathroom. Grace had edged open the door to the empty bathroom when she heard a noise coming from further down the hall.

Someone *was* upstairs. Could that be Jean? There was a light on in the last room, so Grace decided to head in that direction. "Hello?" she called as she approached.

When Grace came to the open door, though, what she saw made her freeze up and pray no one had heard her greeting. That was definitely Jean in the room, with her back to the door, and she had her arms wrapped around someone tall and wiry, with shaggy blond hair.

Christian was aware of her presence in the entrance before Grace could back away unseen. "Who's there?"

Her mouth fell open in panic. Grace turned and fled without offering either accusation or apology.

Chapter 11

It's TOMORROW! Oh My Goodness	
From: Kana-chan	Fri, Dec 5, 11:35 AM

Hi, Megucchi

Sorry I've been mailing you less. I can't believe tomorrow is my exam. I'm crazy! Lately, Otsuka-kun has been asking for a lot of time to study too. I should tell him 'no' more often. But, I want him to do well. It's difficult for me to balance. Maybe I should give up sleep altogether? Hahaha.

But it will be over in two days...I can't wait. I'm ready!!

♡ Kana

Re: It's TOMORROW! Oh My Goodness	12月6日 (土) 10:05
From: メグッチ	詳細を表示

Off-topic. I know you aren't there cause you're at your exam right now, but the absolute worst thing ever is happening. I just walked in on a make out session between Jean and the guy she likes and now she might kill me?

I wish the earth would just swallow me up right now. I am MORTIFIED. Ughhhhhhhhhhhhhhhhhhhhhhhhhhhh T_____T helllllllp.

It was seven o'clock on a Saturday morning that, to everyone else in Japan, was no more remarkable than the Saturday before it. Momokawa Kana was curled up in a knot under her *kotatsu*, the pages of her book crumpled under one arm. *It's so warm here, it's perfect,* she thought she might have thought, though she might have been dreaming, too. Her phone made an annoying noise across the room, but it was sounding far-off somewhere in the dream, and Kana couldn't bring herself to care.

~*~*~

Grace hid in the bathroom. It hadn't been such a great idea, now that she had been able to reassess the situation, but she hadn't been thinking clearly at the time.

If the window had been a tiny bit bigger, she might have been climbing down that tree in the front yard by now. Instead, she huddled in the dark as footsteps hurried down the hallway, followed moments later by another with a more leisurely gait. When she felt certain she was alone on the second floor, Grace reached out and locked the bathroom door.

Her shoes and coat—and her boyfriend—were all downstairs. Scrabbling for her phone, she texted Simon. "Upstairs locked in the bathroom. Come help ASAP."

Next, she sent a message to Kana, more to pass the time until help arrived than anything else. Her head spun and she thought she might throw up. What was taking him so long?

At long last, though, the phone chimed. *Thank goodness.* Grace let out a breath she hadn't realized she'd been holding.

She flipped it open with trembling hands, but the text she read was from Jean, not Simon. Her stomach bottomed out. The screen seemed to be pulsing along with her pounding heart as it lit up the dark room.

"Tell me where you are."

Grace, who hated confrontation so much, became very still.

Jean was looking for her after all. Ready to ignore the message and pretend she hadn't seen it, she almost dropped the phone when it suddenly began to ring in her hand. Taking a deep breath, she tried to answer as casually as possible. "Hello?"

"Hey, it's me. Where are you right now?" Jean's tone was completely unreadable.

"I'm...in the bathroom." Grace's hand hovered over the knob. This was her last chance to make a run for it, if she wanted to try, but she knew she ought to stay and face it. So what if she had embarrassed Jean in front of the guy she liked? It wasn't as though Grace had done it on purpose. And really, it had been for Jean's own good. Grace had been looking around upstairs for the sole purpose of *finding* Jean, after all.

Grace's sense of injustice fought off her flight instinct right up until someone knocked on the bathroom door. She edged it open a crack.

Jean opened the door the rest of the way and hit the light switch with her palm, her face tight and controlled. Grace was certain that had to be a bad sign, so she assumed the most confident stance she could muster.

"That was incredibly embarrassing," her friend said, at length.

Probably not half as much for you as it was for me, Grace thought. "I know. Sorry. It was an accident. I'm sorry."

"Besides humiliating me, you're not supposed to go snooping around people's houses at a party, okay?" Jean's voice rose in pitch. The smell of alcohol hung in the air. "What if Christian had thought you were stealing something? What kind of people would he think I hang around with?"

"Well, I was looking for you. I had something important to talk about."

"For God's sake. Look, I'm sorry I wasn't by your side *twenty-four-seven*. I thought you could survive on your own."

Grace felt as though she had been punched in the gut. "No. It was about something else."

"I think you need to learn to take care of yourself instead of always looking for someone to hold your hand," Jean retorted shrilly. "I thought you said you were trying to change. What happened to that?"

Grace's temper, usually so well-controlled, shot through the roof. The anger bubbled up from a place she had never noticed before, a deep pit in her stomach that had been stewing for three months. "This *is* about that again! This is all about me making you look bad in front of your new friends, and you having to pretend I'm something different than I am! I'm not trying to change myself so that you can feel better about hanging out with me, if that's what you think!"

"That...is so shallow, I cannot believe you would accuse me of it." Jean's voice was razor-sharp.

Grace's was deadly serious. "Yeah? Well, I can't believe you would fly off the handle at me for wanting to talk to you in private, so that's two for two, isn't it?"

Jean, who always looked one hundred percent composed on the stage, in the classroom and at the debating podium, appeared to be having a great amount of trouble calming down. "I don't even know how to respond to that."

Grace, on the other hand, felt as though some dam inside of her had broken, and every thought she had entertained over the course of the evening made itself known in a voice with about as much emotion as a block of ice. "So let's see, first you go out of your way to ignore me at this party where I hardly know anyone, a party where there are Grade Nines drinking hard booze and hitting on other peoples' boyfriends, and you completely look the other way. You're on the Students Against Drunk Driving committee, Jean! What's wrong with you!? Not only are you ignoring all this, but you're half in the bag. Don't bother denying it."

Jean looked stunned. Grace continued without waiting for a comeback. "I don't even know why you asked me to come here. I'm thinking you invited me because you felt guilty for brushing me off all the time, but when you saw me you had second thoughts. You were hoping I'd stay away if you looked busy enough. And then when I hear people gossiping about you in front of our entire graduating class, I suppose I should look the other way instead of going to find you, right?"

"That certainly is what I would have expected from you," Jean shot back. Her knuckles were white on the counter.

"Well, I hope you expected me to leave early too," Grace snapped, pushing past her to yank the bathroom door open. "By the way, I was looking for you because I thought you needed to know that Christian Barber has a girlfriend. And apparently *everybody* knows."

"Don't you even *dare*—"

But she shut the door before Jean could react, and Grace heard Jean swearing on the other side before she could fumble for the doorknob. Grace could barely stop herself from breaking into a run as she flew down the stairs. She pushed past the crowd, took Simon by the wrist, and led him to the porch. She snatched their jackets from the pile, shovelling strangers' coats onto the floor.

"Did something happen?" He gestured with his plastic cup, apparently not sure whether to drink it or set it down.

"No. Yes." Grace said shortly, but wouldn't elaborate until they had stepped out and shut the door. Simon followed her down the driveway, even though he had no idea where she was going. She wasn't so sure, herself. Her cell phone buzzed angrily in her pocket. Grace powered it down without reading the message.

"Jean...?"

"Is incredibly angry at me." Grace felt herself deflate a little. She was still angry, but the adrenaline that had been fuelling her bravado had started to wane. "I saw her and Christian making out upstairs. She got mad that I walked in on them, but I was only looking for her to tell her about Christian's girlfriend —I can't believe he has a *girlfriend* and *nobody* told her—and I totally went off on her. I guess I should feel kind of bad about it, but I don't, not really. I'm just...mad."

"Girlfriend? Yikes. I had no idea. Are you sure?"

"I'm sure. Apparently nobody wants to be the one to tell her about it."

Simon shrugged into his coat, holding the edge of the red cup between his teeth. "Well, good for you for going right to her, then. You don't have to assume you're the one in the wrong, you know. Jean has been acting a bit selfish lately."

"Yeah, but...that's how she is, you know?"

"Is that supposed to be an excuse?"

Grace fell silent, clutching her own coat in her hands. The sharp air raised goosebumps where the arm warmers didn't reach. "Maybe you're right."

Simon slung his arm around her shoulders as they walked down the hill. His touch felt warm and safe, and she leaned against him gratefully, falling into step. "It's going to be okay. She'll be thankful, later, that somebody looked out for her."

"I hope so."

They both fell silent, the snowfall muffling the sounds of a neighbourhood winding down for the night. Simon walked Grace all the way home, even though he lived in the opposite direction. She was freezing in her skirt and tights, but she refused to let on, allowing the snow to collect in her folded arms and on top of her head. When she unlocked the front door and stepped inside the house, her coat, tights and hair were soaking wet.

Simon stopped on the front step, kissed her goodbye, and looked her in the eyes. Grace felt a jolt of apprehension about what might come next, after the long walk in silence, but if he had planned to bring up the *love* issue again that night, he knew that window had closed. "Maybe instead of running to apologize to her, you should let Jean do some thinking on her own, first."

Grace nodded slowly, grateful the conversation was still

about Jean, and not about *them*. "I hate it when she's mad at me. I only tried to help her."

"I guess it's time she found out what it's like to have *you* mad at *her*, instead of the other way around."

~*~*~

Kana awoke feeling more refreshed than she had in a long time. The balcony curtains were open, and the sun streamed through the window, falling right across her face until she had no choice but to open her eyes. Though she felt rested, having slept so solidly, it took her a few moments to become fully conscious, and when she did so a sinking feeling instantly replaced her good mood.

When she rolled onto her back, she discovered she was lying...where? Under the *kotatsu*, Kana thought, as her leg connected with one of the table legs. The pile rug had also been pleasantly warmed by the sun. She wore her blue tartan skirt and blouse, but her vest was balled up under the small of her back. Why was she *under* the table? Hadn't she been sitting at it, going over her adjectives? And now the sun had gone and come up...

What *time* was it?

She scrambled up and across the room, tripping over a pile of books. The clock on the dresser read 7:36.

"No way," Kana breathed, staring at the numbers, hoping they were somehow wrong. The exam, over an hour away by train, would start at nine sharp. Pulling on her cardigan and blazer over the rumpled blouse, she swept her wallet, cell phone, test voucher and the rest of the contents of the table into her satchel and half-ran, half-fell down the narrow wooden stairs. In the entryway she jammed on her loafers and slammed the door shut without calling out a goodbye.

The Momokawa family lived close to Owada Station, but every minute counted, so Kana clutched her bag to her chest and ran as hard as she could, her blazer flapping behind her. She ducked under the closing gates at the level crossing, ignoring the sensors blaring a warning. Swiping her commuter card, she pounded upstairs and threw herself onto the westbound train.

The doors shut a millisecond later, and Kana slumped into a seat, out of breath. She still wasn't entirely awake, and her stomach rumbled. Breakfast had probably been waiting on the table all morning, she thought, with her mother out on the early shift.

The time on her watch read 7:42. Kana ran her fingers through her hair and took out her hand mirror, but found she was much too jumpy to do anything else but stare out the window and periodically check her watch. On the platform waiting for her transfer, she couldn't bring herself to look at her notes or dictionary. Her hands were shaking, and the hunger had already turned to nausea. Her stomach roiled.

The wait for the train felt longer than it ever had before.

For thirty minutes between Omiya and Shinjuku Station Kana clung to her bag and stared off into space. The events of the night before seemed like a fever dream. What happened? Her mother wanted to bring dinner to her room, but Father insisted they eat together at the table. Waiting for the bath. The room feeling so warm. Transitive verbs, intransitive verbs. A ten-minute timer on the clock for her break.

What happened to the timer? Kana looked at her phone, but she couldn't tell whether it had gone off or not. After passing out at the cafe and waking up hours later in Rumi's apartment, Kana wasn't confident that the timer not sounding was a problem with the phone, but more of a problem with the phone's user being too soundly asleep. She hadn't even considered setting her alarm clock, just in case.

The twenty-five minutes it took to get to the campus seemed like the longest in her life. When the train doors finally opened, she charged out with the voucher clutched in her fist.

The university was located close to the station, but when

Kana reached the big gates, they were shut, and though she rattled the bars where the two gates met, they refused to give. She leaned against them, her chest heaving, until one of the men standing on the other side reluctantly came over. By the time he drew close enough to touch her, she clung to the bars, too distraught to look remorseful. "I'm here for the entrance exam."

He reached for her test voucher, already shaking his head. "Sorry. I can't admit anyone who comes late."

"But..." She glanced at the analog clock above their heads. The time read 9:05. "But what about..."

"I'm sorry, Miss, but it's the rule." He handed her back the paper through the bars. "It's unfair to the other students to have people coming and going after the test starts."

"I..." Kana couldn't believe this was happening. All that study, all those late nights all for nothing? "But, what should I do? I had the recommendation. I was supposed to test *now*."

"The general admission period is coming up in February. You can reapply for that instead. It'll be all right," he told her gently, seeing her face start to crumple. "These things happen... students get sick on test day or don't do well enough in the preadmission period, and they still manage to get in on the second wave. I'm sorry."

"But you don't understand! I worked so hard...I truly did my best for this."

"I'm very, very sorry. I'm sure your chance will come."

The second wave would not, she knew, be as easy as he made it sound. Students who tested without early admission not only had a much smaller chance of getting in, but also had to write exams in the other subjects, not just English. She had devoted herself to English study all this time, thinking that would be all she needed.

What was worse, Kana knew she had prepared perfectly. She had made sure that it would be so. Now, being told that all her work had been for nothing, she wanted to burst into tears. She sunk to her knees, shaking, still clenching the bars. The man saw this, and, coming around through the security door, he led her away from the gates and back toward the train station, where he sat her down on a bench. There, he patted her shoulder awkwardly, glancing around as though to make sure no one else saw his attempt at consolation. "Now there, it's not the end of the world, I promise. You're from Koen Academy, am I right?"

She nodded wordlessly.

"Then you know you have a good chance. I wish I could let you in, but you'll have to come back next time. Okay? Are you all right?"

"Y-yes." Though she said this, in truth Kana couldn't bear breaking down in front of this man, this stranger, in front of the school she had hoped she would be part of. She struggled to her feet and bowed several times. "Thank you anyway."

"Don't worry about it." With a last glance back at her, he returned to the smaller door. She could see that he was relieved she had chosen to go.

Kana put the voucher back in her satchel and started to walk, keeping her eyes angled straight ahead. Like this, she walked away from Nishi Gaidai University and past the station, looking for a more private place. She didn't know the area well at all, so she wandered aimlessly for a long time before coming to a tiny park with a sparse patch of grass, a concrete slide and two low-hanging swings. She sat down on one and hung her head, letting the tears of frustration out at last. All of it for nothing! What had she given up all those weekends for? What had her parents been paying for cram school for? She couldn't even imagine her mother's reaction when she would come home to say, "I missed it. I was five minutes too late."

Kana buried her face in her hands and sobbed.

~*~*~

Grace stayed in bed until noon. Her mother's early-morning errands once again worked to her advantage, though she thought had anyone been there, she might have fibbed. Grace had never, ever faked being sick before, not even when she was in Grade Three and learned from classmates how to spike the temperature of a thermometer by placing it on a light bulb. She couldn't bring herself to get out of bed, though she felt ravenously hungry. Perhaps this was another kind of sickness, Grace thought to herself. Not a flu or a cold, but a sickness of the heart.

She dreaded the idea of facing Jean. Somehow, Grace thought, she didn't think she had the resolve to follow through with what she had said to Simon as they walked home from the party. Jean had a stronger personality, and if Jean was mad she would stay mad until *she* made a decision to forgive whoever had wronged her.

Grace wouldn't have been surprised *not* to hear anything from Jean, but she wasn't taking chances. She'd pitched her phone into the laundry basket without turning it back on, where it stayed all day. Opening night? Hah! Forget *that*. Watching Jean on stage would soften her heart, and Grace *wanted* to be mad. Old Grace would have slunk back for an apology, even though she knew it wasn't her fault. New Grace, however, wasn't going to take crap from anyone. *You must not give in!* she told herself.

Her true self, Grace thought, must be somewhere between these two, else she would not be lying in bed half-paralyzed all day.

She was forced to roll out after hearing her mother's car pull into the driveway in the early evening. Then Grace showered, ate a snack, sat down at her computer. At seven-thirty, as the curtain would be coming up at the Arts & Culture Centre, Grace opened her inbox to see seven unread messages from Kana.

"I can't believe it. I overslept and missed my exam. What am I going to do!?"

"I'm so stupid. I am the most stupid person in the world."

"I don't know what to do. I went to the park but should I go home?"

"I can't stop crying. Sorry. I guess you are sleeping. Rumi is sleeping too. I don't have anybody."

"My mother will kill me. Maybe I deserve it. I don't want to go home."

"I wish you were here."

"I give up."

Grace's heart sank. Something just as awful had happened to Kana last night, she realized. No, worse! Entrance exams, Grace knew, were the be-all and end-all for getting into university in Japan. It didn't matter how high your grades were if you couldn't pass your chosen school's test.

None of the messages were all that new, she noticed with horror. The final one had a timestamp of 10:30 PM the previous night. Right after the party. Right after she had messaged Kana from the dark bathroom. Kana had replied to Grace, needing help, and Grace had unknowingly shut off her phone.

Grace hurriedly typed out a response. "Hey, are you there now? I'm so sorry I missed your messages."

While she waited for a reply, she started to search for information about Japanese entrance examinations. The ritual turned out to be even bigger than Grace expected—the rules were different between public and private universities, and she didn't know anything about this place where Kana had applied. Did it mean Kana would have to wait another year? Or would she have to give up on going to the university she wanted? Could she *never* get in?

Grace's heart broke for her friend. She remembered the first time Kana had thanked her for answering a question about English, talking about how much she wanted to be accepted into that school. It was so unfair, Grace thought as she put her head down on her desk. Everything had been ruined so quickly. To think that she had been looking forward to this weekend for so long! Now she and Jean were fighting, and Kana was devastated over her exam, and there was literally nothing Grace could do for either of them. She felt completely helpless, so much that she could barely stop herself from bursting into tears.

Even though Kana hadn't responded yet, Grace wrote another reply. "I am so, so sorry to hear about what happened. What's going to happen next? Is there anything I can do to help?"

She sent the message, but when she laid the phone back down, she knew that from half the world away there was *nothing* she could do.

Grace waited for hours. She took another nap, but slept fitfully, waking up imagining the chime of her cell phone going off. Yet whenever she reached for it, she found she had only been dreaming. Even though morning had come and gone in Japan, and Kana should have been around, Grace hadn't heard back at all. She stared at her inbox, willing a reply to appear.

The only text she received was from Jean. Catty and vitriolic, looking at it made Grace's stomach turn. She put the phone away, trying to focus on salvaging what remained of the weekend.

Grace had her own final exam of the semester on Monday, but she couldn't bring herself to even open a textbook. Her suitcase for Toronto sat on the floor, half-packed. From her computer, Grace sent Kana another message, and then another, but they went unanswered. She began to imagine awful scenarios: Kana's parents had smashed her phone and forbidden her to ever talk to anyone again. Or Kana's mistake had caused her to be thrown out of her school, and she felt so ashamed she couldn't bear to reply. Or the worst; Kana, despairing over the failure, had simply given up.

"Exam hell," was what they called it. One of the leading

causes of suicide in Japan.

No, not for Kana, Grace was sure. Kana acted so differently from the stereotype of the Japanese schoolgirl that Grace had read about in books.

But pressure can get to anyone, she thought. Even the strongest people were susceptible. When it came right down to it, Grace hadn't *known* Kana in a situation like this before, and had no idea how she would react.

She spent all evening at the computer, reading English-language news websites, but found no reports of terrible things happening to teenage girls who had been rejected from their entrance examinations. She did a search for Kana's full name on the Internet, but turned up no results. Grace supposed the ability to read and write Japanese characters would be incredibly handy at a time like this.

Going back through old emails, she searched other keywords Kana mentioned in their messages. *Saitama. Koen Academy. English Club, Shibuya Hoshibacks, Tobu Noda, Nishi Gaidai University. Visual kei, Rumi, Jingu Bridge. Daisuke Otsuka.*

She hadn't expected to get any hits, but to her surprise, the last one turned up a result. She found an English-language blog belonging to a Daisuke Otsuka. Maybe it was a common name, Grace thought, but the blog was real and up to date. Written in a mixture of Japanese and English, it was mostly text with a few pictures. On the sidebar were lots of song titles.

She wasn't sure what to do. Could *this* Daisuke be *that* Daisuke? If wasn't the right guy, Grace would come off looking stupid, but he happened to be her singular link to Kana right now. What if something terrible *had* happened, and she never found out, because Kana's parents didn't know or care that there was a girl ten thousand kilometres away who worried herself sick about their daughter?

And what were the odds, Grace wondered? There must have been hundreds, if not thousands, of Daisuke Otsukas (or Otsuka Daisukes, if you wrote in Japanese order) living in Japan, and more than a few of them had websites and spoke a little English. But how many could there be living in Tokyo, who wrote music and posted photos of ice cream parfaits on their blogs? She copied Daisuke's address into her email client.

Hi there,
My name is Grace Ryan and I live in Newfoundland, Canada. I found your blog while searching for a Mister Daisuke Otsuka who lives in Tokyo and is a high school student.
If you happen to know a girl named Kana Momokawa and know how to get in touch with her, I'd appreciate it if you'd contact me right away.
If I've got the wrong person, I'm sorry! Thank you anyway.

~ Grace (aka Megumi/Megucchi)

Then Grace got into bed, trying to settle enough to sleep, despite the thoughts racing through her head. As she lay awake for hours, she ruminated about all the awful things that had happened. Jean. The embarrassing scene at the party. The stupid musical. Kana. Simon, who could be a ticking time bomb for a meltdown. Her math exam tomorrow. Her parents and their ridiculous infighting. Another Christmas of them each sniping at her over the other. Everything was falling apart.

Her imagination spun out of control, cooking up nightmare scenarios for what might come next. When Grace did drift off, the exhaustion winning out, she tossed and turned all night.

By morning, the reply came.

Hi there Miss Megumi. I have heard many things about you. I know Miss Momokawa of course. But, I have not talked in awhile. She doesn't answer her phone since 2 days. Mails, too. Sorry, I don't have any other way to contact Miss Momokawa.
Are you OK?
DAISUKE

Grace lay back in bed, the wind knocked out of her, rereading the message several times. She felt as though she'd been punched in the stomach. *I'm blowing this out of proportion,* she told herself. *There is no way things could be as bad as that. Hold it right there, Grace, you said you would stop being so fatalistic!*

Yet Daisuke said Kana had stopped responding. Wasn't it natural to assume the worst *could* have happened?

What could she do? From here, from so far away, literally nothing. She had been effectively cut off. Without knowing Japanese, she would never be able to get in touch with Kana's parents over the phone. Her only other link seemed to know nothing.

Grace wasn't sure she could sit idly by and wait for the nightmare to end.

She always hesitated, she realized. She would never do anything meaningful if she kept being this way. It was all fine and good to talk about improving herself, but when it came down to it, Grace was always rendered helpless by her own cowardice. She had proven to herself time and again that this was the way her personality worked.

I thought you said you were trying to change.

Jean, she remembered, had said that. At the time, Grace had been angrier than she had ever been in her life, but now when she thought back to it, Grace felt beset with regret. Jean had been right and she was wrong, as usual. Grace was one hundred percent predictable all the time, and knowing it galled her. She couldn't even manage to keep her own life under control, much less offer assistance to a friend across the ocean.

Then she had an inkling of an idea so outrageous, Grace had to close her eyes again to think it out. It was crazy, and like nothing she'd ever done before—but what was so bad about that? *You're only young and stupid once,* she told herself. *I can't let this go without doing anything at all. Maybe Kana's okay, but maybe I can help. She's my friend!*

Grace leapt out of bed, dumped out the contents of her suitcase and began to hatch a plan.

Chapter 12

Kana-chan,

Hi, it's me again. Hopefully, if you read any of the messages I've sent over the last few days, it'll be this one.

Well, I've been through a whirlwind, and maybe so have you. Never in a million years would I have expected you to ghost me…so I'm positive that's not what's happened. But there aren't that many other possibilities for why you've dropped off the face of the earth.

I hope it's something like, you got grounded, and you won't be able to contact me until you're back at school, so I'm trying to be patient, but I don't *know* and every single minute that goes by while I wait, seems like a thousand years.

I really really REALLY need you to contact me before Friday. I have this crazy plan. I'm sorry if it's going too far. If I hear from you by Friday, it won't be too late to call it off. I'll be watching my phone all the time.

Kana-chan. Your friendship means so much to me, I have to make sure you're okay. Please reply as soon as you possibly can.

~ Megucchi

She wasn't a nervous flyer, but when Grace left her mother behind and rode the escalator up to airport security at St. John's International, the butterflies filling her stomach doubled in size. Ducking into a corner as far from the loudspeakers as she could get, Grace took out her phone and summoned a familiar number. "Dad, hi, it's me."

"Hi, honey," her father replied, his voice tinny. "Shouldn't you be at the airport already? I was thinking about what to do for dinner."

She took a deep breath. "Actually Dad, I'm really sorry, but I have to take a make-up exam. I'm not going to be able to get in tonight."

"What? But I was expecting you. You didn't say anything about this. Isn't the flight leaving soon?"

"I know. Sorry. I have to re-take my English final before I can come."

"Well, when will you come?" He sounded disappointed. Grace felt her resolve waver a fraction. "It's way too late for me to change your ticket. They're not going to give me any money back at this point."

"I know." She'd known from looking on the airline's website. Without the money, he wouldn't even bother calling the airline to cancel, she hoped. If he did, this would all fall apart. "We took care of it over the phone. We already got me a new ticket."

"You did?" Her father sounded surprised. "That's great."

"It's not your fault I have to stay here later, after all," Grace said.

"Okay. When are you getting in?"

"The twenty-fifth." Grace held her breath. "The flight gets in late afternoon."

It was as late a date as she dared try for. The ticket she had *actually* bought would have to be changed, at some point, to match her story.

"Christmas!? That's too late!" he complained. "That

woman! Couldn't she have gotten something earlier? It's *my* turn to have you for Christmas!"

"Sorry," Grace apologized, feeling bad for letting her mother take the blame. "It's not really Mom's fault. I can't write the exam until the last day of the semester." She had to bank on her father's absolute ignorance of the Newfoundland public school system.

"I would have paid for the more expensive flight if it would get you there earlier. Let me change it, at least to the twenty-fourth."

"Dad, no. Let's go with this, okay? It's not like we have big plans for either day. I don't mind spending Christmas Eve..." she paused, "...here."

There was a long, long pause where Grace felt sure her carefully-laid plan was about to fall apart. If her father's annoyance tipped over the edge to the point where he called his ex-wife, Grace would be sunk. She knew her dad, though, and knew he valued her feelings at least a smidgen more than winning the custody battle. After what seemed like an eternity, he exhaled loudly into her ear. "Fine. In the end, it's up to you who you want to be with, after all. It won't be so bad for your mom to have you on Christmas Eve, and me to have you for Christmas Day and New Year's."

"Exactly," said Grace. "And I get to have you both!"

She sensed his ire start to fade with those words. "Okay, honey, I understand. But I'll come get you at the airport, at least, so that we can still make dinner reservations. I'll book something late in the evening."

"That's fine. You can email me." Luckily for Grace, her father never contacted her by phone, and she knew it.

"And I *don't* want to hear any more complaints from your mother about 'her time' at Easter. She owes me."

"Okay, Dad." Grace breathed a sigh of relief. Christmas was saved. "I'll let you know if anything changes. You never know, right?"

"Right," her father agreed.

She felt thankful that no announcements had intruded on their conversation, but there was sure to be a boarding call soon, so once they'd said goodbye Grace hastily disconnected the call. Parent #2, successfully deceived. The rush of adrenaline mostly left her system as she slung her backpack onto her back, but the lingering anxiety remained.

Was this how criminals felt during a heist? How did they manage to pull it off!?

Grace had hardly slept in the four days since she'd come up with this ridiculous plan. She was too jittery to rest, eat, or do much of anything else.

The one thing she *could* do efficiently was orchestrate the logistics. As she'd walked home from the ATM outlet in the plaza the previous evening, and every other evening since the message from Daisuke came, Grace thought to herself that she was being quite brave, if not completely stupid. She'd managed to withdraw a huge chunk of her savings in that short time. Christmas money, wages from two summers working as a day camp counsellor, the allowance she'd been saving for her new wardrobe, and most of the handsome sum from her father that Camilla called "Dad's Negligent Parenting Money." All together, the total she withdrew was enough to pay a semester's tuition. Grace felt bad, but told herself she would only spend what she needed. She'd replace it, even if she had to work in fast food for the entirety of her university life.

In fact, with the money in her pocket, she started to feel giddily confident about the whole affair, about the contents of her suitcase and the extra printed itinerary hidden at the bottom of her backpack.

She was going to Japan.

Grace imagined the reaction Jean would have. No one would *ever* believe Grace Ryan could have done such a thing on a whim.

She'd kissed Simon goodbye after school the previous day, certain deceit must be showing on her face. "I don't know if I can call you from Dad's house, but I'll miss you. So don't worry if you don't hear from me, OK?"

"We can text, then?" He looked at her, confused.

"Oh, of course. I thought you might worry if you didn't hear from me right away. Loads to do when I get there."

This was a clever ploy, Grace thought, in that it was a hint without being a hint. What would he think of those words, a few days from now? Would he remember her saying "don't worry," and read between the lines, when she dropped out of contact? She hoped so. She couldn't stand the thought of him worrying about her. Things hadn't been perfect between them, but he remained her dearest friend. *At this point, he might even be my only friend,* she thought uneasily.

Her mother hadn't missed a beat, or an opportunity to make Grace's father look bad, as she waved their daughter off. "Make sure your dad actually spends time with you, this time. I don't want you sitting in his apartment alone all day, okay?"

"Okay."

"Have a good Christmas. And call me on Christmas Eve—I'll miss you."

"I will," Grace had promised, hoping it was one she'd be able to keep.

It wasn't too late to give up on this crazy plan, but with the money spent and the call to her father made, she had started to feel like turning back *wasn't* an option anymore. Over the course of the last few days, she had imagined all the different scenarios that might occur if her mother realized she hadn't shown up in Toronto. Grace hated being so deceitful—it was the first time she'd told such a huge lie. And what if her parents did get in touch for once? They always depended on Grace to carry their messages—including the rebukes for each other—but what if this time happened to be the exception to the rule? Could the police do anything, given her age? In all the cop shows, the parents of older runaways were turned away. In her sleepy little town, though, if the police got involved, it was sure to be a big deal. It might even be on NTV.

It could have been thrilling to do something so crazy, Grace thought, if she wasn't so worried about Kana at the same time. She felt kind of like she was a heroine in a spy movie as she applied makeup in the airplane lavatory, wishing she had brought something like a wig or coloured contacts.

When they touched down a few hours later in Toronto, Grace had time to waste, so she found spots that seemed out of sight. She called her mother from the bathroom. In a store, she bought a pair of reading glasses to use as a disguise. A flimsy ruse, Grace concluded, but she felt a little more "in character."

She checked in at a kiosk for her flight to Tokyo. She'd had to pick up her suitcase from the Arrivals area and casually take it herself to the International check-in counter, but when she handed them her passport, nothing seemed amiss. She was eighteen, Grace had to remind herself. There was nothing *illegal* about it. And when the gate agent handed back her passport and boarding pass, without even asking to see the prepaid credit card Grace had used to book the flight, the smile she gave the agent was one of complete confidence.

She had been constantly checking her cell phone; if Kana sent Grace a message, she wouldn't have to go through what she was sure would be the longest thirteen hours of her life. But by the time the flight boarded, no calls or messages had come, not from Simon, Kana, or her parents.

She was a little bit lonely, in truth, now that everything had caught up to her, and Grace almost wished someone *would* call —even Jean would be welcome. Instead she walked onto the plane, sat in her seat, waited for the announcements to end and even allowed the aircraft to push and begin its taxi before taking out her phone one last time, just in case. Then, she powered it down.

Chapter 13

Please say you're OK	12 月 12 日 (金) 18:44
From: メグッチ	詳細を表示

Kana-chan,

I'm afraid I'm doing something beyond stupid here. I just need to know you're okay.

Please answer.

~ Megucchi

The trip wasn't short, but she missed most of it. After half a movie and a snack, Grace fell deeply asleep, and there she stayed until a landing announcement broke into her dream. She quickly opened the window shade to look out as the flight attendants repeated the words in French and Japanese.

All she could see through the window was water. If they were over Japan, Grace thought, where *was* it? Though it felt to her like early morning, the sun hung low over the ocean. They dipped lower and lower, and when she felt the knot in her stomach grow unbearable, expecting the aircraft to fall into the sea, land appeared at last under the plane. The ocean was superseded by trees as far as the eye could see.

She stared out, fascinated. This couldn't possibly be Tokyo. It was all forest!

Lush vegetation interrupted by hotels and flat swaths of land; rice paddies, she would later realize. Almost without warning, and so much softer than the landings she'd experienced on smaller planes back home, the wheels hit the tarmac. They rolled across it, toward Narita International Airport.

Grace's heart turned over in her chest. No going back now.

Next was the hardest part, she told herself as she waited to disembark. She had read up on customs policies, and knew she could be refused entry into Japan if she didn't have a return date to write on the visa, so she had bought a round-trip ticket for the cheapest upcoming date—New Year's Day. Grace wrote down the address of a hotel listed in *Friendly Planet.*

At the immigration desk, the official wordlessly marked her passport with a sticker and waved her through. She handed the customs card to another official, at the exit.

Finally Grace emerged into an arrivals hall bustling with visitors and returnees, where she felt her heart rate slow down at last. *I made it!*

The next task would be finding somewhere to stay, but Grace had done her research. She beelined for a hotel desk, and sure enough, spotted signage in English. "Hi, I'd like to book a hotel for a few nights. I want to stay in Saitama. Anywhere in Saitama City would be all right."

"I'm sorry Miss, but we don't list any hotels in Saitama. It's quite far from the airport. We have plenty of hotels within Kanagawa, Tokyo and Chiba, if you want to book with us."

"Chiba?"

The concierge's bright expression didn't falter for an instant. Grace supposed she got clueless tourists all the time. "That's where we are right now. Narita Airport is located in Chiba Prefecture."

Grace blinked. "I thought it was in Tokyo."

"No, miss. The closest past of Tokyo is over an hour away by bus or train. Chiba is southeast of Tokyo and Saitama is northwest. For Saitama, I would recommend choosing a hotel and telephoning them directly. Or, if you want, you can stay in a hotel in the metropolitan area and travel north from there."

"Okay...what hotels are in the metropolitan area?"

The woman opened her binder, flipping through pages with colour photographs. "That depends on what district you want to stay in. We can book a hotel for you in Asakusa, Shinjuku, Ueno, Ginza, Odaiba...any district within the 23 special wards."

"What about Shibuya?"

The concierge checked on her computer, still smiling. She hadn't stopped smiling for even a second. "Normally, yes, but there isn't anything available in our register for Shibuya tonight. We have a select number of hotels, you know. If you go there on your own, you might be able to find a business hotel or a hostel, but..."

"Maybe I'd better not."

"Perhaps you'd like Odaiba? It's very easy to get around there if it's your first time. English-friendly, and lots of sights to see."

Grace wasn't sure where exactly that would be in relation to Saitama, but it was the name of a place Kana had mentioned in one of her final messages, so it seemed like as good a place to start as any. "Okay, Odaiba. Can you book me there? Maybe until Wednesday?"

"Certainly." Beaming, the concierge brought out a sheaf of papers. "Will you be needing a hotel with an airport shuttle bus?"

"Yes, please."

Fifteen minutes later, Grace boarded the cleanest, most immaculately cared-for bus she had ever seen, complete with lace doilies on the headrests, on her way to the city of Tokyo.

She turned on the light over her seat and opened *Friendly Planet*, though it didn't do much to calm her nerves. The book didn't cover the Saitama area either, and when she thought about it, even if she went there, how was she ever going to find Kana? Grace knew Kana's last name, but little else. She didn't even know the name of her high school.

No, Grace decided, she needed a new plan altogether. Now that she had come this far, though, she wasn't entirely sure what that plan was supposed to be.

~*~*~

"Sorry I missed our sessions without letting you know. I'm coming to Tokyo today. Can you meet me at the usual place at 4:30?"

Daisuke was already waiting, uncharacteristically early for him, at the bench by the window when Kana appeared. She was a little winded from her sprint across the intersection.

"Hey." Daisuke smiled warmly, a gesture that usually made her heart skip, but today Kana could only return it with a weak nod. "What's up? I haven't heard from you in days. Thought you forgot about me!"

Kana sat, her posture noticeably slumped. She tried to straighten up before he noticed. "I'm sorry about that...my mom has been making me stay in all week thanks to some... stuff."

"Eh? What's going on? You had me worried, you know. I thought I'd hear from you right after your entrance exam."

"My exam." She looked away. "I...missed it. I was late to the testing site, and I wasn't able to write it."

Daisuke's jaw dropped. Kana, early for everything and who constantly berated him for tardiness, had turned up late for her examination? It was unthinkable. "Are you serious? What did you do?"

"What was I supposed to do? I left without doing anything. My parents are furious. My mother...all that cram school money wasted, she said. My father was just disappointed. And I deserved it. Such a stupid mistake." She delivered the story mechanically, as though it had happened to someone else. Kana didn't want to show him how upset she felt inside.

Daisuke's voice softened. "Hey now, it was an accident. I think? How did it happen?"

Admitting she had fallen asleep while cramming would be akin to admitting she hadn't been taking care of herself; hadn't gotten the rest she'd promised after that embarrassing fainting spell. "I didn't set my alarm correctly. I woke up, but a few minutes too late to get there in time."

He sucked in a breath. "That's awful. But wouldn't your parents have been watching out for you on the big day? Where were they?"

"Mom worked the early shift. She's a nurse. My father was asleep."

"Asleep!?"

Kana set her jaw. "He works away from home, so he's never around. He knew I had my test, but of course he wasn't up at seven in the morning on a weekend."

"Yeah, but if they weren't there to help, they don't have to get on your case. Isn't it partially their fault for not being there? Don't they know you're already beating yourself up over it?"

Daisuke's sense of righteous indignation was in full play now as he came to her defence, but Kana didn't want it. She continued to avoid his gaze, focusing on her hands on the table. "Maybe that's the difference between us. My parents have every right to be mad after everything they've done to make sure I get into a good school."

"But you still *could* get into one. The world doesn't end with Nishidai. I'm sure you could get into *any* university you tested for, and there's still time to try for others."

"That's not the point!" she exploded. "I let everybody down. All this time I put off my commitments to my friends, my regular schoolwork, Luke, my parents. Lately even Megucchi, I only contacted her all month when *I* wanted something. Telling myself that she would understand because it was almost time for my exam. All that for nothing. For a lousy few minutes of sleep."

Daisuke backed off, aware he needed to tread more carefully. "I'm sorry. Of course you should be disappointed. But I'm sure it's going to be all right eventually."

Kana sighed. "The reason I called you here is because I'm not going to be able to see you anymore. Your exam is tomorrow —after that, no more tutoring sessions."

"What? But I thought maybe we could still hang out." He looked pained. "And I could help you get ready for the next exam, right?"

"I know, and I'm sorry, but I can't. I have to get my priorities straight."

"I...understand." Something told her that he felt less disappointed about losing his study partner than he was at not being able to see her. Kana, too, felt a little disappointed, but she had resolved herself. This had all come about because she had been stretching herself too thin; she was constantly committed to one appointment or another, and now where had it brought her? She had put herself in a terrible position for nothing. Now she would have to devote time to not only English, but the other subjects that were covered on the February test. It was better not to be tempted, Kana told herself;

better to try not to care too much about Daisuke and what could happen after his own exam. As much as she hated to do it, she knew she had to say goodbye before that even became a possibility.

"Well, you've done enough for me already, I think I can hack it on my own now," he said at length, putting on a brave face. Kana appreciated the gesture. "As long as it's still okay to message you here and there with a question?"

"As long as it's not all the time." She smiled thinly. "Maybe *you* should find a pen pal."

"Oh!" Daisuke sat up straight. "Come to think of it, your *Miss* Megumi sent me an email a few days ago."

"Megucchi did? What? How did she find you?"

"Looking for you, actually. She wanted to know if I had any way to contact you."

Kana thought back "Oh. My parents took away my cell phone and computer. That was why I sent you the message earlier from my school email."

"Right."

She frowned. "I haven't been able to talk to Megucchi in a few days now. I guess she must have been worried when she didn't hear from me after the test."

"I've got her address in my phone, if you want to send her a message." Daisuke handed it over, with the inquiry from Megucchi on the screen.

Kana noticed that his phone, royal blue, had a tiny doughnut-shaped charm attached to the strap. She smothered a smile. "Sure. Megucchi should be awake in a few hours, so I'll tell her to contact me through our fashion forum from now on."

"Take your time." Daisuke politely looked away.

Kana punched in the reply, feeling guilty for leaving Megucchi hanging. "I shouldn't have told her about the test. She was already having a big fight with her best friend."

"I'm sure she'll understand once she gets this."

When the message had been dispatched, Kana handed the

phone back to him. "Well...I have to go. Good luck with your exam, and whatever comes next for you." She paused. "Sorry I can't help with the last bit of preparation. I hope you understand."

"I get it." She might have been imagining it, but his face hinted disappointment.

Kana supposed that it was wishful thinking. "Goodbye, Otsuka-kun."

"Goodbye, *Miss* Momokawa. Until we meet again."

~*~*~

It wasn't much of a plan, but Grace had little to work with, so when she got up the next day, stretched, and stood out on the veranda of her fancy hotel room, she decided to begin her search with what she knew. She'd read every article published on the English-language news websites, but no news of tragedies befalling Saitama schoolgirls had broken, so Grace allowed herself to hope that maybe the worst hadn't happened. Maybe Kana truly was unable or unwilling to contact her. If that was the case, Grace had no intention of giving up after coming this far. She had essentially one lead—Shibuya.

Grace just hoped that Shibuya was as small in real life as it looked on the map.

At the concierge desk, she asked one of the staff members for directions. The woman explained the route in rapid-fire, American-accented English, drawing circles and stars for Grace on a printed paper map. "Take the Yurikamome Line outside here, to Shimbashi Station, then take the Ginza Line from there, which is the subway. You can take this map. Would you like a train map, too?"

"Oh, I have to take a train?" Grace supposed it was inevitable, but she had never been on a *real* train, only the subway in Toronto. She wasn't sure she wanted to start in a country where she couldn't read the signs.

"It's a little far." The concierge frowned.

"How about a taxi?"

"You can." She paused. "But I don't think it's a good idea. Shibuya is about half an hour by car from here, at this time of day."

"*Half an hour?*" Was nothing in this city close together? Accepting the map, Grace thanked the guide and followed the instructions to the train station, where she stood in front of the ticket machines for some time, wondering what to do next. It didn't seem too bad, she thought. The train line looked artistic, with its little loop after the bridge. She had to take the *Yurikamome Line,* this line, someplace called Shimbashi, right at the end, and then she had to take a subway—Grace opened the folded train map.

She could not immediately come up with a word to describe what she saw. "Daunting" would have been a good one, Grace thought, or maybe "insane." The full map of the Tokyo transit system looked even more like a massive tangle of coloured spaghetti than it had on the back of her guidebook. The stations were written in such fine print they were difficult to read. She spent ten minutes trying to find her present location—it didn't *look* far from Shibuya, but Grace decided that might be bad news rather than good. The concierge would have known what she was talking about, so if *she* said Shibuya was half an hour, then the map couldn't be close to scale.

She would have to deal with the subway when she arrived at Shimbashi, Grace decided. For now she would consider the ability to use the ticket machine a big enough victory.

It was not, she quickly learned, as difficult as expected, thanks to the big ENGLISH button. With so few stations on the line, Grace quickly reasoned out how much money to put in the machine. She bought a ticket and passed through the gates with no major catastrophes. A cool experience, Grace decided as she found a spot in the front car, feeling as though she were seated in the conductor's cabin of the driverless train. They soared out over Tokyo Bay, where she could see boats at the docks from one window, and the metropolis on the other. *Magnificent*, she thought. The view was stunning.

The accomplishment Grace felt over getting there vanished when she exited the gates, however. She didn't have the slightest clue where to find the Ginza Line. She tried to ask the station master, but none of the staff here seemed to speak English, so she fled, embarrassed.

Outside, she consulted the folded map again, hoping some stranger would take pity on her. It might as well have been in Japanese for all she understood it—or even Swahili. Though she didn't want to, she returned to the station master's desk, and asked in clear and slow English, "Excuse me, but where is the Ginza Line?"

"銀座線ですか？あそこです。" He gestured in the direction she had come from, and made a complicated movement with his hands, pointing. "まっすぐ行って, その角を左にまがったら, 階段を降りて下さい。"

Grace could do no more than give him a blank look.

The man held his palm out again to show the way. "まっすぐ行って…"

"Over there?" She pointed in the direction he'd indicated.

"Yes. Yes. そうです. 階段を降りて下さい。"

Trying to look like she understood, Grace nodded hurriedly. "Yes. Thank you." After a pause, she hesitantly stuttered, "*Arigatou.*"

He bowed. "ありがとうございます。"

Turning back, she found what looked like an entrance to the underground. Grace followed signs downstairs and through a long underground corridor, past rows of coin lockers and kiosk shops selling hats and handbags.

Inside the Tokyo Metro entrance, Grace spotted a list of stations and ticket prices. Shibuya was there, written in English, Japanese, and even Braille. When she had taken a few steps inside, she looked up and noticed a sign above her head that read *To Ginza, Asakusa.*

Grace followed the arrow down another set of stairs, relieved. The Ginza Line had less English signage than the high-tech train she'd taken to get this far—it had been a good idea to stay in Odaiba. If she'd gone to a less-tourist-friendly area first she might have found herself in a lot more trouble figuring out the trains!

The Ginza Line seemed older, and a feeling of weariness permeated the stations and the tired-looking cars. Grace hung onto a hard white plastic loop and tried to see the map over the doors, squinting at the small print.

They passed Ginza Station itself within seconds, so she knew she was *on* the Ginza Line, but after more than fifteen minutes, they hadn't reached Shibuya. They were underground, so Grace couldn't see the landscape, either. Studying *Friendly Planet* as she clung to her loop, she listened carefully to each stop announcement, and had taken out the map again when they arrived at a station called Asakusa.

"浅草,浅草です. みぎの扉開きます. ごちゅうい下さい。"

The other passengers all disembarked, leaving Grace behind, mystified. Why had everyone left? Was the train going out of service? She waited, but the announcement didn't repeat.

Wasn't Tokyo supposed to be super tourist-friendly? Grace had a few choice words to say to the people in charge of signage, if she ever met them.

She disembarked and studied the map once again. There, in the top right quarter, was Asakusa. It wasn't anywhere even remotely close to Shibuya.

But why? Grace looked up at the subway car she had gotten off. The electronic signboard over her head showed only a clock and the train's next departure, one minute away. She couldn't read the departure information, and unlike the train in Odaiba, no matter how long she watched the screen, it never changed from Japanese characters to English.

Station announcements were incomprehensible, too. She thought she heard *Shibuya*, but immediately doubted her ears. This was absolutely *not* Shibuya. And now, other passengers had gotten on board the train and started taking seats, so she reasoned that it couldn't possibly be going out of service. Maybe, she reasoned, it was going in another direction. Maybe she would need to change lines after all.

Walking past the electronic display, she found another sign, a white one that did have an English translation. Beside the platform number, it said "For Ueno, Shibuya."

She was still puzzling it out when the conductor, or whoever made the announcements, said something urgent-sounding in Japanese a second time. The repetition caught Grace's ear, even though she couldn't understand his words. "発車します. ご注意下さい."

The doors shut with a hiss, and the train started to move back the way it had come.

It dawned on Grace then that she must have gotten on the train going in the wrong direction, and proceeded to ride it to the exact opposite end of the line. The car lazily rumbled away, leaving her standing on the platform, open-mouthed.

Grace never swore, but now that she was alone in this mystifying country with no one around to help or hear what she said, she broke her own rule. She cursed out loud, over and over, until the taillights vanished into the tunnel.

Chapter 14

Re: Looking for Kana Momokawa

From: otsuka.999991@ao.ne.jp | Sat, Dec 13, 4:37 PM

Hi, Megucchi, this is Kana. I'm sorry I couldn't contact you until now.

A lot of things have happened. I want to explain properly later, but right now, I can't. I met Otsuka-kun for the last time today and I could borrow a phone.

But if you send me your message on SS, I will check it from an Internet cafe sometime.

I hope I didn't cause you a worry. I want to talk to you soon!

Kana

Shortly before two o'clock, Grace finally arrived at her destination.

It's fine, she told herself. She was here now, and that was what mattered. In Shibuya! In the heart of it all, at long last.

When she stepped out of the station onto the street, though, she didn't see the vibrant shopping street pictured in her books or the flashy signs or crowds of trendy teenagers. Opposite the exit were dingy bus stops, and across the street, grey-faced buildings. A highway thronged with cars ran under the raised tracks. Old gum and saliva discoloured the ground. Grace hesitated. She *had* gotten off at the right station this time, hadn't she?

The sign certainly *said* Shibuya, but it didn't resemble the Shibuya that Kana described. Exhaust hung thickly in the air. She wondered if she had come out the wrong exit, and so Grace set off down the sidewalk to circle the building. She hadn't gotten far, though, when she stopped again, incredulous. The underpass, though its concrete walls were painted in soft pastels with stencilled flowers and butterflies, was lined with sleeping bags and tarps. Men with filthy hair and faces lay curled up under blankets along the wall, some fenced in with or lying on pieces of cardboard. One boiled a kettle on a portable stove. Grace, with her foreignness and the purse with all the money she had under her arm, could not help but be frightened. She turned back, feeling afraid and somehow ashamed.

What had gone wrong? Grace studied her map. She'd certainly gotten off at the right stop. This time, anyway.

Walking back through the station, she tried another exit, and felt relieved to find it open into a more commercial area. A handful of small restaurants and a big department store were visible from the door—more lively; less depressed. Nevertheless, Grace couldn't rid herself of the feeling that she had made a terrible mistake.

Famished, she decided to look for lunch before anything else. She hadn't thought too much about eating yet, so eager was she to be on her way, and now her stomach growled in protest.

Grace felt very well-prepared for her first attempt at bridging the language barrier in a restaurant, thanks to *Friendly Planet*. She'd read all about plastic food sculptures, so when she spotted an Italian restaurant with the reproductions of each dish on display in the window, Grace didn't hesitate. She was shown to a table by a smiling young woman with a glass of water and a menu.

Unable to even begin to pronounce anything, Grace pointed at one of the photographs. It looked like spaghetti in a pinkish sauce, so probably rosé, she thought. Not too bad. At this point, she would be willing to take a chance on anything resembling Western food.

While she waited for the meal, Grace thought of her father, the summer days they spent at his condo eating cornflakes and corner store California rolls for lunch. In the evenings, her dad would make spaghetti, Grace's favourite meal. It wasn't anything impressive; Dad's sauce-from-a-jar topped with off-the-shelf Parmesan could be no comparison to her mother's homemade version. His face was so eager for her praise when he served it, though, that she couldn't say a thing.

Grace didn't like that he'd left them; hated that her mother alternated her moods between sadness and anger since. When Dad laid down a plate with home-cooked pasta in front of her, though, she ate without complaint.

She prepared herself for a jar-level experience here in Japan, too. Even if it had mushrooms in the sauce, Grace decided she would eat them. Bad pasta, after all, was better than no pasta.

What appeared on the table, though, took her by surprise. A steaming plate of lurid pink, with something green sprinkled on the noodles. On closer inspection, it wasn't rosé at all. Though similar in colour, there were tiny little balls mixed into the thin sauce. *How weird,* Grace thought, leaning down. They looked like...

Eggs.

Definitely eggs. She wrinkled her nose. Some sort of caviar, like the salmon egg sushi you could get at the Japanese restaurant downtown. Her stomach churned, but she felt so hungry, she wasn't sure what else to do. Would it be insulting to leave the plate totally untouched? It wasn't as though she could explain that she ordered the wrong thing. Gulping, and remembering her resolution to be brave, Grace twirled a bit of spaghetti onto her fork.

Salty. And maybe she imagined it, but it did taste distinctly fishy. She tried to tell herself it wasn't bad, just different, but after that single bite she knew she couldn't eat this, no matter how hungry she felt. Instead, Grace rearranged the spaghetti on the plate and stood up to leave.

She quietly paid the bill and bought a slice of cake from the HamiMart. The convenience store had plenty of other food, food she had already eaten and liked, but the thought of any of it now turned Grace's stomach.

She'd eaten *something*, at least, so it was time to get searching. She continued up the street, slowly, eyes peeled for anything familiar. There was no point in trying to look at everyone she passed, but if she could find a place she knew her friend had been before, maybe Kana would happen by at some point after school.

Try as she might, however, Grace couldn't locate anything the two of them had talked about. Her guidebook was little help. Even when Grace recognized the names of points on the map, she had no idea where *she* was in relation to them. She wandered for some time, until she came to a huge street crammed with cars. Wide sidewalks were lined with shops. This area had a familiar feel to it, and she consulted her book again, frowning. Sure enough, she had managed to leave Shibuya entirely and enter Harajuku, to the north. Sighing, Grace changed direction and headed off down a side street.

There was no lack of interesting things to see, but it was

impossible to enjoy them. Her mission, so far, was a failure. On top of that, here she was in Tokyo, but dressed like she'd come from gym class, without even so much as a decent pair of shoes. Kana would never believe Grace could be the same person who she'd discussed fashion with!

She sat down heavily on a concrete divider across from a second hand clothing shop, watching two girls browsing outdoor sale racks. They were wearing school uniforms with navy blazers, but of course, neither of them were Kana.

This wasn't working, Grace thought. She needed Plan C. She wasn't going to find Kana by walking around. She needed to get herself a better map, and more ideas of locations to investigate. She needed to be able to *sit there* at places like Hoshibacks and Hachiko and watch for Kana. Those were the best leads she had.

A map, and a plan, Grace thought. And a change of clothes, too. She would be embarrassed to have Kana see her, wearing what she wore right now.

Grace had crossed the street and entered the store before she had even thought the whole thing through. The more she watched the girls hold up hundred-yen shirts and skirts, the more it made sense. This was like a sign. Another way to reinvent herself.

She pointed to and bought one of the entire outfits right off the mannequin at the entrance. The clerk disrobed the model in a flash.

Grace squeezed into a curtained area that more resembled a tiny beach cabana than a dressing room, and came out wearing the mannequin's top and skirt, bare-legged, a thousand-yen bill in one hand and her old clothes in the other. She handed her pink graphic tee and boring, bootcut jeans to the surprised clerk. Her Canadian clothes were worth only a few coins, but Grace didn't care. Shrugging back into her parka, she felt quite pleased with herself.

The next destination on her list was a bookstore. With a good English-language local map, Grace hoped to create a plan of attack to make tomorrow more successful. It would be so easy, she lamented, if she had a portable hotspot! Maybe she could rent a fancy Japanese cell phone, one of the ones with rotating screens to watch television on. Everyone here seemed to be doing quite a lot on their phones on the train. Grace felt a little envious of how much better phone technology in Japan seemed to be, compared to back home.

When she had what she needed, she took up a vigil outside the train station, on the street corner, watching people depart and arrive. *This is good,* Grace thought. Hundreds of people were streaming back and forth through this exit.

Somehow, schoolgirls still walked around in short skirts, knee socks and blazers. Grace thought it must have been a fashion point or something, because she wasn't sure she had seen a single student wearing any sort of coat over their uniform.

The longer she watched, however, the more uncertain she became that she would be able to spot a familiar face in the constant mass of humanity. There were so many people, it would be impossible to look at every teenager long enough to take in clues, and this was *one* exit of *one* station. Grace couldn't even know for sure if Kana would be meeting Daisuke in Shibuya today. Tired, hungry and disappointed, she thought about trying to find Hachiko or the Hoshibacks instead, but decided it was time to call it a night. The sun had set, and she felt uncomfortable being out after dark so late in a strange city. Who could have known the days were so short here?

The plan, Grace reminded herself. Now that she possessed an English-language map—an entire *book* of zoomed-in maps—it was time to prepare for tomorrow. She hurried back to the hotel, the chill raising goosebumps on her bare legs. *And tomorrow, I need to buy some tights or leggings. This is* not *skirt season, no matter what the locals are wearing!*

When she flopped onto the queen-sized bed, Grace lay there for a long time. Her first day had been a bust. She had gotten waylaid several times, and though she visited the one place in Tokyo she had been so excited to go, she had left without seeing a single familiar spot. Her first experience with Japanese food (even if it was Japanese-style *Italian*) hadn't gone so well, either. Of all the things Grace planned for the day, she had accomplished none of them.

She frowned and reached for her phone, laying dormant on the desk. Grace didn't dare power it on; if it even worked over here, she didn't want to take the risk that she could be traced. She hadn't had the foresight to print out or forward any saved messages, though, so she would need to rely entirely on memory to find her way around. At a time like this, she thought, it would have been nice to have had Kana's culture lessons close at hand.

Could she be tracked if she used a public computer to look at her email? Grace wasn't sure. She wished she were as tech-savvy as Jean. It might, she'd started to think, be a good idea to reach out to Daisuke again. He would be able to tell her more about where she could look for Kana.

Grace wondered, too, how Simon was doing, and she desperately wanted to talk to him, to have a little reassurance. Simon wouldn't be able to lie to her mother if he were asked, though. It was better for him if he didn't know where Grace had gone. And, she thought, maybe it was better for her, too. She'd come to Japan with the intention of finding herself and strengthening her resolve. Depending on someone else, as she always had, would put her back where she started.

Grace knew she leaned on her friends too much. It was a hard habit to break. Deep down, her fear of other peoples' reactions made it difficult for her to open up. If not for Jean living next door when they were young, if not for Simon reaching out to her, she wasn't sure she would have any friends at all.

Kana was different. Grace wasn't sure how they'd fallen into sync so easily, as though she could talk to Kana about anything

161

without having to worry about being judged. She hadn't told Kana about those fears, though, or why she struggled to connect with people. Grace liked to think that she was content with the friends she already had, and so had never sought out more, but during rougher times like this one, she wondered if the situation was quite the opposite.

~*~*~

Amid her classmates' celebrations over the end of exams and enjoying their freedom (until the next round, of course, the more studious of them reminded each other), Kana felt too despondent to take part. She moved through her days in a zombie state, unable to feel much about anything. Though the initial shock of her exam mishap had worn off at last, she knew she would be in for a difficult few months.

Rumi and the others knew messing around on the weekends was out of the question. Kana had even dropped out of cram school to save her parents' money, though she wondered if the reason her mother readily accepted the proposal was to keep her at home and far away from the distractions of the city.

It couldn't be helped, Kana told herself; she had made her bed and now would have to lie in it. It had been easy over the first few days when she berated herself constantly for the incident, but now that things had begun to return to normal, she missed the life she had been living before. Even the sleepless nights and cram school. She hadn't heard from Megucchi at all, not that she had a lot of time for computer use. Her mother had been merciless the first time she'd seen Kana turning on her PC.

She was on a lonely path now. She wasn't in contact with Megucchi, couldn't go out with Rumi, and had said farewell to Daisuke, possibly for good. As Kana had reached the other side of the crosswalk after their last meeting, turned and looked up at the second floor of the cafe, she had seen Daisuke watching her from the window. She couldn't discern his expression from that distance, however, and thought perhaps he was taking one last look before he put her out of his mind permanently. Not what she would have preferred to believe, but she had to assume the worst. It would fall right in line with the abrupt left turn her life had taken since that awful morning at Nishidai.

Chapter 15

Home > Private Messages > Inbox > Unread

Showing Messages 0 to 0

Unread

makhanikana	*There are no new messages in your inbox.*

Grace became increasingly frustrated with the city of Tokyo, its perpetual state of rush, and most of all her apparent inability to ever get where she wanted to go. The thrill of having the nice hotel room all to herself quickly wore off. She had already spent much more money than intended on train rides, food and clothes. Too hot in her parka and cold in her sweater, she would still need a few more changes of clothes and maybe a fall jacket. That would be expensive, but really, how often would she be in the real Harajuku to buy clothing? Once Grace went back, she would be grounded for the rest of her life, anyway. *A little bit can't hurt,* she told herself, *since I'm already here, right?*

Compared to Tokyo, Saitama was a completely different experience. Grace had no idea where to start to look, only that Kana rode the train called the Tobu Noda to get to Tokyo from her home. The terminal station, Omiya, was the only point Grace could figure was an absolute must-pass for Kana every day.

She knew what Kana's school uniform looked like, so that could be a lead, albeit a small one. Grace arrived at seven in the morning to patrol Omiya Station, hoping to spot any student wearing it. She could only faintly recall the details, but it happened to be a memorable design, with a blue tartan-patterned skirt and a cream-coloured vest. Kana's school blazer had a crest on the front pocket, Grace remembered.

It wasn't a lot to go on, though, and the station was massive. She saw hundreds of schoolgirls, but not a single person was wearing a uniform quite like Kana's. Grace realized too late that she should have been narrowing her search by standing directly on the Noda Line platform, rather than in the concourse.

When it was after nine and school would be in session, Grace had a lot of time to kill before she could try the waiting tactic again. She decided to wander around the local line, looking for other possible clues. It seemed like a waste to not scout out Kana's home prefecture while she was there.

What she *did* know was that Kana lived near a small station, close to Omiya, but not so close to Saitama's urban centres. Grace boarded the Noda Line and took it to the first stop that looked quiet, Omiyakoen.

The landscape here wasn't what Grace expected from suburbia. Near the station, housing complexes in terracotta shades lined both sides of the tracks. She admired the scalloped roofs. There wasn't much to do around here, though. Maybe, she thought, everyone flocked to the main station for their shopping and socializing. It seemed quiet and the homes behind the terracotta structures were more dated. The architecture struck her as being very un-Japanese, unlike the traditional houses she'd seen from the train window on her way there.

Further along the tracks stood a grimy overpass with shallow concrete steps, the fencing below it falling apart. Grace crossed to a footpath along what looked like in summer could be vegetable crops. The house across the way proudly displayed dozens of planters on the outside of its fence, wall and veranda, most filled with flowers, despite the time of year. More plants grew unchecked on the opposite side. Next door, an aging roof dripping with rust protected a car from the elements. A huge stone lantern, reminding her in shape of an inukshuk, beckoned Grace to come closer.

She walked on, passing more homes that were closer to what she would expect to see in a guidebook. Blue roofs, perfectly pruned trees. A rock garden. Bamboo. Yet across the street, wide swaths of land were overgrown and covered with bramble and dead branches fallen from crooked trees.

The path crossed through vegetation for a long stretch, and farmland, with nearly no houses. She felt a little nervous, out there alone, but the tracks helped guide her. Every little while, a Tobu train would roll past, so close Grace could have reached out and touched it.

Her steps slowed as she took in the unfamiliar surroundings. Back home, her community and the ones surrounding it always seemed so small. Her mother had still been young when the settlements all banded together to qualify as a town. Things had changed immeasurably since the 1970s, but compared to St. John's, Grace couldn't help but think of her hometown as *rural*. No public transportation, no mall or movie theatre. One big main road that ran parallel to the shore, with all the smaller roads leading into neighbourhoods branching off. Grace could walk to the next town in less than twenty minutes in either direction. Old-fashioned, biscuit-box-style houses still stood on the main road, their paint peeling with age. Unlike here, undeveloped land at home was heavy with forest. Nothing was compact.

It wasn't exactly metropolitan, but it wasn't like this at all. Belatedly, Grace realized Kana had been born in a place that was much closer to being considered rural than Grace's own home. A sobering thought, given how she had envied Kana for living in a "real" city.

She had to walk downriver, away from the tracks, until she came to a bridge lorded over by an imposing statue of an eagle. This area was decidedly more populated. Grace thought she might be on a main road, so she opted to press forward. Wide sidewalks lined with hedges and concrete scalloping guided her past a shrine and an underused playground.

An even wider road led back to the tracks. Grace followed the road until she could breathe a sigh of relief, seeing the train roll by again. The structure of the road seemed foreign and mysterious. She stopped to stand there, at grade with the tracks, looking down into an underpass at the cars and bicycles travelling below.

A narrow street ran parallel to the line, packed with shops, but Grace couldn't read the names of most. There was less English signage here than any place she'd seen in Japan so far. Still, it had a pleasant, busy, community feeling. Nobody here paid any attention to the foreigner in their midst.

Glancing back at the tracks, Grace saw a train rolling to a slow stop past an at-grade crossing, and she followed it. Across from a "Liquor & Foods Shop" with vintage hand-painted signs, she found little Owada Station.

Schoolchildren were out and about, but it would still be hours before she could hope to spot Kana. Grace looked up; the analogue clock read exactly noon. She'd been wandering for over an hour already.

Other stations on the Noda line were similarly quiet, but after Owada, she started to ride the train between them. Grace was thankful she'd done so, as the distance between stations doubled. By the time she reached Kasukabe, a busy city terminal, it was time to turn around.

She couldn't know for sure if she had passed Kana's home, or walked by Kana's mother returning from the grocery store, or her brother hitting baseballs in a junior high schoolyard somewhere. Grace thought she had gotten a good sense of what life in Saitama could be like, though, and she felt charmed. It wasn't at all like what she had imagined.

Back at Omiya, in a neighbourhood so urban she could have mistaken it for Tokyo, Grace lingered on the Noda Line's open-air platform, watching for students returning home from school. Ten minutes passed between each departure, so it was easy to take a good look the passengers who entered before they boarded the waiting train. She felt certain she would see Kana there, if only she could wait long enough.

The trouble was, standing out in the open as the temperature dropped became more difficult as the afternoon rolled on. Grace didn't have any way to know whether Kana might have her long day at school that day, had stayed late in the city, detoured to cram school or done any one of a half-dozen other options Grace could think of.

Three hours later, as she felt the temperature inching closer to zero, she was forced to throw in the towel. It was too long a day for her to continue waiting there any longer.

Grace inspected the faces of everyone she saw as she left the platform, hoping that each extra moment she lingered would be enough to make it all worth it. At last, her aching feet, growling stomach and frozen digits drew her away from the Noda Line and over to Platform One, where a warm train was waiting to carry her south again.

The next day, Grace couldn't bring herself to return to Saitama, especially not early enough to have a hope of catching Kana en route to school. She slept until after noon, then headed for Shibuya. Kana often spent Tuesdays there or in Harajuku, if Grace remembered correctly.

She now knew the subway and the aboveground trains at Shibuya all had different station buildings and exits, and could use that information to better find her way around. Here, at last, Grace found the statue of the loyal dog, as well as the Hoshibacks cafe Kana and Daisuke often met at. Grace recognized it as soon as she found herself standing in the opposite view, right where Kana would have been looking down on her from across the scramble.

Grace sat down by Hachiko, waiting. She hoped Kana would show up here with Rumi, or even other friends, all dressed in tartan, cream and powder-blue so that they would be easy to spot. Even with all the people crowding around the dog, Grace had a good line of sight on the Hachiko Exit.

Here she stayed for the better part of an hour, before starting to feel a growing sense of anxiety. If Kana planned to come to Shibuya after school, it would have been well past arrival time. Her school was nearby, though Grace had no idea in which direction. What if, Grace thought, they had gone somewhere else today, on her free Tuesday? To Harajuku? Or worse, somewhere Grace could never have guessed? Tuesdays were the only day she knew for certain that Kana had free time after school.

It was risky, but as afternoon turned into evening, she decided to try Harajuku instead. Grace took the train one stop away and headed for Jingu Bridge. This happened to be one of the places she still wanted to see in Tokyo, but she would much rather have been there wearing her most adventurous clothes (still tame in comparison to the usual clientele, probably) and lingering all day, like in her guidebook.

Even though it wasn't a Sunday, there was some foot traffic on the bridge. Teenagers and twentysomethings loitered on either side, most dressed at least a little fashionably. A woman on the corner gave a demonstration with a hula hoop to a crowd of onlookers; closer to the station, a truck with speakers mounted on its top blared incomprehensible messages while a promoter handed out leaflets. A trickle of people flowed in and out of Meiji Shrine; on weekends and holidays, she thought, it must balloon to an unimaginable number.

On the bridge proper, though, there were only a few loiterers, and a disproportionate number of tourists with no subjects for their cameras. A man selling art prints tried to persuade Grace to buy his wares. Overwhelmed, she put some distance between them, sitting on the chain that lined the sidewalk to watch from further away. Rumi and Kana were not among the photographers or the photographed. Grace turned her attention to the station entrance, watching the crowd.

Only when the artist and the hula hoop girl packed up did she stand again and start walking back toward the Harajuku main drag. No Kana. And now what? That had been her best lead.

~*~*~

Kana was so unhappy that she decided maybe it was time to visit the ESS. Again.

Club activities were the only thing that didn't apply to the new "come home right after school" rule. Without cram school, it was also the best free English practice she was going to get. After class let out, Kana followed Yuko and Yoko to the seminar room to test the waters. The second-year students and several first-year girls Kana didn't know were already inside, chatting.

"Sorry to intrude," she volunteered as she stepped inside.

"Momokawa-senpai! Long time no see." Michiko, a second-year, waved her in. Kana waved back, relieved to see that the club leader hadn't arrived yet.

"Hi, Kacchan," Nozomi said, smiling. "We were wondering if you'd be here today."

"You were?" Kana was taken by surprise. She had mentioned going back to the other members in 3–7, but how had word gotten around to the underclassmen? "I hadn't really decided until now."

"Are you going to come back to the ESS?" He looked hopeful.

"Maybe," Kana replied, intentionally vague. "Where's...?"

The other members looked at each other. Kana sensed an uneasy feeling in the air. "Kurokawa-senpai went to look for Luke." Michiko said. "We need him before we start. It's debating, today."

Debating happened to be an exercise the third-years had to do in class, so practising at the ESS was an easy advantage before they started on the real thing. A topic would be set, and the club would divide into pairs to discuss it. Luke often came to chat with them and help out anyone who needed it. Debate practice wasn't anything special, though, so Kana wondered why everyone looked distinctly uncomfortable.

She didn't have time to overthink things, though. Kurokawa and Luke appeared with two other second-year girls and a boy behind them. "*Hi, Kana,*" said Luke in English. "*How are you? I haven't seen you all week.*"

"*I'm fine, thank you,*" she replied, shyly returning his smile. She noticed, though, that none of the others addressed her directly.

Kana had been about to ask Luke how he was in return, when Kurokawa silenced them both by putting her hands down on the lectern and assuming an authoritative pose. "Okay, so as you know, this is our last ESS meeting for the term. Next week, everyone should be preparing for finals, so clubs are all cancelled."

Her words were met with a chorus of groans from the membership. Nobody needed a reminder of how close the end of term was.

"To brush up on our skills before the tests, today we'll be having a conversational debate." Kurokawa looked at Luke, who sat obediently at one of the desks. "Luke-sensei is going to help us today. He'll come to each pair to listen. You can ask him any questions you have, and he'll give us some feedback after the discussion. Does everyone understand?"

There were murmurs and nods from the others.

"Okay then, let's begin. Please find a partner, everyone."

Kana felt relief wash over her when someone else made the first move. Michiko quickly came over to where Kana sat. "Do you want to work together?"

"Sure."

Kurokawa waited until the others had divided into pairs and resettled themselves before she continued. "*Our first topic is 'School Uniforms,'*" she said in English. "*Do you agree, or disagree?*" Then, for the sake of the first-years staring, bewildered, she added an extra tidbit of information in Japanese. "One person will be in favour of uniforms, one person against. One or two sentences each before you switch."

"Hmm." Kana glanced at her partner. "I'm in favour of uniforms. How about you?"

Michiko smiled. "I'm also for. Sorry!"

"Okay. Then let's do rock–paper–scissors."

Kana chose rock, and Michiko paper. "After you," Kana said.

"*I think school uniforms show your pride in your school.*" Michiko's English emerged slowly, but Kana thought her grammar and structure were good. "*And they show...which school you belong.*"

It was Kana's turn to counter with her own statement. "*That may be true, but a bad student in uniform can make your school look bad." She thought of Daisuke, with his unbuttoned *gakuran* and messy dyed hair. "*...Even if that student is smart.*"

Michiko smiled. "*But, if you go to a good school, maybe there isn't any delinquent there.*" Koen Academy was a prestigious enough school that students were rarely caught doing anything more delinquent than jaywalking. There *were* students who rebelled, but you couldn't spot them from a distance, the way you could at a school with a less strict dress code.

Kana considered, then switched tactics. "*In my opinion, a school uniform doesn't....Show. Doesn't show your true face.*" She consulted her electronic dictionary. "*Individuality. Your individuality.*"

Michiko pointed at the green ribbons threaded through Kana's knee-high socks. "*But even today, you are showing it. You are showing...invida...*"

"*Individuality,*" Kana supplied.

She nodded. "*Yes, like here. You are wearing a uniform*, senpai. *But I see your invid-alty.*"

"*But, this decoration is against school rules, is it not?*"

"*Yes. However...*" Michiko paused, thought, and finished the argument in Japanese. "If you're willing to break the rules even a little, that's showing your personality too, I think."

Kana smiled. Michiko's English ability wasn't quite as good as Kana's, probably because she was a second-year, but she was more than capable of holding her own in a debate exercise. "You are right; I think so too. All right, then, *I give up*, I concede."

"All right!" Michiko clapped her hands together. "That's my first time winning."

"*Congratulations.*"

"*Thank you! Your talking points, very good.*"

"*Your points were good, too,*" she gently corrected.

Michiko glanced at the other pairs, still deep in conversation, and at Kurokawa, who chatting animatedly with Luke. She then leaned close to Kana. "Senpai..."

"Yes?"

"Earlier...well, Kurokawa-senpai asked if it's true that you failed the Nishidai exam."

Here was the cause of the awkwardness in the room, Kana realized. Kurokawa had told everyone her bad news. She wondered where the club leader had heard about it, but it wasn't some huge secret. She wasn't the only one at Koen Academy taking the exam, after all, and Kana's teachers all knew what had happened.

Kurokawa was the only person who would be amused to see Kana lose her chance at her dream school.

Kana tried not to let her distaste show on her face. "And what did everyone say?"

"Well, Yoko-chan said that it wasn't *really* true, but something had happened and you had missed the exam." Michiko fidgeted, opening and closing the lid of her dictionary. "She wouldn't talk about it. Everyone else thought...thought it was pretty mean of Kurokawa-senpai to tell everyone, so maybe...well, I thought you should know."

"Thanks." Kana put on a brave expression for her underclassman's sake. "I wondered why everyone was acting so strangely."

"Sorry. But everyone else is happy to have you back. Senpai will welcome you back too, I'm sure."

Kana very much doubted that would be the case. "You don't need to apologize," she replied.

What could the leader's vendetta be about? Kana wasn't sure she'd ever know. It wasn't as though she had any interest in heading the club; she didn't at all, but she wondered if Kurokawa thought she was trying to compete. Or maybe it had something to do with the only-somewhat-friendly class rivalry between them—Kana's class had trounced 3–6 in the Sports Festival, led by Rumi and the other volleyball team girls. 3–6 had come in second for every competition they had been pitted against 3–7. Rumi had beaten Kurokawa herself in a brutal hundred-meter-dash.

Alternatively, Kana thought, perhaps Kurokawa Shiori simply didn't *like* her.

Michiko watched her partner nervously, waiting for a response. Kana nodded again, more resolutely this time. "Thanks for telling me."

"Of course. You're welcome."

Kurokawa's voice broke into the post-debate conversations. "I think everyone's finished, so we're moving to the next topic." She directed her gaze away from the row where Kana sat, but a smile played at the edge of her lips. "Get ready to change partners, everyone. The rules are the same. And the next topic is '*Entrance Examination Hell.*'"

Kana groaned. It looked like Kurokawa definitely wasn't ready to play nice.

~*~*~

The next morning, Grace checked out of the hotel in Odaiba and took the train to Shinjuku. She would miss the balcony and the view, but in the long run, Grace knew this would be better. Or at least she sincerely hoped so, after she opened the door to her new hotel room and found something more resembling her mother's walk-in closet with a mattress stuffed inside.

Everything was compact. The bed was angled perpendicular to a small desk which, even if it weren't attached to the wall, would not have had the space to budge further than a centimetre or two. A half-sized closet stood at the end of the bed, only accessible by standing on the bed itself. A flat screen television perched on the windowsill, rendering the window inoperative. That was fine with Grace, as she could already feel a draft from where she stood.

The bathroom in particular turned out to be a shock compared to the one she had left behind in Odaiba. Everything here was plasticized for easy cleaning and waterproofing. The toilet was as high-tech as the one before it, but the bathtub with the shower hanging above it was scarcely half the size of even the smallest Western-style tub. With these two items taking up most of the room, about half a meter of space remained.

The hotel had thoughtfully provided a pair of "bathroom slippers" to be worn when standing in that small square. Grace shivered and pushed them to the side with her foot.

Aside from the discounted price, her new hotel had little to boast about, but here she had Internet access and the area seemed exciting enough. Here at last was the Japan she had seen in films, with thousands of businessmen in their suits streaming back and forth from the station to the pachinko parlours, and skyscrapers fighting for dominance overhead. Grace had gotten lost no less than four times trying to exit the station, a maze at least a dozen stories deep. When she consulted her map book, curious to see if it had as many exits as Shibuya, she found that there were trains leaving Shinjuku in at least seventeen different directions. The exits were uncountable. A bunch of gargantuan department stores also seemed to be right in the middle of the station, making it nigh-impossible to find her way around without actually exiting the entire building and circling it.

It was daunting. It was loud. But this, *this* was the Tokyo of the movies!

Chapter 16

I miss you!

| makhanikana | Hi, Megucchi... |

I don't know if you got my message before, that I sent from Mister Otsuka's phone. Maybe not. I wonder if you worried about my examination, because my mother took my phone as punishment. Maybe I'll have it back soon. I hope so. I miss reading your messages every day.

I am punishing myself, too. I told Mister Otsuka we couldn't meet anymore, not even to study. To be clear, he can pass his exam easily. He did very well very fast. (Thank you always for your help.) But if I keep seeing him, even sometimes, I'm sure I'll think about him more than now. I think I can wait until February, and if I pass the exam then, maybe something will be possible. Maybe by then, though, he won't want to be friends. I don't know if a boy like him could wait. And he wants to go abroad...for music composition, he says, one must study in Europe. He can't understand the way a girl like me thinks.

Maybe you won't be able to understand either, but this is my way.

I miss you, so I hope you can answer soon.

♡ Kana

With the embarrassment of the club meeting behind her, Kana decided it would be much better to study on her own. She tried to keep her mind off what had happened with Kurokawa—not difficult, given that Kana preferred not to think about her pretentious schoolmate in the first place. She *was* prone to thinking about Daisuke, however, particularly when she stood on the platform, watching the southbound train she would have taken to Shibuya come and go again. It was a little sad, Kana thought to herself, but she had pledged to take responsibility for her actions. Until the next round of exams came and went, she couldn't trust herself not to get too distracted by him.

She didn't blame Daisuke for his demands on her time when they were study partners. After all, he had been paying her for the time, and she had been the one to say "I can do it." It would have been easy for her to lessen the number of sessions they had, but she enjoyed studying with Daisuke, and more importantly, she enjoyed *being* with Daisuke. He was smart, funny, and talented.

That, of course, was also why she couldn't trust herself to be around him. She had hoped—she had even wished, back at that shrine—that after they had written their tests, and the first round of letters came back from the schools they applied to, she and Daisuke would celebrate together, even if it was the same as every day. Over a cup of coffee and a strawberry shortcake or a Mont Blanc. And after that, well, who knew?

Kana had always thought that after the nightmare of third-year exams were over, she could think more seriously about having a boyfriend. It wasn't uncommon to think this way, either; in fact among her classmates it was considered cool and strong-willed to refrain from dating to focus on studying. As long as you sighed every once in a while over how someday you'd have it all, as long as you could hang in there. "Let's do our best!" they told each other, "and after graduation, we'll live it up!"

Sometimes, Kana wished for the sort of easygoing high

school life Megucchi talked about, with seasonal dances and dates and parties, or like the proms she saw on television. Canadian students, she thought, had it easy, not needing to pass entrance exams or SATs. It would be nice to be graded by her teachers who already knew and liked her, and avoid all the long hours of cram school and intense competition. Someday, Kana thought, she would like to go abroad to work, but that wasn't going to be the same as if she'd done something like a high school exchange. She'd never have the chance to try out that culture firsthand.

She didn't like to dwell over what she couldn't have, though. Not under normal circumstances, at least—Kana was surprised how difficult it turned out to be to stop thinking about Daisuke. She hadn't quite realized how much she enjoyed his company until she had given it up. She wondered, not for the first time, if maybe she could be making the wrong call by keeping him at a distance.

Kana also found she was no longer able to concentrate on reviewing during her commute home. It was always so early in the afternoon that she got to sit down on every train, but her mind drifted away to thoughts of Daisuke and Rumi, to Megucchi, and to all the lost freedom she'd imagined she'd have by this time, if only it hadn't all gone so wrong.

When she arrived home, no one was there to greet her, either. Shingo practised with the baseball club until late, and her father had his usual overnights at the office. Her mother sometimes had a weekday off, but went to the supermarket around the time Kana would walk in after her long ride back.

"Normal," in the Momokawa household, was for all four of them to be out until well after dark. Now Kana whiled away hours by herself in her room, trying to focus on subjects that would be part of the second-round exams. Ancient Japanese was a difficult class, and she knew without cram school she would need to keep reviewing daily to maintain her English skills.

She also missed Megucchi. Not just the easy access to answers about English, but her pen pal's own questions about Japanese culture and language. Kana knew she ought to get in contact and update Megucchi on what had happened. If she ever got her cell phone back, there were sure to be a few dozen messages waiting. It seemed odd that there hadn't been a reply to the message she sent from Daisuke's phone, though. Since the weekend, Kana had checked her StreetSwEETs inbox several times, but heard nothing from her pen pal.

When she'd hung up her uniform and changed into lounge pants and a t-shirt, Kana looked at the clock. Nobody was home —where was the harm in sneaking in a few minutes online? She sat at her computer and logged in, but found nothing there. Perhaps Megucchi hadn't gotten the message, and continued to try to contact Kana via cell phone mail?

Kana knew Megucchi often accessed messages interchangeably from both phone and computer. Maybe, she thought, Megucchi didn't realize that in Japan, cell phone provider email addresses went only to the phone. Without her mobile, Kana had no way to get into her inbox to look for replies.

She opened a new window and drafted a message in somewhat messier English than usual, even though she could see from Megucchi's profile that her friend hadn't been online in several days. Maybe she was having some sort of computer troubles, but Kana couldn't help but start to worry a bit.

She sometimes wondered if the cheerful demeanour her pen pal showed in their exchanges was truly how Megucchi always acted. Megucchi seemed to be so shy at times, and critical of herself. Kana wasn't sure why; she was a good friend, and Kana thought she was a nice person. She had a cool-looking boyfriend (Rumi had swooned over that photo of Simon, he was *absolutely* her type) and was so smart even in science and math, subjects that constantly eluded Kana. Megucchi had a cute sense of style and was unquestionably talented at sewing and crafting.

Plus, she wanted to learn all about Japan and studied the language from books, even though she would never have to take a test in it!

No wonder they had hit it off. Kana was abruptly struck with elation, thinking about how nice it had been to have Megucchi as a friend. At first it had been odd to have a stranger asking so many questions about her life, but now Kana felt lucky to have met someone so generous with her time. Kana wished she had asked her friend more questions about her own life.

She signed the message and sent it, feeling uneasy, but there was little she felt she could do. She would have to hope for the best, for now.

~*~*~

In her excitement, Grace had forgotten to be cautious and mark on her map the way she had walked to reach the hotel in daylight. When she returned late at the end of another day of fruitless searching, she couldn't quite figure out how to get from where she stood over to the exit she needed. Compared to this, Odaiba and even Shibuya had been a cakewalk, Grace reflected.

Picking an exit that sounded familiar, she emerged outside of a department store, still lit up like a Christmas tree despite the late hour. The station looked different at night, but this area seemed familiar. She started walking down a street she felt sure she had been on earlier that afternoon. Hungry, Grace kept an eye out for someplace to have a quick bite to eat, but only passed hole-in-the-wall bars and the occasional late-night ramen joint. All the familiar places were closed.

In fact, though it *seemed* like Shinjuku was still lively, Grace realized quickly that the nicer shops and even many of the fast-food places had already shut down for the night. She had envisioned Tokyo as a city that never slept, but here the sidewalks seemed to roll up even earlier than they did back home. A little worried, she walked faster, wishing she'd chosen a hotel closer to the station. Only five minutes, but those five minutes seemed like an eternity.

A short while later, Grace came to a slow stop. The area looked different at night, and she didn't remember seeing this arch lit with neon bulbs, though the buildings lining the narrow road she had just walked along had seemed familiar. Grace pulled her jacket tighter around herself and hurried on, deciding if she didn't find the hotel on the next block, she would turn back.

This part of Shinjuku seemed distinctly seedier than the station area, or at least appeared so after dark. Stopping again, Grace felt absolutely certain she'd gone the wrong way. There were very few people out, and hotels she didn't recognize lined the street. They all had preposterous English signage, like Hotel Heart-Amulet and Hotel Chapeau Honey Neige. No way she wouldn't have noticed these bizarre names the first time. Grace wasn't sure if they were places to sleep, or cabarets, or worse. Everything that wasn't one of the odd hotels appeared to be a bar. She abruptly reversed course.

She had almost made it back to the arches when Grace passed a man dressed in a business suit, his tie loosened and a briefcase in his hand. He stopped when he saw Grace approaching, and crossed the street to intercept her. "Hello. Hello."

"Hello," Grace replied, nervous but surprised to hear English.

"You *skpmrypmohjy?*" He nodded his head and said something Grace didn't understand, that might or might not have been Japanese.

"Excuse me?"

The man stepped a little closer. "Where country?"

"Uh...from Canada."

"Great, great. Canada great. *Esmyvpnosmu?*" The man said something else unintelligible, and made a gesture with his hand.

Grace felt uncomfortable from the start. He was asking her a question, but she didn't really get it, and wasn't sure she wanted to. The motion he had made seemed like it might be obscene. "Sorry, I don't understand…"

"*Vpnreoyjnr.*" The man encircled her wrist with his stubby hand. Grace yanked it away as though she'd been burned, turned, and fled as fast as she could, back toward the neon. She didn't hear anything behind her, and she thought he had maybe had too many drinks to chase her, but Grace was too terrified to stop. She couldn't even glance back over her shoulder. Her footfalls thundered on the sidewalk, and the slaps of her soles made it worse, as though the sound of a girl fleeing would be enough to attract more creepy perverts over for a share. She ran until she was under the awning of Shinjuku Station, and then, once safely inside and hidden around a corner, she crumpled to the floor, trembling.

What a mistake it had been, coming here! It had all been for nothing. She had spent too much money, hadn't even come close to finding Kana, lied to her parents, and now this. Somehow, Grace still managed to feel small and ashamed as she heaved with the effort to catch her breath and keep in the tears. Her knees were too weak to stand on.

Right in front of her, the crowd continued to flow in and out of the station, without directing their attention to Grace for even a millisecond.

She was invisible.

Bit by bit the fear response subsided, but Grace couldn't bring herself to go back outside. Ten minutes passed before she could even stand up without clutching the wall for support, and when she did, she went straight to a grey pay phone and filled it with all the coins in her pockets.

Grace tried to calculate the time zone change in her head. Ten in the morning back home? Eleven? No, that wasn't right, she had forgotten the half hour. Maybe ten-thirty. It didn't really matter to her at that point. No matter what time it was, she was calling.

Grace had to dial several times before her shaking fingers pressed all the right buttons in sequence. The sound of the tones gave way to a tinny ringing sound; once, twice, three times. On the fourth ring she heard a click, and her mother's recorded voice cheerfully requested she leave a message after the beep.

"Hi...it's me. I kind of hoped you'd pick up, but I guess a voicemail is good enough. Called to say hi." She swallowed hard, trying to stop her voice from cracking. "Anyway, my phone's not working right now, so you don't need to call me back. I guess I'll call you again. Miss you lots. I love you. Bye."

Grace hung up the phone and, almost as an afterthought, wondered if she'd made a mistake. The house phone was an old, retro-style handset that didn't have caller ID, but if people began looking for her...

She wondered if either of her parents suspected that she wasn't with the other.

Outside, she did a slow circuit around the station before she dared venture too far from its safety net. Instead of daydreaming or thinking about tomorrow's plans, Grace laser-focused on her surroundings, even when she was back on the well-lit streets walking to her hotel. She tried to look tough, unapproachable as she strode purposefully away from Shinjuku Station. None of the passersby gave her a second glance.

Relief hit Grace like a ton of bricks when the hotel finally came into sight. When she was safely inside, she had to stop and collect herself before passing the young clerk at the front desk. The expression on her face would certainly have betrayed her.

Upstairs, she dropped her jacket on the floor and flopped onto the bed, wanting nothing more than to sleep for a week, but still feeling too shaken up to rest. She double and triple-checked the locks, then showered in the tiny bathroom.

Shortly before midnight, Grace put on a sweatshirt and jeans and went downstairs to check out the public computers in the lobby.

Internet access had been a selling point when she chose this hotel. She hadn't checked her mail since arriving in Japan, and she wanted to talk to Daisuke again and see if he had heard from Kana. He must know *some*thing by now, she thought, though in truth, anxiety tightened her chest. She didn't want to feel any worse than she did right at that moment.

In truth, there had been a few opportunities to peek at her inbox, as she passed Internet cafes by the dozen in her travels. Something stopped her from investigating further every time, though. Internet cafe entrances she'd seen were choked with cigarette smoke and the outdoor signage rarely had more than a hint of English. How was she supposed to book a computer? And if she did, and there was a message from Kana or someone who knew her, what if it was bad news? Grace wasn't certain she could handle hearing the worst under those circumstances.

And what if it *wasn't* bad news? What if Kana had simply been too busy to get back to her? What if Grace was so insignificant a concern that her messages were too much for Kana to deal with all the time?

Plus, what if she had somehow been traced, and opening her mail helped authorities back home find her, and she found herself deported from Japan? Grace hadn't committed a crime, but she wasn't sure what could happen when a missing person was discovered in another country. Who knew what power the authorities here might have?

All these scenarios caused her anxiety. Easier, Grace thought, to rush past the Internet cafes and hope she could find Kana on her own. Now, though, after so many days in Japan that she could no longer afford the nice hotel, the situation had grown more dire. If there were clues to be had in her inbox, Grace needed to look for them, or risk never finding Kana at all.

Connecting to the browser, she opened her email, unaware she was holding her breath as she scanned subject lines. She saw a letter from Simon, with the subject "*I miss you*," that she guiltily skipped. Another alert said she had a new private message on her StreetSwEETs account. Grace never talked to anyone but Kana on StreetSwEETs, so she went to the website straightaway. When her inbox loaded, she saw the message was indeed from Kana.

Grace read the first lines of text all in one glance.

Hi Megucchi,

I don't know if you got my message before, that I sent from Mister Otsuka's phone. Maybe not...

Of course. Of course Kana was fine, as Grace had hoped in her heart that she would be. Everything was okay. Grace let out the breath she'd been holding in a slow exhale.

She felt relieved to see that her friend was unharmed, of course, but Grace also felt almost...cheated. She had come all the way to Japan, and hadn't even managed to find Kana, despite her great detective work. All those hours she had waited by Hachiko, in the cafes, and in the train stations. In the end it had been Kana who ended the search, and without ever even knowing Grace was there!

She could only stay disappointed for a few minutes, though; her great relief that Kana was safe outweighed the sinking feeling that coming here had been a complete waste. On top of that, Grace felt certain Kana was *not* doing all right. That much was clear from hearing she'd told Daisuke to stay away from her. It was the kind of action Grace *herself* might have taken, but Kana wasn't the type. On Grace she had impressed a strong, independent personality who went after what she wanted without hesitation, and carefully balanced her choices. Why drop everything now to study for a makeup test she certainly must already know she would pass?

Grace suspected there could be more to it, but now that she had an opening, she no longer knew what to say. The way Kana had phrased her message, it seemed like she didn't want Grace to question her motives.

She very much wanted to know what was going on. And now, with the search abruptly concluded, Grace would be free to go home, she supposed, but she could hardly do so without seeing her friend in person. But how?

Kana would wonder why Grace was suddenly in Japan, stalking her. She'd feel bad that Grace had dropped everything and flown halfway around the world to look for her. That, or she might think Grace was a strange, desperate girl, one that she might not want to be all that close to.

Grace didn't think she felt ready yet to have *that* conversation.

Kana trudged home from the station feeling more under the weather than usual. Another day of school, then studying until dinner, then studying until bath, then bed. Late December rain ran off her umbrella in rivulets. The damp chill in the air left her legs numb long after she stepped into the house.

Nobody was home. Kana fixed herself a snack and changed into lounge pants, hanging her uniform on a hanger on the wall. She didn't need to open the bureau. She had been changing back and forth between these two outfits for almost two weeks.

It seemed like such a waste to stay in every day like this, she thought sadly, doing nothing but reviewing. Kana was aware that she had been overly strict with herself, more as a form of self-punishment than anything else, but recently started to lose some of her resolve. She felt good about the retest, even the subjects she had been weaker in before. Maybe it would be okay to loosen up a bit. She couldn't forgive herself for what had happened, but she had to keep going. It wasn't like things could go on like this forever.

Under her *kotatsu*, Kana reviewed Japanese literature for the better part of the evening, pausing only to refill her teacup and cut a persimmon from a basket her father had brought home on his weekend visit. When her mother called them for dinner, Kana closed the book with a snap. She had done enough for the day.

After sitting at the table and giving thanks, Kana lifted her rice bowl, then set it down again. "Mother."

Himeko looked up. "Yes?"

"I was hoping that maybe I could have my cell phone back today."

Her mother held her gaze for a long moment. "Why?"

Shingo looked like he wanted to say something, then he quickly reversed course, shovelling rice into his mouth at double speed. He could smell a fight brewing.

"Because I haven't talked to anyone in two weeks. I miss my friends."

"You *did* go to school today?"

Kana frowned. "Of course I did."

"Then you saw your friends?"

"If you have friends in another class, though, there's not a lot of time to see them," offered Shingo helpfully.

"That's right." Kana shot her brother a grateful look.

"I thought you said you were going to study today." Her mother's voice was mild, but Kana still felt as though she had been reprimanded. Himeko's stern face was unsmiling.

"I did. I came home right after school and I've been reviewing since."

"And now you want to waste the rest of the evening playing?"

Kana laid her chopsticks down, but stood her ground. "I just wanted to take a break."

"That's fine, but what's next? Taking a break by going to the city? And if you go, will you come back at a decent hour? You don't seem to be able to say no to people."

"That's not true."

"It is. Your friends always talk you into staying out late."

Kana didn't say anything at all. She couldn't help wanting to please people; her parents had raised her to be gracious. Rumi, being headstrong and blind sometimes to what was going on in front of her, similarly couldn't seem to help wheedling when she didn't get what she wanted. Kana hated to say no.

Himeko seemed to think she'd said enough, so she resumed eating, and the rest of the meal proceeded in silence. Shingo finished in record time and disappeared into his room before Kana had eaten her fish.

When Himeko put the last bite in her mouth, she stood and left the room, then returned with the phone, handing it to her daughter without a word before disappearing into the kitchen. Kana sat at the table alone, divided. She didn't particularly *feel* like having her privileges back anymore, after all that.

But she powered on the phone, finished her meal, then went back upstairs to her room. Maybe her mother *didn't* know how she felt, but at least she might be willing to let Kana decide for herself.

~*~*~

When Grace awoke, she felt calmer than she had been the night before, but still had to fight the urge to run to the airport and catch the first flight back. The weight of worrying about Kana had been replaced with a constant sinking feeling that she had made a terrible mistake, and there had never been any real reason for her to be here.

She'd come so far already. She'd take a day or two to wrap up and do the tourist thing, Grace decided. Once she got home, she would be grounded for so long that she wouldn't be visiting Japan again in this lifetime, and it seemed such a waste that most of what she'd seen had been the inside of subway stations and the seediest parts of inner Tokyo. Aside from the miniature Electric Town, not much interested Grace in the area around her hotel. She wasn't entirely sure she liked Shinjuku at all anymore.

Now that she had come to terms with the transit system, though, she didn't mind going a little further afield.

She had been looking at Tokyo Tower from across the bay for days, but hadn't gotten up close, so Grace decided it might be a good place to start. According to the guidebook, even though the Skytree would be much taller when it was completed, Tokyo Tower was still one of the biggest tourist attractions in the city. It happened to also be a popular field trip spot, so Grace was pleasantly surprised when the lobby turned out to be empty. Perhaps it wasn't the season, she mused, taking it as a sign that her luck might be improving. She could watch through the window as the elevator climbed to the observation deck, then stepped out into a scene that seemed so familiar, from a movie she'd seen or the anime shows that aired late at night at the hotel, that she couldn't tear her eyes away.

The experience was similar to the CN Tower she'd visited in Toronto, but with much bigger windows. Uniformed students clustered in groups around the binoculars. Suddenly shy, Grace hung back from them, watching schoolgirls take photos of each other.

As she circled the observation deck, Grace was astonished by the sheer size of the metropolis. From Odaiba she had seen the skyline, but the bay lay between her and it, so it had seemed much smaller than expected. This, though, was exactly the mental image she had created of Tokyo before she arrived; vast, expansive, with towers and office buildings and public bath chimneys rising haphazardly in every direction. Grace picked out the shapes of Shinjuku skyscrapers in the near distance. Further away, Mount Fuji peeked out, barely visible among the clouds. She had come on a clear day, and marvelled at actually being able to see it from so far away.

On the bay side, Grace could see the first hotel she had stayed in, and the bulbous TV station headquarters. She walked the entire way around the tower again, wishing she had brought a camera. This, she thought, would be something she wanted to remember. Tokyo was so amazingly vast, and maybe it was a little too busy and grey for her to want to live in, but she hoped to be able to recall what it felt like to be in the middle of a place so incredibly different from home.

For the first time since she'd arrived in the city, Grace felt as though she'd done something worthwhile.

Before taking the elevator back downstairs, Grace opened *Friendly Planet* to look for other places to spend her day. Not too far away from the Tower, she wandered the streets of Ginza, looking at the exquisite Christmas decorations in high-class shops. She went to Akihabara, the so-called "Electric Town," and browsed cheap electronics, then sat in massage chairs among the businessmen at a department store.

The next day, Grace returned to Shibuya and let loose. She wore the best clothes she had to browse in the 109 building, trying to look like she shopped there all the time. She still felt a bit nervous, wearing trendy clothes and sparkly hair accessories, as though someone she knew would appear from around the corner and call her out for being a fake. It was nice, Grace thought, that here, no one stared at what she was wearing and laughed behind her back. Here, she felt only out of place because she happened to be a foreigner, and the shop girls still smiled politely, so what did it matter?

Christmas was only a few days away, now, and Grace knew it was past time to try to get her ticket back to Toronto. She almost dared to think she might get away with this whole adventure *without* her mother ever finding out she'd been gone. *I could show up at Dad's on Christmas Day, like I told him I would, and neither of them would ever know. Wouldn't that be wild?*

She felt a little proud of herself, having gotten this far. Arriving on schedule in Toronto on Christmas Day, though, meant spending Christmas Eve here by herself. It was tough to imagine missing the usual ritual of hot chocolate and the wood-burning fireplace of her mother's house, but also the walk down to Yonge and Queen with her father to look at Christmas window displays, like they'd done every year she spent in Toronto. She would need to spend Christmas on the plane, Grace realized, to get there on time. Wouldn't she? Time zone changes were so complicated!

It would be better to go home early, she decided, and tell her dad the ticket had been changed after all. He would be happy and she'd be happy. Nobody would have to know she'd been gallivanting around Asia for a week. It was nice being here for the season, but she didn't want to spend Christmas in Japan if she could help it—even though it was impressively festive. Meiji Street was decked out, and the illuminations on the Shinjuku Southern Terrace and Odaiba were breathtakingly beautiful. Religious references were noticeably absent, but Grace thought it was fine that way, seeing how there were very few Christians in Japan, as far as she knew.

Shibuya, too, had been dressed up since she arrived, but Grace hadn't had time to truly appreciate it until after her search had ended. A huge tree had been placed in the garden in Hachiko Square that was brightly lit at dusk, and decorations hung on light fixtures all the way up Center Street. Someone had even dressed Hachiko in a Santa hat and garland.

She lingered by the statue, people-watching, as she had done so many times before. The metal supports behind the statue helped Grace rest her weary legs. She didn't think she had ever done much walking in her life as over the last few days. Maybe that was how everyone here seemed to stay so thin, Grace thought, as a gaggle of girls in short shorts and knee-high furry boots swept past, looking as unaffected by the December chill as if it were July. Grace shivered, unmistakably cold in her skirt and black leggings, but she felt *fashionable*, she told herself. She wiggled her toes inside her warm boots and kept thinking about home.

The events of the party now seemed ages away. Grace felt guilty, wondering how Simon and Jean were doing. She'd skimmed one or two of the pleading messages Simon had been sending, but hadn't known what to say. She didn't have an excuse for why she'd been ignoring him after getting Internet access. She thought about maybe responding when she returned to the hotel that night, even if she had to fib a little about why she hadn't responded in a week. The thought of turning on her cell phone when she landed in Canada and seeing all the missed texts and calls put Grace's stomach into knots.

And then there was Kana...she would have to tell Kana soon that she had come to Japan, but without saying why, Grace supposed. In spite of how nervous she felt, Grace wanted to meet her friend in person. She couldn't go back yet, not without having seen her pen pal.

Grace was mentally composing the many things she might say to open the conversation, when two meters in front of her, an unmistakably familiar figure appeared.

It was Kana.

Chapter 17

The big smoke	Fri, Dec 19, 9:55 AM
From: simon_says_something_clever@geemail.com	To: megumi_709

Hi Gracie. I just wanted to say that I miss you so so much. I sent some texts before and tried to call, but it goes right to voicemail without even ringing. I even tried to use a read receipt. Maybe you had phone trouble or got grounded or something? That doesn't sound like your dad, but totally grasping at straws here, since you usually eat and sleep with your phone in your hand. To be honest, I'm worried.

I don't feel right about it. Is everything okay? If something is wrong, you know I want to talk about it.

I think it would be a good idea to have a phone call if you can. I can call you at your dad's place if you give me the number.

Love always
simon

For a second Grace thought she must be mistaken. There were thousands of Japanese schoolgirls who wore blue tartan skirts and cream-coloured cardigans, and millions who were on the tall side and had long, straight black hair, but there couldn't be too many who threaded ribbons around the tops of their socks. The figure who'd caught Grace's eye stood with her back to Grace, watching the station exit, and she'd only caught a glimpse of the face for a split second, but she felt positive. Grace had watched hundreds and hundreds of people meeting at Hachiko since she arrived, and never once had she looked at one and been so certain.

Kana stood close to the statue, and shuffled further away to give a pair of tourists room to take a photo, setting her satchel down on the ledge to fix her pale blue scarf.

This was a sign, Grace realized. She could stow the reading glasses, approach her friend with a casual wave and shyly introduce herself. Maybe she could say it had been a surprise, though fibbing about that part might backfire when Grace returned home and was inevitably grounded for life.

She stood up, clutching her purse in her hand, but Grace couldn't force her legs to move. The thought of walking up to Kana without any preparation paralyzed her with fear. What if Kana reacted negatively? What if she realized Grace wasn't the confident speaker from their text exchanges, but in reality a shy and awkward girl?

Worse, what if Kana *herself* wasn't the person Grace had expected her to be? It seemed better to keep Kana the way Grace had always imagined her, instead of letting a chance face-to-face encounter change that.

She knew chickening out at this crucial moment would be a step backwards. Here, she had conquered travelling by train, ordering food in a foreign language, staying alone in a hotel, creepy businessmen and more.

Why should it be so difficult to go up to Kana and say hello?

Grace wasn't even sure. She only knew that she could not

make her legs move to close the gap between her and her friend, who still stood so close Grace could grab her by the back of her blazer, where if Kana were to turn around she wouldn't be able to help noticing this wide-eyed foreigner lurking behind her.

Instead Grace drew back and watched as Kana waved to someone. A shorter girl approached, clad in bright purple corduroy short-shorts trimmed with white fleece. It wasn't Rumi, not with that long curly bleached hair.

The stranger spoke with Kana for a few moments near the statue. Then, as the pedestrian crossing changed to green, they walked off together.

Gathering her shopping bags, Grace ran after them, but stopped to stand at the edge of Hachiko Square, watching Kana's scarf disappear into the throng. The countdown steadily ticked toward zero. Someone hit her elbow and muttered in Japanese.

The crowd around her ebbed and flowed as all sides rushed forward and past, until Grace was the only one left standing there.

~*~*~

Miki seemed to like sweets as much as her brother. She ordered a strawberry shortcake, as Daisuke always did, and a coffee with three sugars. Kana tried not to wince as she watched cubes plop into the cup.

"So, what can I help you with, *Miss* Momokawa?" Miki inquired, laying her spoon daintily on the saucer. "Sorry. That's about as much English as I can manage."

"It's okay. Actually, I'm having some trouble and I wanted to ask you for your opinion."

"About Dai-chan?"

Kana smiled at the nickname, but shook her head. "No, it doesn't have anything to do with Otsuka-kun. Well, not much, anyway. It's just that I'm kind of...confused...about what I should be doing right now."

"What do you mean?"

Kana twisted the fringe of her scarf into a knot. It was hard to look Miki in the face and talk about her shame so bluntly. "I messed up with my entrance exam, and I didn't plan for any other schools, so now I have to wait for the next round. I told Otsuka-kun I wouldn't be able to...to work with him anymore. And I told all my friends not to bother asking me to go out."

"Ah."

"I even quit cram school to save my parents the money, so I go right home and take out my books thinking it'll make them happy...and I honestly do want to get into Nishidai...but *I'm* not happy. Miki-san, you go to a good school and you work; how did you manage it?"

Clearly, the older girl hadn't expected their conversation to go in this direction. She paused for a long moment, thoughtfully stirring her coffee. "I've gotta tell you, it's not easy. Especially if you're really passionate about your hobbies. Like I am, and I think you are, too."

"Yes."

"Well...I think you already know this part, but when I was in junior high and high school, I was a Gal. If you know anything about that...well, we spent a lot of time hanging around, generally embarrassing the adults." She smiled fondly. "Everything was about clothes, makeup and brand names. We'd crowd together into two tables at the fast food places—the twelve of us in my circle—and trade makeup tips and Print Club photos. Every day after class I'd take the train to Shibuya from Kamata and hang out with my friends."

"I read about what Gals were like back in the heyday." Kana said. "The scene was so different back then."

"I was there when it was just *the best.* In those days, Gal culture was at the height of power. Wherever we went, we ruled." She laughed. "We made our own rules."

"I wish I could have been there."

"It was amazing. But my circle and me, we were all about ourselves, and honestly we didn't give a damn about anything that wasn't part of the lifestyle. It probably sounds silly to you, because you're such a good student, but I liked it that way.

"The thing was, my mom died when I was young, and my dad never remarried. He put me through high school, even though I didn't want anything to do with it. I only wanted to be a Gal, and maybe get a job at Maru-Kyu someday. I wanted to hang around Shibuya until I got noticed, got famous. Instead, Dad made me take all these high school entrance exams, and I ended up at a public school near my house."

Kana nodded, fascinated. Miki kept talking. "Dai-chan was in elementary school then, and it's kind of embarrassing to say it, but I wasn't a good big sister." She looked sheepish. "I wanted to be a normal teenager, you know? I didn't want to be the girl that didn't have a mom. So I bought my lunch from the convenience store on my way to school every day, and packed it to pretend someone had made it homemade for me. My dad used to give me some money; I think he knew I was wasting it, but he never said a thing. I guess he didn't really know how to raise a teenage girl and he felt guilty about it."

Kana felt captivated as Miki told her story, surprised she hadn't known the Otsukas were a single-parent family. She'd pictured Daisuke as the type of boy who came home and got a good-natured scolding from his mother for his hair and dress. When she thought about it, she had no recollection of him ever mentioning his parents.

"Things went on like that until my last year of high school. The teachers were harping on us about exams, but my friends and I couldn't care less. We still wanted to get the dream job, working at a shop here, selling clothes. I'd thought about maybe studying journalism once or twice because I was into writing, before I started thinking about fashion, but I never gave it much thought. I figured I could stay at home with Dad and Dai-chan until my lucky break came along."

"But...?"

"It's coming!" Miki's dazzling smile never faltered. "So, one day at the beginning of my third year, I faked being sick so I could go home and get dressed up for the night. I wanted to go to karaoke with my friends and I was super into this cute guy working part-time at the KaraBan. Nobody should have been home, but when I got there, Dai-chan was in the kitchen by himself, making instant ramen. I guess he must have been eleven or twelve at the time. Still in elementary school."

Now Miki laid the cup down and looked at the milky coffee. "Well, he wasn't supposed to be there, so I got annoyed. When I asked him what he thought he was doing, why he wasn't at *kendo* or something, he made some lame excuses. And I told him if he was cutting practice and eating salty junk like that, he was going to end up getting fat." Miki's cheeks coloured under her makeup. "I mean, I was seventeen and he was my little brother, I wasn't exactly nice all the time. But it turned out he quit *kendo*. He'd been coming home every day and eating the only thing he could cook, ramen. Because he had been missing lunch every single day, all that time, ever since I stopped making his lunch box."

Kana gasped. "Oh, no..."

"Yeah. So *that* was great. All my fault. I found out later that he used to hide up on the school roof so his classmates wouldn't ask why he didn't have anything to eat. I wondered why he never told Dad that nobody was cooking for him, but I think it was because he didn't want to get me in trouble. That was the kind of kid he was; quiet, sweet. A far cry from now, I guess." She laughed to herself. "Anyway, it was kind of a wake-up call for me. I started getting up early again to make sure he had something to eat and time to play after school and join clubs. I... didn't want him to end up in the same kind of spot I did with my non-Gal classmates. Sometimes I wonder what would have happened if I didn't get my act together back then, if he could have been someone totally different."

"And then you decided to go to university after all?"

"That's right. After the whole thing with Dai-chan, I kind of saw that I had been letting him down, and started to think that I must have been disappointing my dad, too. He worked such long hours, after all, and he kept telling me I should go to university. So I started studying, and I got a part-time job to help me save up for it. I'm not like you; I don't have the brains for a scholarship." Miki laughed. "And in a low-level school like mine, it was tough to learn the right things in class. I was working really hard every day with discount study guides to catch up, and of course I was in the same boat as you when it came to my hobbies. Couldn't stop them altogether."

"So you kept being a Gal?"

"Did I ever! I was the most studious one in town. I think I got asked on more dates than ever after I became a nerdy Gal."

Kana's hands were wrapped tightly around her cup. She was so absorbed in the story that she hadn't touched her milk tea. "That's amazing. I would never in a hundred years have guessed that you didn't study at all."

"I flunked almost every high school entrance exam I took," Miki admitted. "And it made things a lot harder for me in the end. Your school *actually* teaches you what you need to get into Nishidai, even if you need to push harder to get to the top. That's the difference between our situations. But you know what? I know you can do it. Every time you come into the cafe with Dai-chan, even when you guys are supposed to be taking a break, you're a hundred percent focused on everything you say. I had enough English to get into my school, but I can't follow half of what you guys are saying when I pass by your table."

"Well, Otsuka-kun is actually very good at English." Kana replied, a little flattered.

"He is, right!?" Miki couldn't be modest when it came to her little brother's skills. "He's fantastic. And so are you."

"I don't know. Maybe it was enough to pass the early test, but everything is different now." She shifted uncomfortably in her seat.

"So your solution is to drop everything else, until you get so down on yourself you can't focus?" Miki leaned her chin on her hand and looked at Kana, perplexed.

"That isn't what I mean."

"Okay, then, what do you mean?"

Sighing heavily, Kana laid both hands on the table, staring down at them. "I feel *guilty* about doing anything else. Like I should have earned any rest I get. My mother is getting on my case, too, because she thinks I'm wasting time."

Miki cracked a smile. "That's her job, kiddo. She doesn't know any other way than to nag. But the job of a high school student sometimes involves pissing off one's parents. I wouldn't worry too much about it."

"You wouldn't?"

"Definitely not. I remember what my mom was like when I was in junior high."

Kana took a deep breath. "I'm sorry about your mom. That must have been hard."

"It was really hard," she replied softly. "But I got through it. And I think she'd be happy for me now. I found a balance."

"A balance," Kana repeated.

"Yeah. Because if all you do is study, you'll start hating it, and it'll be even harder. You have to find something in between. I think you're the type that always listens seriously to your friends and your parents, but not everything they want for you is going to be what's right for *you*. You have to follow your own beat."

Kana thought back to the weeks before the exam, and the way she had conceded to Rumi and Daisuke every time they needed her. Maybe Miki was right, maybe she needed to learn to say no to people. If she had levelled with her mother at the dinner table the other day, maybe she wouldn't have spent all that time moping.

"I think you're right," she said at length. "I was trying to keep everybody happy. Even though I was the only one who wasn't."

Miki grinned and put the last bite of shortcake in her mouth. "And you know, maybe if you stop being a hermit, my brother will stop moping around all the time and get his own plans back on track."

Kana felt her heart speed up. She hoped it didn't show on her face. "You're joking."

"He's been so down since you stopped seeing him."

She couldn't help but feel a little pleased that he was thinking about her. Maybe she hadn't lost her chance after all.

"Hey," Miki interrupted. "I know that look. I didn't say it to make you feel guilty. I only want you to know that he wants to see you. I gotta look out for my little brother, right?"

"I know. I understand."

"Hang in there, kid," Miki said good-naturedly. "Listen—it's getting late here. I have to go, but come talk to me anytime if you need help. I'll listen anytime."

"Thank you."

Outside, Miki grasped Kana's hands, the gems on her decorated thumbnails glittering. "Please at least talk to Dai-chan. It would make him so happy. Okay?"

Kana looked down at the stones as she spoke. The false nails were manicured and decorated with such care, painstakingly inlaid with gems and tiny plastic bows. Somehow, Miki found the time to be a full-time university student, work part-time, make lunches for her little brother, and still manage to pay close attention to the style that defined her. Kana wondered if the nails had to be taken off for her job and reapplied later—she had never noticed her friend wearing such a manicure at work. But they were Gal nails through and through. It seemed like something that was important to Miki, something that Miki made time for. Even when she had very little extra time to work with.

"...Okay. I'll contact him." Not just because Kana owed his

sister now, but if Miki could slice out the time to meet Kana on what was obviously a busy day, Kana could make the effort to see Daisuke, too.

"I'm counting on you, gorgeous."

"Thanks again."

Miki hurried up Center Street, leaving Kana alone. On her new schedule, normally she would be most of the way home already. Today, though, she didn't rush back to the station. Kana had already found hope in Miki's advice, but the question that remained was what she would do about it. She needed to think.

Satisfied that she had done what she'd come to Shibuya for, Kana returned to the scramble crossing and went into the underground. She wondered, if she retraced the route Daisuke had taken them on a few weeks before, up to the seventh floor of Aqua City, would she find him there?

The sky was almost completely dark by the time Kana reached the shrine. Even though she held out that little bit of hope she might run into Daisuke, she felt more relieved to find the roof mostly empty.

She stood with her arms resting on the tall railing, her satchel at her feet, a chill breeze from the bay whipping through her hair. Buildings on the Shinagawa side and civil twilight worked in tandem to light the cloudless sky.

The last time Kana had been here, she'd thrown a coin into the offering box and made a wish that her feelings for Daisuke could be mutual. The situation had changed so drastically since then.

Though Kana wasn't religious or superstitious, she had always liked the idea of luck and charms, and sometimes the wishes made on falling stars that sailed above her grandparents' house in rural Kyoto had come to pass. They were simple whimsy, but those early wishes tempted her analytical personality with a belief that maybe such things could be possible. In junior high school, Kana had tied lucky charms to her school bag and prayed that she would get into Koen Academy. Not so long ago, the wish she had made at Meiji Shrine had brought Megucchi to her. Why should Kana be surprised that the wish she had made with Daisuke might also come to pass?

Maybe, she thought, it was because in the past she had made wishes that she could accomplish on her own, and deliberately put herself on the path to making them come true. Daisuke was different, a sudden fancy beyond her control.

Kana had never considered herself a believer in fate or a subscriber to the theory that everything happened for a reason. She found, though, as she looked back at the offering box that contained hundreds of five-yen wishes, that maybe those things weren't so much more far-fetched than buying a lucky charm and praying for success. Maybe the universe was telling her to accept what she was being given instead of fighting it.

Kana crossed the roof to the shrine, withdrew another fifty-yen piece, tossed it into the box and rang the bell. She didn't make a wish; rather, she simply stood in front of the *torii* for a long time, considering carefully. When she turned back to the skyline, she thought that maybe, just this once, it would be all right to let what would be, be.

~*~*~

Long after Kana's swishing blue scarf disappeared from her view, Grace sat beside the statue, hoping her friend would walk across the square again.

Unwilling to direct her gaze away from the crowd even for a moment, Grace had only her thoughts to distract her. She found herself wondering how Jean and Simon were doing. Simon, in particular, was a cause for worry. When Grace left Canada she had felt the same as always, yet the longer she went without seeing him, the less she thought about him. Not a good sign, and it made her nervous about what might happen when she returned home.

Home was closer than ever, now that Grace knew Kana was all right. Hadn't she done everything she needed to, now? She'd seen the sights, tried the food, bought plenty of clothes. She had listened to brave fledgling bands play on street corners, bathed in a public bath, eaten fried octopus dough balls, and watched Tokyo Tower light up from the bottom. It wasn't bad for a single week, and Grace felt she had gotten a little closer to Japanese culture than the typical *Friendly Planet* tourist. She'd turned a disaster into a successful trip.

So far, at least—meeting Kana would be the last thing left, as soon as Grace worked up the nerve to send an invitation. She was acutely aware she'd squandered a perfect chance already. Here she was patting herself on the back for getting this far, when the most important part was yet to come!

Today, though, didn't look like it would be the day for her to make two fateful encounters in a row. Tired, hungry and disappointed, Grace walked across the square, ready to throw in the towel. She glanced back for one last look, then swiped her train card to open the gates.

Chapter 18

I'm sorry	2008 年 12 月 20 日
From: thehealinglight@saftbank.ne.jp	土曜 午後 12:18
To: otsuka.999991@ao.ne.jp	Reply

Otsuka-kun

I got my phone back, so you can contact me here again now.

Long time no see. About before, I'm so sorry. I shouldn't have stopped working with you on such short notice.

I guess your exam must be over by now. I hope it went well!

Momokawa

Re: I'm sorry	12 月 20 日 (土) 12:58
From: otsuka.999991@ao.ne.jp	詳細を表示

Hey, MISS Momokawa! That's great to hear, but you don't need to apologize to me. I understood your reasons. I'm still happy to hear from you again.
My exam is over, but I don't have the result yet. How did it go? Hmmmm... I wonder!? I'll let you know as soon as it's announced. ROCK AND ROLL!
Otsuka DAISUKE

Re: I'm sorry	2008 年 12 月 20 日
From: thehealinglight@saftbank.ne.jp	土曜 午後 13:05
To: otsuka.999991@ao.ne.jp	Reply

OK, I'll be waiting!

Momokawa

She rose so early on Saturday that even Shingo was still asleep, and Kana felt better than she had all week.

She fixed herself a slice of toast with honey, sat down at her table and did practice questions all morning. She had set an alarm, this time not to gauge her answering speed, but to stick by a limit on when to stop. She felt ready to toss out last week's strict schedule for a new approach; one that permitted both study and fun. She hoped, if she could pull it off, it would leave her feeling better about herself at the end of the long days.

When the timer chimed, Kana changed into a black mock turtleneck one-piece and tights and went downstairs, where her mother was making lunch. She'd been aware of the smell of curry rice in the air for some time.

Himeko gave the pot a final stir. She looked up, surprised, when Kana entered. "I was about to call for you."

"It smells delicious." Kana helped her mother take out plates. "Is it ready?"

"Let me get you some rice."

"What about Father and Shingo?" Kana asked.

"Your father took Shingo to his baseball game." Himeko replied.

"Oh." So they were alone. Maybe it would be better this way, Kana thought.

She allowed her mother to put two scoops of rice and two of curry on the plate before taking it to the table. When they were both seated and had said a thank-you, Kana ate hungrily, breakfast seeming like a distant memory. The curry, mild and sweet with lots of potatoes, was just the way she liked it.

After she had eaten every bite, Kana waited for her mother to finish as well, knowing there was something each of them wanted to say. She could feel it in the air.

Once Himeko had laid down her spoon and dabbed at her mouth with a serviette, she immediately stood and began to clear the plates without a single backwards glance. "You want to go, don't you?"

"Yes," Kana whispered, setting the teapot on the counter.

"What about your test? You're not ready yet."

"No, I'm not." She took a deep breath. "But I'm going to be ready. I'm the one who's taking the test. I'm the one who knows what my abilities are."

"Kana...."

Kana sighed and sat back down at the table. "Mother, I know you're worried, but I can't stay in my room and study *all* the time. I want to make you happy, but it's too much."

"I thought you would at least keep it up for a little while. I didn't think you'd go back to your old ways so fast." Himeko hadn't finished clearing the table, but she stood over her daughter disapprovingly.

"It's not my 'old ways.' I would never have overslept on the exam day if I hadn't stayed up every night reviewing."

"I know."

"I was prepared for it. Honest. But I was so exhausted."

"Yes." Her mother smiled indulgently and set the dishes down. "You were out with your friends far too much."

Kana shook her head. "That's not what I mean. I was out too much, worked too much, went to cram school too much, studied too much. Wasted too much time. All of it was too much. I need to cut back on everything, *including* studying. And if I *just* study, I can't be happy."

"Kana..." Himeko sat down slowly. "I try not to push you too hard, because I know you have the motivation, but you must stay on top of it. Even if you were ready for the first exam, that doesn't mean you automatically pass the next one. It's harder when it's more than your best subject."

"I know."

"I was a high school student too, you know." Himeko regarded her daughter seriously. "And I wanted to have fun. But I also wanted to go to university, and have a career. I had to give up all my free time to get into nursing, you know, so of course I worry about you getting into a good school. That's all. I want the best for you."

"I'll do it," Kana promised, "but I'll prove to you that it can be done without studying every moment of every day. I promise I can do it."

Himeko seemed to hesitate, wrung her hands and focused on them, not saying anything for a long time. Kana wondered if maybe her mother remembered her own high school days, and the then-rare decision to take up a career that would be lifelong. *You can't take back youth*, Kana wanted to tell her, but she knew it wasn't her place.

After a long pause Himeko sat back and said, "All right, you win. You'll have your semester grades soon?"

"Yes. On Wednesday."

"Then you can have your privileges back, but on Wednesday I want to see proof that you can handle this. When you get your grades back, they will be Nishidai level. When I see them, we'll talk again."

Kana hadn't expected to win the argument, but now that she had, she regarded her mother with a new respect. "I promise I won't let you down."

As she shut the door behind her, Kana felt as though a weight had been lifted from her shoulders. Maybe her mother didn't understand why Kana dressed or acted the way she did, but that was fine. As long as she could be trusted to handle this situation on her own, Kana thought it would be all right.

She had picked up her phone at last from where it lay on her desk, and powered it up on the train out of Saitama. Two weeks without checking had caused a lot of messages to pile up.

Kana counted thirty-five alerts coming in before the deluge stopped. She scrolled through the list. Some of the messages were from Daisuke, some were from Rumi, but most of them were from Megucchi. Kana noticed right away, though, that the most recent message she had gotten from her pen pal had been dated a week before.

Frowning, Kana opened up the oldest one, then skimmed through the rest. The tone escalated in concern with each one. Her final message pleaded, *"I just need to know you're okay. Please answer."*

Kana swallowed hard, guilt settling in her stomach. She should have gotten in touch right away, instead of waiting. Megucchi hadn't replied to her message on StreetSwEETs either, days later. She hoped Megucchi wasn't angry.

Kana typed out an apology and sent it right away, even though it would be after midnight on the other side of the world. She didn't want to wait any longer to fix everything that had been going wrong. After meeting with Miki, Kana at last felt she had the power to do something. More power than she had been able to muster up since this whole disaster began.

At Rumi's house, Kana laid out her terms. "I want to see you and hang out like before. But if I go out on Saturday, I stay home Sunday, and the other way around. I'm going to set my own curfew. And when I say 'I'm done, I'm going home,' I can't accept any arguments. I hope I don't make you feel bad."

Rumi laughed with relief. "It's absolutely fine. I was afraid you were going to tell me we couldn't be friends anymore."

"What!?"

"Well, we're so different, you know?" Rumi gritted her teeth. "I don't like school, and I know your mom thinks I'm a bad influence. I thought she would tell you to cut me off."

"I could never do that. You're my best friend."

"Kacchan. You take academics way too seriously for my taste." Rumi met her gaze with grim determination. "If you really wanted to, I think you *could*."

Kana tried to laugh off the accusation. There had been a few days, after the exam, where it had been easy to think that her social life was over forever. Maybe she had been dramatic, she thought, but maybe not.

"Does this mean you'll be seeing Otsuka-kun again too?"

"Otsuka-kun..." Kana looked at her hands in her lap. "I sent him an apology on my way here. I hope he'll forgive me."

"Don't be silly! Of course he will. He's so into you. Did he get into his fancy music school?"

"I haven't heard back from him yet. I'm not sure when he'll have the results."

Rumi gave her a knowing smile. "And when he finds out... what's your next move?"

Kana feigned ignorance. "What next move? There isn't a next move."

"What? No way." She sat back in disbelief. "You don't like him anymore!?"

"I do, but I don't want to make a move when I don't know if I have time to even see him as a friend. I have too much going on, so I'm going to leave it alone for now."

"No, no, no! He'll get away if you're not careful," Rumi admonished.

"I wonder." Kana's phone trilled. The sound made her jump —she had almost forgotten she had it back. Kana checked it, reading Daisuke's reply to her earlier message.

"This week. And school is finished on Wednesday. Shall we meet? We can have coffee and cake. If I pass the exam, I'll buy."

"*Wednesday?*" Rumi didn't have to look at a calendar to check the date. "That's Christmas Eve."

"....Oh. Maybe it is."

"How romantic!" Rumi clasped her hands to her chest. The ultra-feminine gesture looked out of place against her ragged-edged punk rock t-shirt. "Lucky! I've never been asked on a Christmas Eve date. He sure is smooth, isn't he?"

"I guess so." Kana felt rooted to the ground. Surely he had *known* it was Christmas Eve? No holiday in Japan could be more devoted to romance, save Valentine's Day. She wondered if Daisuke hadn't made some kind of mistake and forgotten Wednesday happened to be *that day*.

"Kacchan." Rumi grasped her by both shoulders. "You...*are*

going to say yes, aren't you?"

"Um." Kana stared down at the phone, not sure what to do. "I guess it couldn't hurt just to have coffee. I owe him."

"Yes! Good! Tell him you'll be there!"

"Okay, okay!" she grumbled, secretly grateful for the extra push. When she had typed a reply, also in English, she had to double check to make sure it was perfectly reserved and not too eager-sounding. "*Sure, send me a message. Good luck!*"

Rumi was already up and rummaging through the closet as though picking out her own clothes for the big day. She turned, making starry eyes at Kana. "Ah, and maybe after coffee, he'll invite you to see the Christmas illuminations in Ginza, and give you a special present he's been holding onto...maybe he'll even write you a song!"

"*Rumi!*"

"Yes, yes. I know! No boyfriends, no romance. Not until graduation." Rumi made a sour face and hung a black bomber jacket back in her closet. "If you get into Nishidai's next wave, though, I don't see why you need to wait!"

Kana sighed. It was much harder to explain to someone why the finish line was *after graduation* and not *after entrance exams*. It wasn't as though Rumi's logic didn't make sense. After all, the exams were the important part; once you got into your chosen school, the rest would be all a formality. "Hey. Are you listening to me?"

To her credit, Rumi seemed to recognize that she was pushing in exactly the way Kana had warned she would no longer tolerate. "Ah," she said, sitting heavily on the bed. "I'm sorry. I promised, didn't I?"

"You did."

"Well, maybe I'm a little envious. Could be, you attract them because you're not available, who knows. I wish I could have it so easy! I mean, I don't know how I'd feel about this cake addiction of his; that's kind of feminine. Boys aren't supposed to be sweets fanatics. But I could get over it."

"I think it's kind of cute." Kana ducked her head, aware that Rumi's words had softened her resolve the tiniest bit.

"I can't wait to hear about it as soon as you get back from seeing him. Promise you're gonna keep me updated?"

"I will."

"And speaking of days out, if you set a curfew, what do you think about going to Harajuku the day before that? On the holiday?"

"I *will* be on my curfew that day, but since finals are going to be over, I was expecting you to ask. What do you want to do?"

Rumi considered it for a moment. "Maybe look at Christmas illuminations? I don't know, maybe it would be nice to go shopping in Shinjuku, too. They have a Christmas tree set up already on the plaza. I'll get you a present if you get me one."

"Sure. That'll be fun."

"We can do a gift exchange. I'm sure Sae and the others will join in. I wish my parents would buy me a lot of gifts for Christmas," Rumi said wistfully, resting her chin on her hand. "When I was little they got me some things, but not so much now. I don't think it's fair to outgrow Santa Claus."

"You've got it lucky," Kana countered. "My parents didn't bother with Santa at all. I get a gift from them, but that's it. Kind of jealous of Megucchi; she must be getting ready for Christmas now."

"How nice..." Rumi sighed. "I bet she's got a tree in her house and everything. I wonder if it's a *real* tree like on television? You should ask her to send a photo."

"Sure," Kana agreed, feeling somewhat uneasy. She remembered that the message she'd sent Megucchi from the train earlier had gone unanswered. It seemed out of the ordinary for her friend not to reply at this time of day.

"I can only imagine it...a tree as tall as the ceiling, and a huge dinner with lots of friends and family over, and everyone exchanging gifts..." Rumi trailed off, her voice dreamy. "Wouldn't I like to have that kind of Christmas!"

~*~*~

"I'm sorry, there aren't any open seats left this week. I can change your ticket for you, but not to *before* Christmas."

"You can't be serious." Grace's knuckles turned white on the counter. "But I absolutely, absolutely have to be home by then!"

"I have Executive Class class available for Christmas Eve, but not economy." The agent didn't look any happier about it than Grace felt, especially after the long ride to Narita Airport to talk to someone.

"But I have a ticket in economy already, for next week. I only want to go a few days before, that's all."

The woman shook her head. "I can change your booking to Executive Class class, ma'am, but you do have to pay the difference. I know it's high. If you come to the airport on the day you want to leave, we may be able to get you in economy on a flight if someone doesn't show up. It's a very busy time to travel."

"I guess I have no choice...?" Grace bit her lip. She didn't have enough money to stay in Japan much longer, but she also couldn't afford the prices the agent quoted. Worse, if she didn't show up in Toronto on Christmas Day, her father would go ballistic. There was no way Grace would be able to talk her way out of that.

"I'm sorry." The agent looked helplessly at the line of people behind Grace. She obviously wanted to move on before it got any longer.

"I understand," Grace replied, though what she really wanted to do was run through the gates and onto the next flight, seat or no seat. Instead she sat in the Arrivals area for a few minutes, trying not to burst into tears. She stayed there for a long time, nursing a paper cup of hot chocolate from the vending machine until she felt she could leave without embarrassing herself. It was ridiculous to get so worked up, Grace told herself; she could probably get on a standby flight. It was only a matter of coming back the next day, and the next, if need be. She had at least until Christmas Day to pull it off.

Missing Christmas with her father would be a surefire way to bring his wrath down on her mother—and once that was underway, there would be no way for Grace to keep her adventure a secret. She shoved her passport back into her bag and took off the reading glasses, turning them over in her hands. She had gotten herself into quite a fix by leaving the ticket until the last minute. Maybe if she had come even a few days ago, she might have gotten something affordable. As it was, Grace wasn't sure what to do about the money issues—she might even need to check out of the Shinjuku hotel and find something cheaper, like a youth hostel. And instead of taking the limited express train, she would have to try to use the cheaper local trains to get back to Tokyo.

Grace found her way back to the station under the airport and looked at the fare display, wincing at the cost. Commuting to the airport every day to wait on a standby flight wasn't going to be cheap. If this was the only way to get home, though, she would have to start.

The local train didn't go directly to Shinjuku, either, so it took two hours to get back to her hotel, where she lay on the bed for some time, stomach growling. The day was still young and the weather nice, and Grace had intended to explore some of the areas in Tokyo she hadn't visited yet, but now she couldn't seem to find the motivation. Her heart felt incredibly heavy.

She went down to the lobby instead, to check her messages. There were a few from Simon, and one from her mother. Heart in her throat, Grace opened Camilla's email and read it through, but it was nothing more than a short "I miss you," and the usual demands that Grace not allow her father to neglect her while she was visiting. She typed out a short reply and promised to call soon.

After that, Grace went to StreetSwEETs. She opened the private message Kana had sent and reread it several times.

Perhaps, she thought, she should tell her friend what had happened, in case she needed help. The idea of admitting she had come all this way only to get herself in serious trouble seemed a little embarrassing, though. Grace felt particularly ashamed of having to seek help *now* when she had worked so hard to be strong all this time.

Would it be an admission of defeat to go to Kana at this point? Maybe. Grace decided to keep her money problems a secret for the time being, but she did type up an invitation to meet with Kana. She felt awkward writing it, but sent it off before she could overthink it too much. If she planned to be on a plane by Christmas, there would be no more time to hesitate. Grace would not be able to forgive herself if she left Japan without seeing her friend face-to-face.

Once the message left her hands, she turned to the next big decision on her list—whether to request backup. The chances of getting back to Canada before Christmas didn't look good. Grace had started to think that maybe she should call her father and tell him the whole thing. She hesitated, though, at the thought of him insisting she come back right away, business-class ticket or not. She had already done enough financial damage.

The uncertainly she'd feel over the next few days would be punishment, Grace decided, for spending the money she'd worked so hard to save. She wouldn't tell her parents unless she had no other choice. And she wouldn't run to anyone else for help, either. She felt more than a little scared, really; so much that her hands shook, but inside the old Grace had been a person who hated giving up, and the new Grace was determined to carry on smiling.

Chapter 19

Home > Private Messages > Inbox

Re: I miss you!

megumi_709	Dear Kana-chan,
	This will probably come as a bit of a shock, but right now... I'm in Japan! It's a long story.
	I'll be going home very soon, so I hope we can meet each other before that time...sorry it's so sudden.
	If you want to, can we get together tomorrow? If you're free in the afternoon, choose the time.
	Meet you by Hachiko...?
	~ Megucchi

Home > Private Messages > Inbox

Re: I miss you!

makhanikana	Whaaaaaaaaaaaaat!?!?!?!?!?????!??!?!?!??!?!?!?
	�(ˊ □˙ *)川
	Σ(▼□▼メ) I'm shock!
	I can't believe it! Yes, of course I can meet at Hachi!
	Can you come after school?? 15:30? I'm sorry if it's so late. But I'll be waiting for you!

Kana was astonished to see the message in her inbox when she arrived home from her day out. When she read its contents, she felt even more flabbergasted. What sort of errand could have brought Megucchi to Tokyo so suddenly?

Kana couldn't wait to find out. For all the strange events that had happened in her life over the last weeks, it was about time good things started coming her way. As Kana settled into her evening routine, she felt a great deal of relief to have the pressure of worrying about Megucchi lifted from her shoulders. Kana had dearly missed their daily messaging. And the chance to meet in person so unexpectedly was enough to lift her spirits even more. Tomorrow would be fun!

Later, as she sunk into the large metal bathtub, Kana felt more calm and peaceful than she had in many months. Now that she had spoken to Miki, her mother, Rumi and Daisuke, she felt sure everything was finally turning around. Kana would have to keep working hard to get through her finals, depending on stronger subjects to make up for her difficulty in the sciences, but she still had hope that she could make it to the top of the curve. She wouldn't allow her mother's reluctant blessing to be revoked before it had even started.

~*~*~

Like a boat cut loose from its moorings, Grace drifted down Omotesando, her eyes trained more now on boutique windows than on the people passing her by. She wished again that this whole thing could have been a pleasure trip rather than a stress-laden search. Now that she was free to finally do as she wished in Tokyo, there was hardly any time left, and she still felt a little out of place.

Grace's confidence had been having trouble catching up to her new image, as though someone might laugh at her not because she was wearing fashionable street clothes, but because she didn't quite know how to.

The combination of frayed jacket, baggy retro t-shirt, shorts over grey tights with boots and suspenders was something she never could have found the courage to wear at home, but Grace still had trouble feeling confident in them. She wasn't Gal or visual kei, Lolita or angel, brand, *decora* or punk or goth. She just wore something she put together on a whim. It felt kind of freeing, but also on some level embarrassing.

So convinced was she that her clothes were not trendy enough to be noticeable, Grace was taken by surprise when a man with a camera approached her and asked something in Japanese. "すみませんが, 写真を撮ってもいいですか?"

"Excuse me?"

"Can—I—take—picture?" he asked in laboured English.

"Oh, uh...sure. Thank you." Maybe, she thought, he was a country tourist who had never seen a foreigner before. She'd heard that kind of thing happened in rural towns, but it seemed a little weird for Tokyo. Grace stood still and upturned her lips into what she hoped was a cool, carefree smile.

"OK, チーズ."

The flash went off, softened by a white bulb on top of the camera. He took one more photo, then held out a clipboard with a pen attached on a string. "Please—this." Pointing at the first space with another pen, he marked an x beside it. "Your name. Here."

"Okay." Would he send her the photo? That would be nice, Grace thought. She didn't have a single picture of herself on this trip. She wrote her name in the box.

He moved his pen tip to the next space. "Age."

Now she felt a touch of apprehension. This guy wasn't trying to recruit her for some nebulous trafficking ring or something, was he? Was it too late to tell him she didn't want the picture after all? Maybe he planned to hold Grace's photo hostage unless she paid him a stack of money, like those green-screen photographers at famous landmarks she'd gone to with her father.

"こちらはブランド. Brand," the photographer said.

Confused, Grace looked up. "Brand? What brand?"

He gestured at her, moving his open palm down from shoulders to boots. "This one, brand."

She drew a blank.

He touched his own jacket. "This one, brand, Devil-May-Care." Then he touched his shirt. "T-shirts, brand, Superb."

Branding, she realized. What kind of tourist photographer asked you what brand of clothes you were wearing?

Grace suddenly had an inkling of what was happening, though she got so excited at the realization she could hardly speak. This casually dressed guy had a lanyard with a name tag around his neck, and while she couldn't read the Japanese characters on it, there was one word she knew very well. "Wait, wait, wait! Are you from *SwEET* magazine?"

"そうそう、スイーツのカメラマンです. From *SwEET*."

"Oh my God." There was no way *she* would be in the magazine, was there? Grace thought she could feel her blood pressure bottoming out. A photographer from *SwEET*! This couldn't be real!

Grace wrote something in the brand and hobby boxes, paying so little attention now that later she would not even remember what she had put down. She scribbled her email address as though on autopilot. Not for the last time, she deeply regretted not being able to speak more than a handful of words in the language, but tried to thank the photographer with what she knew. "*Arigatou!* Thank you so much, I'm so happy! *Ureshii! Arigatou!*"

"ありがとうございました!" He bowed and presented her with a business card she couldn't read. Grace giddily accepted it with a bow of her own, even remembering to take it with both hands.

Waving goodbye, the photographer turned away to look for his next subject.

Grace stood still for a long time on the sidewalk. Unbelievable! Even if her picture wasn't really printed in the magazine, she felt flattered to think the photographer had picked *her* out of the fast-moving crowd flowing down Omotesando and asked her to pose. Thinking she was one of *them*.

Amazing, Grace thought, what chance could bring you sometimes. If the rest of the day went as well as it started out, she thought she might be convinced that miracles were possible after all.

~*~*~

The afternoon brought on a sharp wind that cut through Grace's grey tights and made her shiver. The denizens of Hachiko Square were, as always, unaffected; even the trendsetters in their short-shorts and schoolgirls wearing skirts with knee socks. Grace wondered how they did it.

Not long after, one of those schoolgirls approached Grace, her familiar face wearing a shy smile. "Megucchi?"

"Hi there," Grace managed, still doing her utmost to look cool as she hopped down from the railing. "It's, it's great to see you!"

"You, too. I hope you didn't wait long." Kana's voice hit a little lower than Grace imagined; her English had a touch of Australian to it. She remembered Kana mentioning a summer studying abroad.

Grace tried not to wave her hands around too much. "Oh no, I just got here."

Kana stood a tiny bit taller than Grace, which came as a surprise after Grace had been towering over high-schoolers she passed on the streets. The raven-haired girl wore her school uniform, with a cream-coloured cardigan under an unbuttoned navy blazer, and the blue ribbons threaded around the tops of her knee socks matched the colour of her scarf. Two crisscrossed blue bobby pins held back her sideswept fringe. Her hair looked exactly the same as it had been in that *SwEET* photo, reaching most of the way down her back. Kana carried her satchel on her arm, and a metallic purple cell phone in her hand. She looked Grace over, and said something that made her friend glow with pride. "Wow. You're so cute!"

"Hah, I should say that about you! Your school uniform is so adorable!"

"Thank you!"

They grinned at each other for a few moments, neither seeming to know where to start the conversation. "I was so shocked to hear you were in Japan." said Kana at last. "I'm very happy, though! Did you come here for a holiday?"

"Something like that," Grace replied, grateful for the reprieve. "But I can't believe I'm finally seeing you in person! I've been so looking forward to it."

"Me too! I didn't think I would get to meet you so soon. It's so exciting."

The fact that Kana felt as excited as she did made Grace twice as courageous, and a little more of her reserve fell away. She pointed at the pedestrian crossing light, which had turned green. "Do you want to go somewhere and warm up? Maybe we could have coffee or something?"

"All right," Kana agreed, obviously grateful for the suggestion. The wind blew colder than it had over the previous few days. She led the way across the street, hurrying to reach the corner before the music stopped. On the other side, she paused. "Do you like sweets? We can go to Miki-san's cafe."

"Sure."

Kana continued to lead the way to the cafe—one that Grace had passed by many times that week, never realizing it was the place where Daisuke's sister worked. Miki wasn't in that day, though, and a young woman with vivaciously sparkling eye shadow took their orders. Grace, conscious of her finances, had a cup of tea. "I ate a while ago," she lied, thinking back to the rice ball that had been her breakfast.

Kana had no reason to suspect otherwise, so she went ahead

and ordered a Mont Blanc for herself. "This shop has the best *monburan*," she said, pronouncing the name of the sweet with a heavy accent. Grace wasn't sure what that was, and decided to wait until the waitress brought it out. It looked like it had been made with the modelling clay shaper she owned when she was five. "I just love *marron*," Kana confided as she took a bite.

"*Marron*? What's that?"

"Isn't it English?" Her friend looked puzzled.

"I don't think so?"

Kana opened her bag and took out something that looked like a cosmetics case. When she turned it around, though, Grace realized it was a tiny computerized dictionary. "Oh. *Marron* is 'chestnut.'"

"So it's French. I should have known that." Grace covered a smile. "My French isn't what it should be."

"なるほど!" Kana laughed. Both her laugh and her native speech were a little higher-pitched than the tone she used to speak English. "*Monburan* is also French. French is so common for names of sweets."

"Oh, yeah?"

"Oh, yes. It's so elegant, don't you think so?"

Grace laughed, too. "I never noticed!"

They talked for a few more minutes about desserts, the conversation flowing. Eventually the topic turned to English, then Daisuke, then fashion. Grace couldn't believe how easily she could speak with Kana. She had imagined their first meeting would be awkward, perhaps even ending with hardly any words exchanged. But Kana was as fluent a speaker as she was in writing, though she left the dictionary on the table where she could reach for it now and again. When this happened, she grinned and apologized to Grace. "Megucchi, my English is so terrible, isn't it?"

"Not at all!" Grace reassured her. "If you want to see something terrible, my Japanese vocabulary is only about fifteen words. And I got most of them from watching late-night

TV in my hotel room."

"Hmm, that might be an interesting way to learn, why don't you try it?"

Grace thought Kana's accent was adorable, and she unconsciously added bits of Japanese here and there.

Her English had good structure, but she also seemed to know the strangest words. When Grace would comment on an odd vocabulary choice, Kana would sit up looking alarmed and say, "It's a word I memorized for the test. Is it wrong?"

"Ah, no, that's just not how I would have said it." Then Grace would paraphrase, and Kana would nod and say "I see!" as though she had made an important discovery. Grace thought it was funny, but couldn't say so out loud. She didn't want Kana to stop.

Eventually the conversation turned, as Grace had feared, back to her visit to Japan. "Where are you staying? When did you arrive?" Kana asked.

"I stayed at a hotel in Odaiba and now I'm at one in Shinjuku. I got here...about a week ago. I'm sorry I didn't try to reach you before."

"Oh no, my mother took my cell phone, so I couldn't receive mobile emails," Kana explained, in what Grace thought was a very grave tone. "She was so upset about the exam."

"I can imagine. You must have been, too."

"I was." Her face was unreadable for a moment, then she put on a big smile. "But, Odaiba, how great to stay there! It's fun. Actually, I went recently to Odaiba too, to Aqua City."

"Oh, really? What for?"

"Just to think." Kana seemed reluctant to say anything more. Instead, she changed the subject. "Then, are you here with your friends? Or on a class trip?"

Grace had been about to ask what kind of school sent their students overseas for field trips, but remembered Kana talking about a class trip to Hawaii, and thought better of it. "No, I came alone."

"Wow, so brave!" Kana looked impressed. "To get around Japan without speaking Japanese is hard enough, but to do it alone must be even more difficult."

"It wasn't so bad," Grace said, but inwardly she felt pleased and proud. "In Tokyo, anyway. I managed to find my way around."

"I wondered if you would really be able to find Hachiko in the middle of all those people!" Kana grinned.

Grace had deliberately chosen the statue, not because she could easily find it now, but because she had spent so much time in the popular meeting spot that she wanted to be able to say she had met someone there, too. It was a little embarrassing, and she thought to herself that a few weeks ago she would never have said such a thing out loud, but now found herself wanting to tell Kana. "Can you believe it? I saw so many people meet here that I wanted to 'meet you by Hachiko,' too!"

Kana smiled. "Megucchi! I never thought you would be so funny. I'm surprised."

"Funny, me? Seriously?"

"Seriously!"

Grace decided to take it as a compliment, and they changed the subject again and again, talking about Canada, fashion, and boys. Outside, the sun dropped from the sky and Shibuya came alive with neon, but Grace took no notice of anything aside from the table she shared with her friend—she had never felt so animated in her life.

When they'd lingered in the cafe too long, Kana took Grace to an arcade with a Print Club machine so they could commemorate their meeting. Grace had seen the photo sticker machines everywhere, but had been too intimidated to try one on her own. Kana, however, knew what she was doing. She spun through the menus with practised ease, and showed Grace how to decorate their photos with a stylus on the touchscreen.

When the photos slid out of the printer, Kana inspected them, nodding in satisfaction. "These are great. Megucchi, you pick three big ones, and I'll take the other three, okay?"

"Are you sure? We could choose one by one, you know."

"I'm sure! I want you to choose your favourite. It'll be your memory of our meeting in Japan!"

They cut the sheet in half, and Grace tucked the photos into her map book and placed it in her bag as carefully as if they were worth twenty thousand yen rather than the two hundred she'd paid. She watched Kana manoeuvre a crane game, and tried one herself, but neither of them were any good. Laughing, Kana put her coin purse back in her school bag and they left the arcade to find something else to do.

Outside, the street teemed with late-evening shoppers and students celebrating the end of exams. Even for a weeknight, the karaoke boxes were busy, but Grace and Kana found one with an open room. Grace had never done karaoke before, and didn't feel at all ready to try it—she felt awkward enough about her singing voice, even without an audience. But her friend seemed so enthusiastic that Grace went along without complaint, accepting an English songbook as big as a telephone book. Together with Kana she sang old favourites, and even a song by herself. When they received the call that there were five minutes remaining in the karaoke session, Grace was surprised to find she felt reluctant to leave.

"Otsuka-kun has a very nice singing voice," Kana remarked wistfully as they drank back their melon cream sodas. "I haven't seen him in a while now. It makes me a little..." she paused, looking for the word. "...waku-waku. My heart beats."

"It's too bad I won't get to meet him."

"Ah, that's right, you won't meet him. I won't see him until Wednesday. What time will you leave Japan?"

Grace hadn't told Kana that she wasn't actually booked on any flight yet. "I need to go to the airport early in the afternoon tomorrow. I'll leave Shinjuku around twelve."

"I guess there isn't any time to introduce you. It's too bad. We have a holiday tomorrow for the Emperor's birthday, so it would have been a good chance."

"Sorry. You can tell him hello for me, I guess." Grace wanted to meet Daisuke; wanted to spend more time getting to know Kana, but she could feel the anxiety of the upcoming airport run bubbling inside her. She wanted to leave, even though she had been having so much fun moments before.

Kana smiled. "I will."

Grace checked her watch. The hour hand neared eight. She didn't want to say goodbye, but she couldn't contain the nervousness that had started to creep up as soon as Kana asked about the flight. She felt conscious of the fact that it was still a weekday. Kana had already done more than enough by agreeing to meet on a day when she was so busy. "You have tomorrow off?"

"Yes, for the Emperor's birthday. I did say I wouldn't be too late tonight." Kana looked torn. "But I don't want to leave early when you'll be here for just one more day."

"Absolutely not. Don't worry about that," Grace said firmly. The last thing she wanted was for Kana to lose her newly-won freedom. She too wanted the night to continue, as she was having the most fun she'd had in Tokyo yet, but it wasn't worth the cost. Grace hadn't forgotten what it was that had brought her to Japan in the first place. "You head on home. I need to get back to my hotel and pack, anyway."

"I could go with you to the airport, if you want. Tomorrow."

"No, that's okay," said Grace. It seemed like a waste to be leaving when Kana had the whole day off, but the airport run was something she wanted to do alone. "I can handle it myself. Thanks, though."

Kana smiled. "All right. Megucchi, really, I had such a good time. I'm so happy we could meet."

"Me too."

"Here, let me give you my number. If you need anything, you can call me."

Grace knew she would never use it, but she opened her

notebook and let Kana write the number on the inside of the front cover. Her handwriting was cute; a neat and deliberate script. Grace smiled at it before putting the book away.

They walked together to Shibuya station, where inside the gates, Kana gestured at the stairs to the clockwise platform. "This way."

Even though Grace needed to travel north as well, she felt incredibly nervous about parting in a hurry on the crowded Yamanote car as the train pulled into Shinjuku. Would she be able to hug Kana goodbye on the train? What if people stared at them? Grace tried to excuse herself, even though she had already paid her fare. "I have to do one more errand, actually, so I'll go the other way from here...so we should say goodbye here at the station, I guess."

"Oh. Do you need my help? I could come with you."

"No, it's okay. You need to get home. I'll be fine on my own."

Both girls paused, there at the bottom of the stairs. Grace suddenly felt awkward, not sure how to say goodbye to a friend she had technically only met today, but felt as though she had known for a long time. Would Kana feel strange if they hugged? Would she think it strange if they didn't? She had read in her books that Japanese people were not as touchy with one another. Did she dare hope that Kana, who travelled and homestayed and spoke English like a native, would be any different? The old Grace would have hung back and waited for someone else to make the decision. Instead she shyly approached Kana and put her arms around her friend.

Kana, to her relief, hugged back. "I'll miss you. Let's meet again someday."

"I'll miss you, too," Grace declared.

They split, and walked up two different sets of stairs, coming to stand directly across from each other on opposite platforms. Kana, wearing a broad smile behind her houndstooth scarf, waved at Grace as her train approached. Grace started to choke up a little, but she put on a smile too, and watched her friend's image flash through the windows as the first train pulled into Shibuya Station. A second later, her own train came whizzing by, hiding them from each others' sight.

Grace didn't let herself cry, but hid her face from the other passengers by turning her head toward the window. The night scenery flashed by.

The train had gone three stations away before she managed to compose herself enough to disembark and turn around. She wished she had said something like, "Come visit me in Canada." Maybe Kana might want to do that, as Grace wasn't going to be able to come back to Japan for a very, very long time once she returned home. Even if she managed to get back without anyone finding out about her escapade, she would have to work every single day for the rest of her school career to make up the savings she'd spent. Any hope of getting her degree without taking out a student loan had vanished over the last week. Was it worth it?

It was, Grace decided. It had all been worth it, for today.

At the hotel, she packed her suitcase full of the things she had amassed since arriving. Most of it was clothes and toiletries, with a few peace offerings for her parents. The task of packing was hardly long or arduous, but when she had finished, she sat down on her bed, exhausted. It felt as though she had packed her whole adventure down into one suitcase, never to think about again.

Chapter 20

Home > Private Messages > Inbox	
"Aite yokatta"	
megumi_709	Kana-chan, I wanted to say thanks for today. I was so glad I could meet you. I couldn't have left Japan without seeing you in person. Take care, and I'll message you soon. ~ Megucchi

Home > Private Messages > Inbox	
Re: "Aite yokatta"	
makhanikana	Hi, Megucchi ❤❤❤ It's me who should be thanking you. Thank you for coming to see me! I was so excited and happy. I wish you'll come back to Japan again soon. Or, let's meet in Canada next time!? (˚□˚) I'll be waiting!! ♡ Kana

When Grace awoke, she thought she might be ready to say goodbye to Japan at last. She wished she had more photographs to remember it all by. The Print Club pictures were tucked into a pocket on the inside of her notebook.

She checked out of the hotel and took the Yamanote Line, jostling for space among suited salarymen and office workers. For once, she didn't mind being on the standing room only train, even though she had to press into a corner to protect her luggage. She bought a ticket for the Keisei Line and a rice ball at the convenience store. As she ate, Grace made each bite slow and chewed carefully. This, she told herself, might be the last rice ball she would eat for a long time. As the high-rises of Tokyo gave way to the open fields and squat little houses of Chiba Prefecture, she thought again that this would hopefully be the last time she would take the train like this, with the soothing announcer's voice saying, *Aoto, Aoto desu,* loud enough to nudge dozing passengers awake. Now she could pick out words that meant something, instead of every announcement being a string of gibberish. *Migigawa no tobira o akemasu, gochuui kudasai.* Careful, the doors will open on the right.

At Narita Airport, she rolled her suitcase up the escalator and walked across the terminal, breathing in the scent of coffee from the cafes, absorbing a few last snatches of unrepentant Japanese. When she had at last come to stand at the ticketing desk, the same agent who had been there a few days before was back. The woman nodded at Grace as she approached. "Ah, it's you. You were looking to change to an earlier flight, right?"

"Yes," Grace replied. "To Toronto. But I guess I could connect somewhere if there's open seats."

She shook her head. "Unfortunately, yesterday's direct flight was cancelled due to some weather. Everyone from that flight is trying to get to Toronto now. Even Executive Class is full."

Grace made a face. "What should I do?"

"I can try to get you on the connecting flight through

Vancouver, though we've already moved a lot of the passengers over there. The direct to Toronto is basically impossible, I'm sorry to say. There are so many passengers waiting from yesterday that I can't transfer anyone else to it. Why don't you come back to this desk around four-thirty? If anyone cancels or doesn't check in for Vancouver, we may be able to do something for you."

"Okay." Grace sighed and left the desk. She stored her luggage in a coin locker and prepared to while away her time in the airport shops, hoping that by six she might be somewhere over the Pacific.

She returned to the desk exactly on time. The friendly agent wasn't anywhere to be seen, so Grace held back, waiting for the check-in line to dissipate. When all the other passengers and their luggage had left to go through security, she approached the new agent. "Um, hi. I'm waiting on standby to go to Toronto, maybe through Vancouver? Has anything opened up?"

The new agent, a man, gave her a cool look without consulting his screen. "Was your name called? What's your last name?"

Grace had heard many other passengers being paged, but her name hadn't been among them. "It's Ryan."

He pursed his lips. "I'm sorry, but so far everyone is checked in and we still have quite a few standby passengers waiting for both flights."

"Oh. I see."

"I'm very sorry, I don't have any seats to put you in. We had a flight cancel yesterday." He shook his head. "You might have better luck tomorrow, though. There are still standbys on the list, but not as many as today. I'm very sorry, once again."

She let out a long breath and willed her lower lip to stop trembling. "I guess."

"Good luck." He smiled sympathetically.

"Thank you."

Grace walked back to the waiting area, dejected, and now uneasy. There *was* a chance she could still be home on time, if she made it to Toronto the next day, but it wasn't looking good. With no hotel and little cash flow, she would need to spend the night in the airport. A cheap meal from the convenience store followed a long evening of browsing overpriced souvenirs, and after wasting as much time as she could playing arcade games, Grace looked for a quiet corner to get some rest. She was acutely aware that there was a single day left before her deception would be exposed.

Curling up on a chair with her head on her backpack, Grace nodded off, feeling as though the day had ended much worse than it had began.

~*~*~

Dressed for the festive occasion, Kana and her school friends met in Shinjuku to look at Christmas illuminations, admiring the tens of thousands of lights that decorated the Southern Terrace. Kana was blown away by the amazing display. She had never been to the Terrace at night, with its glittering view and holiday music setting the mood for pedestrians to stroll. Every tree had been wrapped in them; every manicured hedge carefully outfitted with different coloured strings of lights, creating a wave effect of green, yellow and purple.

Even though it wasn't quite Christmas Eve, couples walked hand in hand everywhere, sitting outside the restaurants and coffee shops, enjoying each others' company. A long lineup snaked around the outside of the "new" doughnut shop—Kana had gone with Rumi the year before, but the lines were still nearly as long as opening week. They were doing brisk business, it seemed, even though today was the Emperor's birthday.

Kana thought about buying Daisuke a little gift. Part apology for the way she'd acted, and part congratulations for if he had good news for her tomorrow. Nothing special, she tried to tell herself. A way to say "thanks for your hard work, and Merry Christmas." And maybe a little, "Sorry for running away when you needed my help." She didn't think Daisuke had it in him to hold it against her, but still she felt low for cutting him off so suddenly. What had been too easy to do at the time now seemed like a horrific slight. It was one Kana hoped to make up for.

She had her answer when Rumi and Michiko led her to a stationary shop to exclaim over the cute calendars, and Kana found herself standing in front of a shelf of hardcover journal-style notebooks. They weren't expensive or special, just plain books with lined paper, but one in particular caught her eye. Kana plucked the black notebook, its piano design embossed with silver, from the top of the display. It had a rubber band on the cover and a loop to hold a pen. She remembered the scraps of paper Daisuke carried to their study sessions, torn and crumpled, with lyric translation notes written everywhere. It would be nice if he had someplace to keep them all, she thought.

This sort of gift seemed feminine, almost bordering on uncool for a high school boy, but Daisuke was hardly your average boy, no matter how cool he tried to act. He was an *artist*, Kana told herself as she brought the book to the counter. The saleswoman wrapped it in silver foil and sealed it with a snowman sticker, and Kana glanced back at her friends before she slid the package into her bag, a little sheepish.

She didn't want Rumi to know yet that she was reconsidering what she had said about going out with Daisuke. In truth, in the days since they had arranged their Christmas Eve meeting, she had thought about him more than ever before. She didn't want to get her hopes up, but Kana had found that no matter how hard she tried to tell herself that seeing him on Christmas Eve wasn't going to be a big deal, it was starting to become one.

~*~*~

"It's completely full again," the agent apologized. Her name tag read *Tanaka*. "But if someone doesn't show up, we'll do our best. I'll page you, so stay in the area, okay?"

"Okay. Thanks." How many times had she heard that, now? Though she tried to control her expression, Grace wanted to cry. She went back to the chairs to wait, dragging her suitcase behind her, aware of the agents watching her as she sat where she could easily see the check-in desk. Grace felt too sick with nervousness to eat or even sit still. This would be her last shot—it was already Christmas Eve on both continents, and here she was, still in Japan. As she had the day before, Grace watched the clock tick by to almost five. She knew very well what time the flight would be boarding, closing up, departing. Most of the agents at the desk left to go airside. Nevertheless, she sat and sat until there could be no doubt the plane was well on its way without her aboard.

Maybe she was imagining it, but Grace thought she spied the remaining two check-in agents glancing over at her, then quickly looking away again. They were obviously nervous about delivering another rejection. She didn't want to approach them again, but she also couldn't leave without going back to the desk.

She steeled herself with a smile that she hoped didn't look as fake as it was. She felt dangerously close to tears, this time. "No good, huh?"

"I'm so sorry. There isn't anything I can do." Ms. Tanaka didn't even need to look at the computer. She bowed deeply. "Do you want me to transfer your reservation to tomorrow? To stand by again?"

"Tomorrow's too late." Grace's words came out in a whisper.

"I know. I'm sorry," she apologized again. "It's Christmas, after all. But you have your ticket for next week."

Next week? Grace wasn't sure she could make it that far on rice balls alone!

Chapter 21

Re: GET	12 月 23 日 (火) 15:40
From: otsuka.999991@ao.ne.jp	詳細を表示

GET the result! Let's meet by Yurakucho Station east exit. Area map is across from the department store. See you 19:30. Are you OK?

Otsuka DAISUKE

Re: GET	2008 年 12 月 23 日
From: thehealinglight@saftbank.ne.jp	火曜 午後 15:45
To: otsuka.999991@ao.ne.jp	Reply

Otsuka-kun

I'm looking forward to it! 19:30, Yurakucho East. I've been there before.

Did you choose this place because of the *puchi-taiyaki* shop? (·ω −)〜☆

If you didn't know it was there, I'll guide you this time~

See you soon!

Momokawa

"It's a pass," Rumi said loftily as Kana joined her in their homeroom class with a broom in her hand. "That's about as much as I can ask for."

Kana had a spring in her step. "Same here," she said. "A pass is a pass." She had done well in most of the exams, though her grades had certainly suffered in the math and science departments as a result of neglecting them for so long.

Her English Communication grade had to be near, if not at, the top of the class. Luke hadn't said anything about it, but he had looked up from his work to grin at her when he spotted her hovering near the entrance to the staff room.

Rumi gave Kana the side-eye. Her hands were dusty with chalk from the erasers. "Oh, please. Don't pretend like you were anywhere close to the bottom."

Kana wasn't sure what to say. She busied herself with sweeping the area below where Rumi clapped erasers out the window. "Well, you know. The usual stuff wasn't great, especially math. Ancient Japanese was okay."

"English?" Rumi grinned.

Kana ducked her head. Her pleasure at seeing the results in English and her humanities subjects had only lasted a few moments. She felt only relief at having it over with.

Kana couldn't remember a time when she hadn't berated herself after a test for the questions she had messed up. It was freeing, now that she didn't quite care as much as usual.

"Yeah, I thought so." Rumi bumped Kana's shoulder with her own, grinning. "Hey, I know you have plans tonight, but I guess you don't have time to go home first, right? Do you want to come to Shibuya with Sae and me, in a little bit? We're going shopping." She paused. "Not everybody has a Christmas Eve... plan." She stopped short of the word *date*. Kana was grateful; more than one of their classmates were still within earshot.

"Well..." It wouldn't hurt to have a distraction for the next few hours, she thought. Kana had considered sending Daisuke another message that day, but she didn't want to look too eager.

She wanted to hope that he was thinking about her, but at the same time, she felt nervous, anticipating what he might have planned for their date, not really a date. Was it a date?

Her best outfit, folded neatly, sat in a paper shopping bag beside her desk.

"You can say no," Rumi hurried to add, mistaking Kana's wandering thoughts for hesitation. "You don't have to if you aren't in the mood. It's no big deal."

Kana's heart warmed, and she almost agreed. "I would love to...but I'm going to say no. I need a little time to think before I see him. Next time?"

"Next time."

Kana waited for the familiar twinge of guilt she felt whenever she told her best friend 'no,' but this time, it didn't come.

~*~*~

Pausing against the haphazard tableau of Spain Hill, Grace shoved her hands into the pockets of her coat. The air felt crisp, with no signs of snow. Maybe that was normal for Tokyo, but in Newfoundland a green Christmas was uncommon, and Grace felt decidedly *un*-Christmassy as a result.

After waiting all day and not making it onto a flight, she had returned to the hotel with her bags and booked herself in for another evening. She couldn't stay in the airport a second night, not on Christmas Eve. Not tonight, of all nights!

Grace felt a twinge of resentment toward the couples passing her on the sidewalk, and tried to force it down. Nobody out here was spending the evening alone, that was for certain. Even Kana was probably with Daisuke by now, sharing his good news over a cup of coffee. It seemed silly to be jealous of her friend at a time like this, but there it was. Grace felt beyond fed up with her string of misfortunes at the airport, and very nervous that in a few days she wouldn't even be able to afford an *onigiri*, much less a bed to stay the night.

She wondered how Simon would be spending his evening. The winter formal had come and gone a few days before. Had he gone without her? Did he dance with other girls, or stand against the wall, watching Kirk and his friends with their dates?

Had Jean found out the truth about Christian Barber?

Thinking about it made her more homesick than ever.

Grace lingered near the entrance to a department store, wondering what to do. Shibuya was as it ever was, bursting at the seams with people, music and advertisements blaring over the loudspeakers. Every store had a Christmas tree to rub salt in the wound, but at least it was all familiar sights and sounds at this point. Shibuya almost felt like her home away from home.

Here, too, couples held hands everywhere she turned. It was a sight she wasn't quite used to in Tokyo.

There was no obvious way out of the predicament Grace would be in when her father rolled up to Pearson Airport to collect her, less than 48 hours from now. She was as good as dead, at this rate.

She spotted a red phone booth about halfway up the hill, and Grace felt a stab of temptation as she passed. At this point, it didn't matter if anyone found out where she was, did it? She squeezed into the booth and rooted around for the slip of paper with her long-distance calling card numbers.

Seven-thirty in the morning back home—Simon wouldn't be up, not during school holidays. She wasn't entirely sure she was ready to tell him yet, anyway. Her mother would be awake, though, working a half-day. Grace missed her family more than she was willing to admit.

She dialed the house number with shaky hands. The phone rang twice, and then Camilla Ryan answered, sounding groggy. "Hello?"

"Mom."

Her mother became instantly alert. "Gracie? Are you okay? Isn't it really early for you?"

"It's early," she said, realizing how unprepared she was to be caught in a lie. "Sorry. I wanted to catch you before you left for work. And I missed you." Now that she had her mother there on the phone, Grace missed her more than ever, and felt a sharp pang of guilt at the untruths she'd been feeding her parents. And her friends, and Simon, and...

"Aw, honey, I miss you too. For some reason..." Camilla trailed off. "Even though you're with your dad, it feels different this time. Maybe it's because you're growing up, getting ready to graduate. I wish it'd been my turn to have you for Christmas this year."

Grace found herself reassuring her mother. "It's okay. I'll be home soon, I promise. And I'll be home for Christmas next year, even after I graduate. It's way better there, than," she almost choked on the last word, "here."

"I'll feel so much better when you get back. I've had the sense that something's wrong the whole time since you left. Oh, Gracie, I'm so glad you called. Even if you woke me up. I have the day off today, you know."

She smiled at the childhood nickname. "Sorry, I thought you were working the morning. Go back to sleep, then. I just wanted to call you...Merry Christmas. I wanted to be home for it, I swear."

"I know, honey. Merry Christmas. I love you!"

"See you soon. Love you." Grace's voice cracked. She hung up the phone before she could actually start crying. With the receiver back on the cradle, Grace had to lean heavily against the side of the phone booth and compose herself before she could leave.

She felt a little better. Less tempted to return to the hotel and sleep off the rest of the evening. Instead, she walked down the other side of the hill and stepped into a convenience store. Picking out two packs of disposable hand warmers and a bottle of warm couldn't-quite-read-what-kind-of-tea, Grace brought them to the counter. Then, she reached for her wallet.

It was not, however, where she usually kept it. The outside pouch of her purse was empty. Grace patted her coat pocket, frowning. The clerk continued to smile at her expectantly. She smiled back and held up a finger to signal *one minute, please.*

She set her bag down and quickly rifled through it. Grace carried a small purse, a single compartment with an outside zippered pouch. The wallet, a bulky thing, would have been impossible to miss.

Alarmed, Grace checked her coat again, and then unzipped the garment to make sure she hadn't stuck it into some other pocket she'd forgotten she had. But the top she wore wasn't made for carrying extras, nor was her grey skirt.

Grace closed the bag slowly, her mouth dry.

"だいじょうぶですか?" the clerk asked in Japanese, her voice not unkind.

"Sorry, I...I'll come back later," Grace replied, embarrassed. She managed an apologetic bow and hurried out of the store with her coat flying open. Where had her wallet gone? She hadn't needed it since arriving in Shibuya. The last time she used it had been leaving the station, swiping her train card. Could she have been pickpocketed? Surely not, not in Tokyo! Her heart was in her mouth. She *had* put it in the outside pocket, hadn't she? That spot was prime for the taking, if someone could open the zipper without Grace noticing.

She backtracked, down the street bedecked with holiday lights, weaving around the couples on their Christmas Eve dates. She hadn't gotten all that far from the station, but if it *was* lost rather than stolen, what were the chances someone had been honest enough to turn it in?

She tried to convey to the man in the stationmaster's office that she had lost something, and though the older gentleman had little English, he seemed to get the idea from the look on her face. He put his hands up and shook his head in a "no" gesture, then asked her a question in Japanese. Helpless, Grace could merely shrug and reply that she couldn't understand him.

"*Wakarimasen.*"

"こばんはどうでしょうか？"

"*Nihongo wakarimasen,*" she stammered, trying not to panic.

Looking concerned, the stationmaster left his little window and came out to lead her to the exit. He pointed at a small door close to the street. "こばんに行ってほうがいいです。"

Grace more or less got the point and followed the man's gestures to the corner police box. They sat her down and had her draw a picture of her wallet and make a list of the contents. The biggest loss was what little money she did have...the wallet, built like an oversized coin purse, had her train card, all the cash, and the vanilla credit card she needed to pay for the flight change fee. Her passport, thankfully, was safe in her purse.

There wasn't much else she could do. The policeman wanted Grace's contact information, but she had none to give him. She didn't even have the phone number of the hotel. With a helpless shrug, she tried to tell him there wasn't anywhere she could be reached, but the officer insisted. Out of ideas, Grace gave him the only number she knew—Kana's. Making an *x* with her hands, she hoped he understood he shouldn't use it. "Emergency *only*. Don't call!" She would have to come back later on her own and check for herself.

With no train card or money, it wasn't like she had many other options.

Time was of the essence. If it had been stolen, well, there wasn't much she could do, Grace realized. If it fell on the ground, maybe there was still a chance of salvaging this mess. She started to retrace her steps from the station to the phone booth.

It's probably still on the ground somewhere, or someone put it on a flower box or something. She had seen lost items—gloves, children's shoes and toys, once even a folder of papers—laid in a visible place for their owners to return for. Shuffling hastily back up to the phone booth, however, Grace couldn't spot it on the sidewalk. Pedestrian traffic and darkness made it hard to see anything. She picked her way through the crowd on Spain Hill with her eyes glued to the road.

When she reached the convenience store, Grace tried to signal her dilemma to the clerk by looking around, on the floor, holding her fingers and thumbs in the shape of a square. The young lady shrugged helplessly and shook her head.

Grace tried not to cry. There wasn't much money left in there, but it was all she had. Without her train card, there would be no returning to the hotel. She *needed* that money to eat and pay for a bed after tomorrow night, and get to the airport.

Grace counted the loose change floating at the bottom of her purse—less than ninety yen. Not even one Canadian dollar.

Her hands were shaking and she felt as though she might faint. Stepping outside, Grace gasped a few breaths of the brisk evening air, trying to calm down. She didn't know what to do.

Could it have really been stolen?

She didn't want to believe that. Theft was the *worst-case* scenario here, she reminded herself. There was every reason to believe she had dropped it. Right? She'd taken the Yamanote Line to Shibuya Station, check. Taken the wallet out of the zippered pocket, check. Tapped her card at the Hachiko Exit, check. Opened the map book to think about where she might go to eat. Walked across the square to the scramble crossing. Didn't remember zipping up the purse, though. Was the wallet still in her hand? Or in the purse? She'd shoved the book into her left coat pocket at the crossing. There had been a big crowd waiting for the light to turn green.

After that, Grace didn't think she'd touched anything in her purse or pockets until using the pay phone. If she'd dropped it, that could only have happened at the crossing, the red phone booth, or somewhere in between.

Every moment she spent doing nothing caused the elephant standing on her chest to become heavier. Steadying her resolve, Grace forced back tears and ran down to the square to search again.

She did another circuit of scramble crossing, train station, police box, Spain Hill, phone booth. Then another, and another. The initial panic slowly subsided into miserable acceptance. It might not be found, Grace realized. She didn't feel like crying anymore, though. She felt...empty.

A tiny playground was wedged between the two sides of the street near where she stood. Grace walked over and sat on the swings. The fixtures were built directly on green-painted concrete. It seemed appropriate to Grace that this would be the kind of playground you'd find in the middle of Tokyo—in the middle of the road, bereft of grass. She suddenly felt angry with herself, and so too with this city that she had been so enamoured with. One misfortune after another, and was it worth all of that heartache to spend one afternoon with Kana? Grace needed to believe it was so, or she didn't know how she would be able to stand up and keep going.

She felt desperate to be home—not at her father's place in Toronto, but *home*. Climbing up on the monkey bars, Grace noticed for the first time that the light pollution from the city blocked out all the stars. She felt her dread worsen.

Looking at places in the sky where familiar constellations should have been, the stars she and Jean had gazed at so many times on the grass in the Yetmans' backyard, Grace wondered what kind of day it was back home. Maybe it might even be snowing now, and her friends and family were waking up excited for their turkey dinners. She thought, if she had enough credit on her phone card to place another call, she would have liked to talk to Simon tonight.

It was almost scary how little she'd even thought about him since she came here. Grace felt ashamed of herself, but she hadn't even missed him. *What an awful girlfriend I am*, she thought, blinking back unexpected tears. She hadn't replied to any of Simon's messages. She had failed him, just as she'd failed Kana. This trip, she realized, hadn't really been about Kana at all. It was all for herself.

That kind of made everything worse.

Grace covered her eyes with her hand, blocking out the glare. Even Simon was probably angry, by this point, and he was the most easy going guy she had ever met.

Maybe, she thought, that might be part of why their relationship wasn't working the way it was supposed to. She'd believed she could like Simon as more than a friend, but so little had changed between them since they started going out. She didn't *feel* differently about him, even after six months of dating. In fact, since meeting Kana, she had spent even less time with Simon, and rarely thought about him when they were apart. It wasn't a good sign.

She stared down into the space between the monkey bars. What *did* she feel for Simon? He was a lot of fun to spend time with. She liked hearing about his friends on the basketball team and going to their games. She liked when they had a date at the coffee shop in town and sat in the big armchairs with glass mugs of hot chocolate, talking. Together with Jean, they had lots of fun on the French class trip to Saint-Pierre, and seeing movies as a trio in town on weekends. Grace wasn't so sure, though, that she had been having *more* fun with Simon since they began dating. Hanging out alone together was no different for her than hanging out with him in a group.

Her heart felt about as heavy as her stomach had for the last few hours. She lowered herself down between the bars, where the metal numbed her hands, but it was a good kind of feeling. It reminded her to come out of her thoughts. Grace hung there for a few minutes, then dropped lightly to the ground.

What would Kana be doing right now? She must have heard whether or not Daisuke had passed his exam.

Grace wondered if Kana would tell Daisuke how she felt about him. The real-life Kana she met this week seemed different from the outgoing one who had corresponded with Grace online—more hesitant, more cautious—but Kana was still, Grace thought, at least that much more brave than herself.

Chapter 22

Re: GET	12 月 24 日 (水) 18:55
From: otsuka.999991@ao.ne.jp	詳細を表示

Σ(·□·) Σ(·□·) Σ(·□·) Σ(·□·) Σ(·□·)
Please teach me!! Taiyaki-sensei

Re: GET	2008 年 12 月 24 日
From: thehealinglight@saftbank.ne.jp	水曜 午後 19:38
To: otsuka.999991@ao.ne.jp	Reply

OK! Keep some room in your stomach!

I'm waiting for you ♂_♂ Did you stop for taiyaki???

Re: GET	12 月 24 日 (水) 19:40
From: otsuka.999991@ao.ne.jp	詳細を表示

I'm arriving now! 2 minutes more. Don't leave! (T ▽ T)

From the moment she saw the message with the meeting place, Kana had a sense that something was out of the ordinary about Daisuke today. It was rare, for one, for him to suggest meeting her anywhere but Shibuya. She thought it meant good news for his exam results, but didn't want to get her hopes up too soon, so she agreed to his suggestion to meet outside Yurakucho Station. The roof over the escalators sparkled with tinsel and blinking blue and white Christmas lights.

Kana played with her phone as she waited, trying not to look nervous. She and Daisuke had met like this dozens of times. It didn't mean anything. Except maybe it did, because tonight was Christmas Eve, and Kana wore her best poet dress, the tan one with the lace and ruffled skirt, and had curled the ends of her hair before school that morning. The wrapped journal was tucked into her purse.

They had agreed on seven-thirty, and it was already twenty to eight, but Kana wasn't particularly worried. Waiting for Daisuke was something she'd become accustomed to. She tried to act casual and engaged in looking at a weather report on her phone.

"*Hello there, Miss Momokawa,*" he said with an easy smile, two minutes later, as promised. "Sorry I'm late. Thanks for waiting."

"Hi," she returned, suddenly shy. It wasn't the first time she'd seen Daisuke in street clothes, but could she be imagining that he had dressed up more than usual? He wore a tight long-sleeved shirt and jeans, a bronze necklace and stylized belt buckle. At least his hair was its usual wavy mess; it was getting to be longer than it had been the whole time she'd known him.

"*Shall we go to a cafe? Are you hungry?*"

"Sure." Of course the plan would be a cafe! Kana had to laugh, but at least they were changing up the location from their usual go-to spots. She followed him across the square and into a tall, glass-fronted building. On the second floor was a fancy, upscale place with high ceilings and a trendy green-and-white colour scheme.

When they had ordered cakes and drinks, and sodas had been delivered to the table, Kana looked expectantly at Daisuke. "Well? Don't keep me in suspense."

He held his hands up. "Whoa, are you excited to hear about this or something?"

"Of course I am!"

He grinned. "And here I thought you wanted to see *me* after such a long time."

Kana hoped her cheeks were not as red as they felt. "Well?"

"Okay, okay. I'll tell you. I got my exam results back."

The way his expression changed made Kana apprehensive. "And?"

"And...I didn't make it."

"Oh, no...." Kana swallowed the sudden jolt of apprehension that had run through her. She had truly expected good news. "I'm so sorry. You worked so hard."

"I want to say *easy come, easy go,* but honestly, I was disappointed." He shrugged with a wry smile. "Especially since I was so close, I think. My English got better, but not good enough. Not for that school."

Something didn't add up. He still looked too happy to be delivering such unfortunate news. "Okay? And then...?"

Daisuke grinned. "Aha, and then! *Then,* I got a phone call from Satou-sensei."

"Your music teacher?" Kana remembered one or two mentions of this man from Daisuke's talk about the brass band club at school.

"That's right. He called my house to ask if I passed. He knew the results were out."

Kana was impressed. None of her teachers would have called her at home to see how her test had gone. Koen Academy brimmed with smart and competitive students, though, and it was easy to get lost when so many kids with similar talents were all trying to get into top schools. At a place like Daisuke's where most of the graduates would start working right out of high school, a kid trying for a scholarship abroad would stand out.

"I told him I didn't get in. He seemed disappointed, too."

"Of course."

"But then, he told me about this job."

Now she was *really* confused. "What?"

"A *job*. Sensei is on the director's board of an orchestra here in Tokyo. They tour abroad, but they also bring in guest performers from all over the world. They're having a big name violinist flown in from Amsterdam in the spring to perform *concerto*, but none of their pianists speak English or Dutch. They wanted to assign him an afternoon practice partner to work with temporarily who could communicate." Daisuke smiled modestly. "He recommended *me*. He said I had the best conversational English he'd heard in all his years teaching there."

Kana couldn't stop herself from clapping her hands together in excitement. "That's amazing!"

"Yeah! And it came completely out of the blue. I'm not supposed to say anything, but if I do all right with this, I can stay on for interpreting and maybe even audition as a pianist backup. Satou-sensei put in a good word about what I'd been doing in the brass band club."

"Wow! Congratulations. I'm so happy for you!" Kana couldn't contain her excitement. "It would be so great if you got in and could tour with them and everything."

"For sure," he agreed. "It's not exactly what I wanted to do, but it's enough for now. It'll help me get a foot in the door. I might apply for a music program here in Tokyo instead."

Her mouth dry, Kana tried to direct her gaze at his glass of cola and not at his eyes. "Here? But what about Europe? And songwriting?"

She couldn't miss, though, the way his eyes got a little distant. "I guess Europe will have to wait a while. Maybe I can apply to do a summer exchange or something."

"I'm glad you're staying, though." The words were out of her mouth before she had a chance to think them over. Kana immediately ducked her head and pretended to be very interested in the table.

"You may say that now, but you might not be so happy to be stuck with me." Daisuke's smile was easy, but she thought she detected a note of surprise in his voice. "I'm going to need to brush up on my conversational English even more before I start my new job. All the stuff that I'll need for real life conversations. It's important I have someone I can trust to practice with before the violinist arrives."

"You want me to keep tutoring you?" Kana couldn't help but be shocked and—dare she say it?—relieved.

"You don't want to?"

"Of course I want to!"

She might have agreed too fast, she thought, but Daisuke looked unfazed. "That's great, really great! Thank you!"

"It's my pleasure." She meant it. She had missed their meetings; missed *him*.

"So, then, can we pick up where we left off? As teacher and student? Not tonight, of course. After."

"After...?"

"Oh, come on. Today, let's be *us*. After all, it's Christmas Eve."

Could she be imagining it, or was Daisuke blushing...?

~*~*~

It was time to make a tough decision. Stay in Shibuya, or go back to the hotel? Neither option looked particularly appealing to Grace.

She stood in front of the police box again, deep in thought. There would be no way to return here quickly if she went back to Shinjuku. If she *did* go back, and have the hotel contact the policemen who'd been helping her, she would have to stay in the hotel waiting for a call. There would be no chance of going to the airport.

I could stay here, and if it's not found, walk to the hotel in the morning, she thought. *Give up on the wallet if it isn't found by check-out time. Try to find a way to the airport from there.*

Not a great plan, she knew. Without the money, though, she was sunk.

Call home? Also a no. Not yet. *Tomorrow,* Grace decided, her mouth dry at the thought of admitting what had happened. If she didn't have it by noon, she would call her father and ask for help.

It wasn't a great plan, but at least it was a plan. Even having that much decided helped calm Grace's nerves.

Staying out all night came with its own risks, she was well aware. She remembered seeing drunks half passed out by station exits later in the evenings. And unlike the men who slept in cardboard boxes under the highway, Grace would be a highly visible target. With her wallet missing, she couldn't afford to lose her passport, the one item of value she still had.

She would look for someplace safe to wait until daylight, she decided. And then what? Grace wasn't sure. When the sun rose, she could search the streets again with better light, but for now, she was exhausted. A few hours sitting down would help. She hadn't eaten since early evening, and though she'd taken a drink from a park fountain, she felt thirsty again. She had been on her feet all day.

As she walked away from central Shibuya, Grace felt her palms start to sweat again despite the cold weather. *I must be crazy,* she thought. *How on earth did I end up in this situation?*

The street wasn't as busy or brightly-lit as other parts of the area; in fact, Grace had never been through this section of the neighbourhood, though she recognized that the parkland had to be Yoyogi Park. That might be someplace she could rest awhile, where she could hear if anyone tried to approach—maybe, she thought, she could climb a tree or something. When Grace came to an entrance, though, the gates were firmly closed for the night. Disappointed, she backtracked to a row of bushes by the perimeter fence. They were well-manicured and large enough to block the wind.

This seemed like a safer spot than most, Grace decided. She could hide here for a while and wait it out. Nobody could get behind her, and anyone approaching would have to climb over the retaining wall first.

Careful to stay out of view, she settled herself behind a hedge, grateful for the chance to sit down out of the ferocious wind. The park was utterly serene behind her, the trees and bushes as close to a sense of safety as she could hope to get.

Grace took a deep breath. She could get through this, she told herself. Nothing had happened so far that New Grace couldn't handle. This was just like any other day on her ridiculous Tokyo adventure. She'd done a dumb thing, but she would figure out a way out of it. In the morning, Grace would either have the wallet or be calling her father.

She very much hoped for the former.

It wasn't as cold as it had been the last few nights, but it wasn't so warm, either. She wished she'd been able to buy those hand warmers back at the convenience store. Though Grace knew she shouldn't sleep, there wasn't anything to do, and her eyelids were as heavy as lead.

She decided to lay down and rest her eyes. Retracting her arms inside her coat, Grace drew her legs up to her chest, pillowing her head on her purse. *Not bad,* she thought. Here didn't feel totally safe, but it would have to do.

~*~*~

Stuffed with cake and cream soda, Kana and Daisuke walked along the main street in Ginza, discussing everything from Chopin to chopsticks. Kana wasn't sure where they were going, but she didn't care all that much.

She thought about the journal in her purse, looking for the right time to give it to him. He'd still use it, she hoped. It could still be a "congratulations" gift, if she wanted it to be.

Or maybe something more, now that he planned on staying in Japan, she thought.

The evening was drawing to a close. She was supposed to be home by midnight. There was still time, but she wanted to give him the journal now, while the mood was right, against the romantic Ginza backdrop. Just in case it ended up leading to a long conversation.

Kana had her hand on the gift when her cell phone began to vibrate next to it. She frowned, wondering who would be calling so late in the evening. On the display she saw an unfamiliar number.

"Hello? This is Momokawa...no, Momokawa Kana...Grace? Oh, for Megucchi..."

Kana covered her other ear with her hand to muffle the din of the street. Daisuke paused at her side, waiting for the conversation to end, and when it did he looked concerned at the expression on her face. "Who was that?"

"The Shibuya police box. They found Megucchi's wallet." Kana furrowed her brow, confused. "She went back to Canada a few days ago. But he said it had been lost today."

"Maybe it fell somewhere where it was hard to reach, and was *found* today?"

"Maybe. But she gave them my number." Kana looked at the phone, perplexed. "They wouldn't tell me anything else over the phone."

"Can you get in touch with her?"

Kana was typing as she spoke. "Come to think of it, I haven't heard from her since she went home. I hope nothing happened with her flight. Do you think we should go over to Shibuya and check it out?"

Daisuke took her arm and steered her around so they were facing an underground entrance to Ginza Station. "Let's go."

Despite the late hour, perhaps because it was Christmas Eve, Hachiko Square was crowded with people and the roads thick with cars. When Kana and Daisuke arrived, the officer on duty informed them that Grace had filed the lost item report hours before.

"But that's impossible," Kana said, bewildered. "She left Japan already."

"Nevertheless, a Canadian girl came here earlier this evening, saying she'd lost a wallet." The officer looked equally confused. "Everything inside matches the description she gave."

Daisuke, who had never even seen a photo of Grace, scanned the crowd through the window. "Did she say to call Momokawa-san if it was found? Did she say anything about where she was going?"

The officer looked uncomfortable. "She didn't speak any Japanese, but it didn't seem like she wanted me to call. She came back twice, and she said she'd come back again. It's been a few hours, so we decided to call after all."

"How weird...I wonder where she could have gone?"

"Maybe she went to look for it," Daisuke suggested. "On the ground somewhere."

"This late?" Kana glanced at her watch. It was after ten. "Where was it found?"

"In the crosswalk. A young lady found it and brought it here."

"I wonder if she went back to her hotel," Kana mused. "She said she was staying in Shinjuku."

The officer shook his head. "I don't know. She didn't know the address of her hotel."

"Right, but she could get back to the hotel from here. She would know the way. Unless...you're probably not supposed to tell me what's inside, but was there a SUICA card?" Kana didn't remember Grace stopping to buy a ticket on the day they'd met. She must have tapped a card to pay her fare.

The officer sucked on his teeth. "Well…"

"That must be it. Come on, let's go look for her." Daisuke inclined his head at the window. "She might be searching for it somewhere nearby."

"You're right. Please, would you call me if she comes back here?" Kana asked the officer, who nodded and held the door open for them to leave.

"Don't worry," Daisuke said, obviously trying to calm her nerves. "I'm sure we'll find her soon."

Kana frowned and fidgeted. It seemed to be taking forever for the light to change. "It's not just that. Why didn't she tell me she was still here? Something must have happened."

"Maybe she was too busy with whatever she came to Japan in the first place for?"

"But she said she was going home 'tomorrow.'" Kana was genuinely confused. "And I thought we had a good time. I don't think she'd lie to me."

"Maybe she didn't want to trouble you?"

"Maybe…"

"Don't worry about it." Daisuke patted her shoulder, and Kana jolted—it was the second time he had touched her that day, and she still wasn't used to it.

They split up to take opposite sides of the street. It was wide, and the amount of foot traffic was enough to warrant a pair of eyes on each side. Kana kept a watch on the people passing her, as well as sneaking quick glances at Daisuke, who seemed to be sizing up everyone around him. Luckily, Shibuya was not as popular a tourist destination for foreigners on Christmas Eve, and it was easy to spot the Caucasians in the mix. At the end of the road, none of the passersby were the girl they were looking for.

"How tall is Megucchi?" Daisuke intoned when they were standing side by side again.

"A bit shorter than me. Maybe taller than most Japanese girls."

"No easy way to pick her out of a crowd, huh."

"I think you could. Compared to a Japanese person, she stands out. She has that brown hair girls at school like."

He knew just the shade she meant. Daisuke's school had plenty of rebel students who flaunted the "no dyed hair" rule.

They turned down a side road, and walked along Inokashira Street. Here, the department stores were closed for the night. Kana kept glancing at her watch, until Daisuke took notice. "What's up?"

"I'm supposed to be on the train by eleven," she admitted. "It'll take me an hour to get home, and I said I'd be back before midnight."

"Oh, no..."

"What if something's happened to her? Why would she leave Shibuya without coming back to the police box?"

"It'll be fine." He tried to smile as easily as usual, but Kana could see that Daisuke was worried too. She felt a rush of gratitude—after all, he and Megucchi didn't even know each other, but his concern was clearly genuine. She hoped he wasn't irritated that this had interrupted their evening.

Kana checked her phone for the hundredth time, but there were no missed calls or messages. "What should we do?"

He carefully considered his reply. "You should go. It's a long way back from here. What are you doing tomorrow?"

It was the first day of winter vacation. "Nothing," she said. "No plans."

"Then go home, and come back in the morning if you need to." He led her back to the intersection. "The officer will call you if she shows up, right? So you go, and I'll stay here at least until the last train. I still have a few hours."

"You'd do that for Megucchi?"

"I'd do it for you." He seemed to stop there, unsure what to say. "So by extension, yes, I would do this for her."

"Otsuka-kun..."

"In exchange, call me by my first name, why don't you?" He

grinned, but he avoided looking her in the eye.

Kana's heart jolted. If she agreed to call him by his first name, she would be removing the formality from their relationship. Admitting she wanted them to be closer than they were.

It was a big step. Kana felt her cheeks flush. "Do you want to call me by my first name, too?"

"That would be great. *Miss* Kana."

She laughed. "Just 'Kana' is fine, *thank you very much.*"

~*~*~

When Grace awoke, she felt pins and needles all over. Her legs had gone numb from being in the same position for so long. At some point, she'd crawled most of the way into the hedge, then woke up shivering. There was no way she was going to be able to spend the night out here. How did rough sleepers ever manage to survive out on the streets in winter?

Grace had never in her life felt exhaustion this absolute. Maybe because she had stayed the previous night at Narita, she was ill-equipped to last another evening without a bed. She couldn't remain here, she realized.

It was tough to muster the drive to move out of the little nest she'd made in the bushes, as lacklustre a shelter as it had been. When feeling returned to her legs, Grace crawled out, peeking over at the street. Not a sound could be heard anywhere nearby.

She felt decidedly uneasy in the silence. She knew the way back to Shibuya, but it wasn't a familiar route. Slipping back down to the sidewalk, Grace ran full-tilt along the perimeter of the park until she reached the main Harajuku strip.

Here, there were still restaurants with their lights beckoning. She used one to wash her hands in hot water, waiting over a minute for feeling to return to her fingers.

It wasn't even midnight yet.

Grace wanted to put her head down on a table and sleep. She

had no money to spend there, however, and so she left with a growling stomach.

Outside, there were still people around, but that wouldn't last forever. It would be better to go sit outside a police box or a train station, and try to stay awake until sunrise, though the idea made her sick to her stomach. She was so exhausted she wasn't sure she *could* stay awake.

Despondent, Grace sat down heavily on a railing and began to cry. The overwhelming situation was simply beyond what she could handle. Save for begging the police officers for a ride, she was out of options.

Unwilling to let anyone witness her misery, even if she would never see any of these people again, Grace buried her head under her arms.

As expected, Harajuku flowed around her, unyielding. For a few moments.

Then someone really did reach out, touched her shoulder, and spoke to her in English. "Hey, are you okay?"

Grace raised her head and tried to focus through tears. "Uh..."

"Do you want a tissue?" The voice belonged to a bespectacled Caucasian woman with long, curly brown hair.

Her companion, a redhead who also wore glasses, offered Grace a tissue packet. She accepted it gratefully. "Thank you."

"Do you need some help?" The brunette leaned down closer to her. "If you're lost, we can help you out."

"No, it's...well, I lost my wallet, and that's all the money I had, so I'm not sure where to go now..."

The women exchanged glances. "Oh, man," said the shorter one. "That sucks. You lost it around here? Do you know where the *koban* is?"

"No, it was in Shibuya. I went to the police box but it didn't turn up. I guess it got stolen." She laughed, a hollow sound, and choked on a hiccup. "Not much they can do with a hundred bucks, a few foreign cards and a SUICA."

"I'm sure they'll find it," the taller woman said reassuringly. "People here are super honest. Are you an exchange student? Or do you live here? Stop me if I ask you too many questions. I'm Em, by the way."

"Maybe not weird her out too much with an interrogation," her companion said. "We're high school teachers, if that helps any."

"I don't live here," Grace said softly. "I'm visiting."

"Okay. Why don't we go inside and warm up?" The redhead pointed at the same restaurant where Grace had washed her hands a few minutes before. Grace detected a hint of something familiar in her accent, but couldn't quite place it. "My name's Ashley. And you?"

"Grace," she stuttered.

"Nice to meet you, Grace. Are you hungry?"

Her stomach was gurgling. "Yeah."

"Okay. Come on, then. My treat."

Grace couldn't believe this was happening. "Are you sure?"

"Absolutely."

They led her in and sat down at a table, where Grace began to pour out the story not only of what had happened to her that day, but the whole fiasco of the last few weeks.

Her new friends seemed bewildered, but also impressed. The two of them were neighbours, they said. They lived in Osaka, teaching English, and had arrived in Tokyo that morning for a vacation.

"I like Japan, but I can't imagine moving here without being able to speak the language," Grace managed to say in between bites. This rice casserole might be the best thing she'd ever eaten in her life. "I wouldn't have the guts."

"Are you kidding? You came all the way here by yourself, that's pretty gutsy," Ashley said with a laugh. "I would never have been able to do that. And trying to sleep in the park? Nope, nope, nope. At least when *we* got here, we had jobs and apartments."

"Gutsy, maybe, but that was dangerous," said Em. "Personally, I think you should go back to your hotel tonight and come back in the morning. You can call the *koban* from there; the staff at the hotel will ask in Japanese for you."

"Ah, but...without my SUICA..."

"Don't worry about that. I can spot you." Em was taking thousand-yen notes out of her pocketbook.

"No, I couldn't..." she trailed off. Grace was ashamed to admit she *could*. Returning to the hotel and sleeping in a bed sounded like the best thing ever. These girls had already bought her dinner and listened to her story, though; she couldn't ask for anything more.

Ashley shook her head. "You absolutely can. I've been helped out by plenty of strangers in Japan. If we had the time, I'd tell you the story of the umbrella-toting taxi driver who drove us to the base of Mount Fuji."

"If you told her *that* story, we'd be here all night," Em said with a grin.

"Besides, what are we supposed to do, tell you to go sleep on the sidewalk? Or join the tents over in Miyashita. We'd be buying the newspaper for the next week to make sure we didn't get you killed."

"And I think you should contact your friend in the morning," Em reminded her gently. "Even if you do find your wallet. It helps to have someone to lean on."

"Okay..."

Em handed Grace three thousand-yen bills. "Take this, and don't worry about it. Really."

Ashley pressed more notes into her hand. "Just in case."

"And here's my phone number, too." Em pulled a notebook from her huge messenger bag. "You can call me if you need anything. Do you know how to make a pay phone call here?"

"We'll be in Tokyo until the fifth of January."

Grace was on the verge of tears again. "Yes. I'll call if I need it. Thank you..."

Em put on fingerless gloves. She checked her watch and shot her companion a glance.

"It's pretty late. We have to get the Chiyoda Line back to our hostel," Ashley said. She pushed her glasses further up on the bridge of her nose. "You should go, too. You don't want to miss the last train."

"Okay. Thanks."

The women got up and paid the bill while Grace stood silently behind them. The trio then stepped outside.

Omotesando wasn't yet quiet, and the huge Christmas tree in front of Laforet still glittered breathtakingly with lights and hundreds of pink and silver plastic balls. Grace took a deep breath and felt the pressure in her chest ease the slightest bit.

"Do you know the way?" Em pointed up the street, toward the train station. "JR Harajuku is up the hill, there."

"Yes. Thanks so much, both of you. I really appreciate it."

"But be careful. I'll be checking the headlines." Ashley smiled so that Grace could be sure she was joking.

"I'll be careful. Thank you again. See you!"

"Bye!" The pair kept waving as they disappeared into the subway.

There was enough time to reach Shinjuku before the trains stopped, but Grace still didn't feel right about leaving without returning to the police box first. Maybe, she thought, now that she had a little cash, she could find someplace nearby to stay until morning. She could check for the wallet and go home on the first train.

Turning around, Grace headed back in the direction she knew best, grateful to be walking under bright street lights again. The district was still busy despite the late hour. Many of the revellers out so late on Christmas seemed to have been drinking, so Grace steered clear until she spotted an Internet cafe on the other side of the street.

Somewhere in the back of her mind, there was a memory about Internet cafes. Ducking into a door frame, Grace opened the trusted *Friendly Planet* book that had never yet let her down.

There it was, Internet cafe: Cheap and popular choice for people who miss their last train home.

How serendipitous to find one here, right when she needed one! The process couldn't be that hard to figure out, Grace thought. She'd been shy to try one before now, but after all this, how bad could it be?

Easy, was the answer. She paid a pittance for a tiny private room with a padded floor to sit on. Five hours of computer time and all the coffee she could drink. Shrugging off her coat, Grace considered using some of the time to check her mail and online haunts, but she was too exhausted, and the dimly-lit space was blissfully warm.

Grace thought about what she would say to her father when she called, but decided it could wait. It wasn't going to be a pretty scene, whether she was delivering the news that he didn't have to come get her at the airport, or asking him to bail her out. Grace tried not to think about it for the time being. She pillowed her head on a beanbag chair and pulled the coat over her body as a makeshift blanket. Her body was ready for real sleep, and as far as Grace was concerned, the sooner this night was over, the better.

As she drifted off, she wondered how everything was going on the other side of the world. This would be the first time she would wake up on Christmas Day away from her family.

It was an unforgettable Christmas, that much was for certain. If she got through this whole mess somehow, she was going to have one heck of a story to tell.

Chapter 23

Home > Settings > Private Messages > Sent Items	
Something happened!?	
makhanikana	Megucchi
	If you get this, contact me right away by phone or email.
	I'm so worried about you! (T⌒T)
	♡♡♡ Kana

Nothing yet	12 月 24 日 (水) 23:55
From: otsuka.999991@ao.ne.jp	詳細を表示
MISS Momokawa, sorry I don't have good news for you yet. The trains are stopping soon. I hope you got home OK? Did you hear anything?? Otsuka DAISUKE	

Kana jolted awake shortly after six, though she hadn't set an alarm. Maybe, she thought, it was the *lack* of sound that had made the night so fitful. She had slept with her phone's manner mode off, right beside her pillow, but the entire night had slipped by and she hadn't heard from Grace, the police, or even Daisuke.

Kana quickly got up and changed without even putting away her *futon*. It was early enough that no one in the house was awake yet. Her mother had worked a late shift the previous night and gotten home later than Kana had. Her father's holidays wouldn't start until the weekend, so he was probably sleeping on the couch in his office in Gunma, as he often did during the week. Kana felt a pang of regret that she hadn't managed to spare more than a few words for her father the last few times she'd seen him. She had been too busy with her academic troubles, and he, reluctant to interrupt.

Even Shingo had a break from the baseball club until after the new year. Tiptoeing quietly past her brother's room, she crept down the stairs, pulled on boots over her leggings and a pea coat over her sweaterdress, then hurried to Owada Station.

Weekends weren't busy on her local line, especially so early in the morning. Kana was able to sit, but found she was far too alert to nap. Even though it was too soon to expect him to be up, she sent Daisuke a message.

She was surprised when, a moment later, the phone vibrated in her hand with his reply. "*Good morning. Meet you by Hachiko?*"

"*OK. I'm on my way.*"

Kana was impressed, too, that he had managed to get to Shibuya so early. She spent the long ride fidgeting, waiting for the rest of the world to start waking up.

The Square was nearly empty, but a few people lingered around the statue, and that was where she found Daisuke sitting on the metal railing with one knee drawn up to his chest, head down. When she spoke his name, he didn't move, so she laid two fingers on his shoulder. "Daisuke-kun."

"You're here." Quickly he sat up straight. "Sorry. I didn't find your Megucchi yet."

"I figured. Thanks for trying."

He looked as exhausted as she felt. "I went by the police box a couple of times, but she hasn't come by at all. Not since last night, before we arrived."

"A couple of times?" Kana blinked. "When did you go home? On the last train?"

He tried to brush the question off. "I didn't want to waste much time."

Now she noticed he was still wearing yesterday's clothes. "Wait. You *did* go home, didn't you?"

"Well..."

"Seriously?" Her hands flew to her mouth.

He sighed. "Seriously. I thought she'd be easier to spot if she was still wandering around after last train, but I didn't see anyone that could be her."

"Daisuke-kun..."

He shrugged. "Don't worry about me; I'm pretty good going without sleep. You haven't heard, either?"

"No. Nothing at all."

"What do you want to do?" Daisuke gulped down the last of his canned coffee and stood. "Should we go look?"

"Yes," Kana said with finality. "Until we have some clue, I want to look. Even if we have to walk all the way to Shinjuku."

"Okay, Boss. You got it."

They returned to the street. Kana was aware of the jitters in her stomach, not only out of concern for Megucchi. She was nervous about what seemed to be happening between the two of them. Daisuke had gone far out of his way to help her, giving up his entire night to look for her friend! She didn't want to read too much into things, but that seemed like too big a favour between student and tutor. Particularly one who had been ignoring him for weeks. She wanted to think that it meant something; the way she had hoped him asking to meet on Christmas Eve had meant something. Now that he'd given her signs, though, she was anxious about what was supposed to happen next.

The journal was still in her purse, waiting for the right moment. The festive mood they'd shared in Ginza was long gone.

Daisuke, seeming fully awake, led her toward Miyashita Park. "I've been starting with the JR tracks and walking most of the streets back and forth from the station until I hit Bunkamura. Then I come back and do the other side of the line. I haven't looked much around the south exit, but there isn't much there for her, I think."

He had a method. Kana sensed that Daisuke had traced this route quite a few times in her absence. She managed to stammer, "Wow, you covered quite a lot."

"I don't know Shibuya as well as you do. I was just kind of walking around, heh."

The streets they checked were empty of pedestrians; those out this early were employees sweeping the sidewalks outside of businesses and cleaners removing stacks of trash from the curb. Shibuya looked a lot dirtier in the early morning light. Kana frowned, searching the faces of each passerby.

They walked fairly far without seeing anyone who looked out of place—in fact, once they had turned off Fire Street, there were no other people around at all. So when Kana spied a figure in a purple coat and plaid scarf ambling slowly down the hill, even from so far away, she had a hunch.

She caught Daisuke by the wrist and hurried to pull him forward. "Down there!"

"What? Is it her?"

"I'm sure it is!"

They ran down the hill, though Kana let go of her companion as soon as she realized what she'd done. She was glad he couldn't see her face, in case it had turned red.

The girl was inching along, peering at the ground. She looked so involved in her search that Kana slowed to a stop more than two meters away, not wanting to startle her. "Megucchi?"

Grace looked up, startled to hear her nickname. "Kana-chan!"

"*It is you. I knew it.*" Kana switched to English, overwhelmed with relief. "Are you all right?"

"I'm okay." Her friend looked astonished. "What are you doing here?"

"We've been searching for you everywhere. A man from the Shibuya Station police box called me."

"They *called* you? They found it!?" Grace's face lit up. "Oh, thank goodness. I was on my way down to the station."

"Now? Where have you been all night?"

Grace flushed. "I went to an Internet cafe and ended up passing out. It's a long story."

Daisuke laughed. "That is like me. All the time I miss a train."

Now that he had spoken up without warning, and in English, Grace's mouth fell open. "Oh! Hi there. Sorry, I didn't...uh..."

To his credit, Daisuke just smiled and stuck out his hand for her to shake. "I am Otsuka Daisuke."

"Grace Ryan." She accepted the handshake. "So this is the famous 'Mister Otsuka.'"

"I am famous?" He glanced at Kana. "That's great. I like it."

"*I would say* infamous *more than* famous," she quipped in Japanese. Daisuke looked delighted—at the joke? Or at the fact that she had talked about him?—and let go of Grace's hand.

Bashful, Kana turned her attention back to her friend, who looked only slightly the worse for wear after the long night. Her hair was tousled, and she had a leaf caught in her scarf and a smudge of something on her cheek, but seemed otherwise unhurt. The idea of sleeping in an Internet cafe sent chills down Kana's spine. Grace certainly had a particular sort of courage, or maybe it was something that came from her culture, Kana wasn't sure. She had to admit she admired her friend's spirit.

Grace seemed energetic, if bleary-eyed. "Thanks for coming out to look for me. I appreciate it. I'm so sorry I got you involved."

"No, not at all. I wish you had told me that you were in trouble."

"I'm sorry." She pursed her lips. "I was going to call you today and tell you. Honest."

"I wish you told me that you were still in Japan," Kana said frankly. Would her friend be embarrassed? Angry?

Grace, though, laughed along with her. "Believe me, I didn't mean to be here. It's a very long story."

Daisuke gestured further down the street. "Before you tell a very long story, shall we go to the police box? Miss Ryan?" To Kana's amazement, he seemed to be following the rapid-fire English with ease. She couldn't help feeling proud at how far he'd come in such a short time.

"Oh, yes, please." Grace looked relieved. "But you don't have to call me that. You can call me by my first name, Grace. Or Megumi, or Megucchi even, if you prefer it. I know 'Grace' is hard to pronounce for Japanese people."

Kana smiled. "That's right. Until the police officer called, I had almost forgotten that 'Megucchi' wasn't your real name."

Daisuke was already nodding, grinning his familiar grin. "OK. Miss Megumi."

"That'll do." Grace laughed.

The trio walked together to the pedestrian scramble. The square was still mostly empty, and to Kana it felt like any other day, not like Christmas Day at all. A shame, since it was the first time in her life she'd really wished to have a Christmas date.

They all forgot about the holiday, though, when a stack of paperwork was placed in front of Grace at the police box. She filled out the forms without complaint as Kana translated, and fifteen minutes later they were walking out of the tiny office with Grace's wallet safely back in her purse. Despite the remarkably brave face she'd been putting on for the officers, her friend looked about ready to burst into tears by the time they handed her the pouch. Everything was inside, untouched. Kana promised to write a thank-you letter for the woman who had turned it in.

All three of them were still running on empty, so Daisuke led the way to the cafe where his sister worked. Miki let them enter early when he rattled the locked front door. Glammed up in over-the-top eyeliner, she regarded her little brother with surprise. "I figured you had to be out with a girl when you stayed out so late on Christmas Eve, but I wasn't expecting there to be *two* girls."

"Ha ha." Daisuke tried to look offended, but failed. "I'm starving. Can we eat?"

"We're not open yet."

"I'm ready to sit here until you are."

Miki sighed. Kana had to hold back a laugh at the way she immediately indulged him. "You're lucky I'm the one opening today."

While Miki readied the shop for the day's customers, Grace spilled her entire story for the second time, even the unfortunate circumstances that had brought her to and kept her in Japan. Food started appearing on the table, and the story went on and on as they stuffed themselves with a Western-style breakfast. Grace ate voraciously—two big meals in such a short time was more than she had been able to afford in several days.

Kana was more shocked than anyone to learn the truth about the visit to Japan. "No. You came all the way here because of *me*?"

"Stupid, I know." Grace laughed. "I should have thought that through a little better."

Daisuke, on the other hand, looked so awed that he forgot what language they were supposed to be speaking. "*Amazing. That is so amazing.*"

"*It is not! Imagine what's going to happen when she gets home!*" Kana chastised, but honestly, she too felt it was a little bit amazing. Nobody had ever done anything like *that* for her before. She felt bad that Grace had gone through so much for her sake, though, and Kana hadn't even known it until now.

"It's definitely crazy," Grace said. "Hopefully someday I'll be able to tell my kids about my amazing adventure as a hobo in Japan."

"'Hobo'?"

"The classiest in Tokyo."

Grace seemed like she wanted to explain what *hobo* meant when Miki came back to the table with coffee. Kana had never been so excited for an Americano.

Grace and Daisuke on the other hand had become sluggish, looking as though they wanted to nod off, so Kana stood up as soon as she finished the drink. "Megucchi, I'll take you to get your luggage, and then we can go to my house, all right?"

"Sure," Grace agreed sleepily. The long night had caught up with her.

"*And you need to get some rest.*" She said in Japanese, looking pointedly at Daisuke, who was staring blank-faced out the window.

He jumped when she addressed him. "*Ah, okay. Right.*"

All three reached for their wallets at the till, but Miki waved it off. "*I'll let you off with the bill for today. I want a proper explanation when I get home.*" She eyed her brother. "*All of it.*"

"*Tomorrow,*" Daisuke corrected, stifling a yawn.

They went back the way they had come, down Center Street. At Shibuya Station, Grace got into the line to use a machine. "I need a minute to charge my SUICA."

Daisuke and Kana stood back; exchanged uncertain glances. Kana recognized an opportunity when she saw one, but didn't want to make the first move. Luckily, Daisuke did it for her, switching back to Japanese. "Listen, I kind of wanted to spend today with you...not as good as Christmas Eve, I know. But I guess we can't."

"Sorry." She felt just as regretful as he sounded.

"You should take care of *Miss* Megumi first."

"Thank you for looking for her...you didn't have to do that." She was beyond impressed at his dedication. It would have been easy for him to go home and give up.

"But you're glad?"

She nodded.

"Then it was worth it," Daisuke declared.

Was this the right moment? Kana wasn't sure, but there weren't many moments left before they would have to part ways. Shyly she handed him the foil-wrapped package. "This is for you, by the way. Merry Christmas."

He seemed surprised, but he accepted and opened it. When he held the journal in both hands, he flipped through its blank pages with a broad smile. "Wow, this is great. Thank you."

"You're welcome. Congratulations on the job."

"Listen...Kana..."

It was the first time he'd said her first name. She couldn't help but notice that he hadn't called her *Miss*.

For once in his life, however, Daisuke seemed to be at a loss for words. "I've been wanting to ask you...er, that is, to tell you..."

Grace returned with her train card in her hand, interrupting whatever it was he wanted to say. "Thanks for waiting."

The moment was gone. Grace didn't seem to notice; Daisuke and Kana both looked away nervously. As if on autopilot, they entered the ticketed area, then seemed to remember they needed to go in opposite directions. Kana felt a sense of *déjà vu*; although this was not the exact spot where she had said goodbye to Grace before, it was close. Daisuke put on a smile for Grace. "We will surely meet again, Miss Megumi."

"Yes, I definitely hope so!"

Then he switched languages again, addressing Kana alone. *"Will you meet me again sometime, when you have time?"*

"I think so. When?"

"Take your time with your guest first. No rush."

She nodded wordlessly, not trusting herself to speak.

"You tell me the day. I'll be waiting for your message." With that, he turned and darted up the stairs.

"There's a Yamanote train coming," Grace noted, inclining her head. Shaking off her reverie, Kana hurried up, with Grace a few steps behind. They made it to the top just as the train arrived. Inside the car, Grace looked at Kana curiously. "What was that? Did he ask you out?"

"I'm not sure," Kana confessed. Even though Daisuke had spoken in Japanese, she wasn't surprised that Grace had figured out the exchange.

Grace fell quiet for a while, watching Shinjuku come into view through the window. Then she led the way to the hotel.

Neither spoke for a long time. Kana thought maybe she ought to try to make conversation, but she had a lot on her mind right then, and it seemed Grace did, too. Her suitcase sat inside the door, fully packed; the bed unrumpled.

"Thanks," Grace said as she laid the key on the check-in desk.

The weather started to warm up, and Kana looked up at the cloudless sky as they turned back toward the station. "After all that," she said at last, "he didn't pass his exam, either."

Grace rolled her suitcase up the street with practised ease. "Daisuke didn't?"

"No."

Her frown deepened. "Wow. Sorry to hear that."

"Yes. It might be all right, though." She paused. "He got a job offer here in Tokyo. So he's not going to go to the university."

"That's too bad. He studied so hard, after all."

"He did." Neither of them were in a hurry anymore. Kana seemed lost in her thoughts for a few moments before speaking again. "He got a lot better at English. Only a couple of months of tutoring, and he sounds so good."

"But not enough?"

"No. Not enough."

Grace fiddled with a key chain on her bag. "He seemed really nice. And cute. Sorry, I guess you don't say guys are *cute* here, do you? He was *cool*."

"I understood you."

"What about Europe? Estonia, or wherever he wanted to go?"

"I don't know. It looks like he'll stay in Japan for now." Kana tried to ignore the way her heart beat faster when she thought about it. She didn't know for sure what Daisuke felt, after all. But what he had said about wanting to spend Christmas with her...that was something. She wanted to know what it was he had intended to tell her at the station.

Grace looked thoughtful. "But that's great, for you, anyway. If you like him. You *do* like him, right?"

"I do." She was surprised how much she meant it.

Chapter 24

From: megumi_709@geemail.com	Wed, Dec 31, 6:35 AM

Hi Simon,

I'm so sorry I never got back to you until now. I've had a lot on my mind, but that's not an excuse. I'm sorry I keep letting you down. I'm even letting you down by sending this in an email, but every time I try to get my own thoughts together, it comes out totally wrong. Don't panic—this is not a breakup email. (Gotta draw the line somewhere, right?) But something's not right, and I have to tell you about it. I don't think I can change.

I think it's a problem that's so much bigger than my best guy friend becoming my boyfriend. More even than not knowing how to be with a partner. The more time passes, the more I think that maybe romance isn't for me. Maybe I can't be "more than friends" with someone at all.

It doesn't mean I don't have feelings for you. I just know that they aren't the same feelings you have for me. And you don't deserve to wait while I figure out what's going on in my own head.

I understand if you want to break up. And I hope that if you do, we can go back to the way things were before...which is basically exactly how things are right now? Hahaha. Yeah. That's kind of the issue right there. u.u

I'll be home next Saturday, so if you want we can go out for coffee, maybe on Sunday? We can talk about it, if you want to.

Miss you.

~ Gracie

After the stories of how Kana was kept under her mother's thumb, studying day and night, Grace was shocked by how welcoming the Momokawa family acted toward the total stranger in their midst.

They lived in a roomy house, big by Japanese standards, though far enough from central Saitama that Grace could see they had traded convenience for space. Closer to the "real" Japan than anything Grace had experienced so far. They even had a little stone pond in the gated driveway, and a well-kept *bonsai* tree on a table in the tiny yard.

Grace didn't say anything to Kana when she stepped onto the familiar platform at Owada Station for the first time. Who knew she had gotten so close to finding the Momokawas on her own, without even realizing it? That little detail, Grace decided to keep to herself.

Kana's family didn't seem at all surprised by the sudden appearance of their guest; in fact, her mother fell over herself taking care of Grace, and thanking her for "tutoring" her daughter. Kana handled all the translations. Himeko had countless questions about what Grace had done in Japan and whether she liked it.

Grace wasn't sure *what* Kana had said to her parents, but they seemed perfectly content to have her, when they were around, at least. Himeko worked odd shifts, not always during the daytime. Her father, Kazuki, was absent when Grace arrived and didn't turn up at all until Friday night. It seemed like a strange situation to Grace for him to be sleeping at his office, but Kana didn't seem bothered. She also had a little brother, Shingo, who played baseball and practised his English on their visitor.

The girls spent their days in a much quieter fashion than Grace had gotten used to. She had envisioned Kana's life as an everyday rush in and out of Tokyo, singing karaoke, shopping and hanging out in the fashion hot spots. Grace had been so envious of her friend, being able to visit the exciting places described in *Friendly Planet*. Life in Saitama, though, was even slower than back home. In the daytime they watched videos, looked through Kana's magazine collection, and went out on walks. On a few occasions they went to Tokyo and hung out with Rumi or visited sightseeing places, but for the most part, the pair stayed at Kana's house. Grace felt grateful for the change of pace.

She had to call home on that first day, starting with her father. Grace usually felt a little awkward on the phone with him as it was, but having to deliver this news caused her guts to seize up in knots.

He picked up on the second ring. "Hello?"

"Hi Dad, it's me." She took a deep breath. "I have, uh, bad news for you. Is this, is this a good time to talk?"

"Oh, boy." Grace could hear noise in the background. She almost hoped he'd say no, it *wasn't* a good time, and she would have an excuse to put this off a little longer. "All right, hit me. Let me guess, you're staying home with your mother after all."

"Not...not quite." For a heartbeat she felt tempted to go along with his suggestion, but she steeled herself. It was time to stop taking the easy way out. "The truth is, I went on a little trip by myself. I tried to get back in time to meet you on Christmas like we planned, but things went wrong. I'm really sorry, but there's no way I can be there tomorrow."

He went quiet for a few seconds. Grace could hear her own pulse pounding in the earpiece.

"I guess that explains the wacky phone number," her father said at last. "Where are you?"

"In Japan." She hurried to add, "And everything is totally fine, I'm safe, I'm staying with my friend's family. But there was some messiness with the ticket. I'm supposed to get to Toronto on January first."

"I can change it," he said without missing a beat. "What airline? I'll call them right now."

"Dad..." This part was almost as hard for her to say as the

initial news. "Would it be okay if I stayed here a few more days? I'm sorry. I know we agreed it was your turn. This is all my fault though, not Mom's. She didn't have anything to do with it."

The wait for a response made Grace's stomach churn. Her father didn't deserve to miss out on his holiday, either.

What he said next, though, wasn't what Grace expected at all. "Well, of course, if that's what you want. Don't waste your trip after travelling all that way."

Astonished, she clutched the receiver tighter. "Really? Are you sure? Aren't you mad?"

"I'm disappointed, of course. I'm not *mad*." Her father *harrumphed* in his professorial voice. "I would be more disappointed if you were choosing Christmas with your mom over me. It's not fair, you know. But it's not like she and I can go on like this much longer."

"What do you mean? 'Like this'?"

"You're going off to university in the fall," he said gently. "I can't expect you to keep up the custody arrangements your mom and I made when you were ten. It's already past time for you to decide where, and who with, you want to spend your time."

"Dad..." Her heart swelled.

"Though I'll admit I'm surprised *she* agreed to an overseas trip. Your mom can be a little protective."

"She didn't *exactly* agree." That would be a longer story than Grace wanted to tell when her calling card minutes were ticking down. "I have to talk to her, too, and I don't think she's going to take it as well as you did. I'm honestly shocked. I expected grounding for life."

She could hear her father's smile. "I guess that's up to your mom. But for me, I'm actually sort of impressed."

"What? Why?"

"Well." He hesitated. "You're usually so shy. You never wanted to go on any trips with me before when I invited you. So of course I wouldn't expect to hear about you jetting off to

Asia."

Grace managed a faint giggle. Maybe she would live through this encounter after all.

"I'm not happy to hear you weren't truthful with me," he said firmly. "I wish you had told me before that you wanted to skip Christmas. But you also have the right to choose. And I think it's great that you're getting out there and seeing the world. There's so much of it beyond the island. A lot of people never leave home."

"I know," she said. It wasn't so long ago that Grace thought she'd be one of those people.

"I'll go to bat for you with your mom, if you like. We can wait until you get here."

She felt a little of the weight lift off her chest. "That would be good. I'm not looking forward to that conversation."

"Try to give her a little credit, Gracie. She knows what's coming. We may not be able to get along anymore, Camilla and I." He paused. "But I still know her better than anyone in this world. She'll be as sad to have an empty house as I am."

"Come on, Dad." Grace could feel a flush of embarrassment heat her cheeks. "Besides, I'm probably applying to go to MUN in the fall. Mom's house isn't going to be empty so soon."

She thought he might protest, ask why she wasn't applying to universities in Toronto, but he didn't. Instead, he surprised her again. "Well, I hope if you've gotten bitten by the travel bug, you'll want to go somewhere with your old Dad sometime. That would be a nice way to get together when you're out on your own, spending your holidays with whomever you like."

The idea of taking a vacation with her father sounded a little exciting. Now that she had been as far as Japan, Grace realized, none of the holiday destinations they'd discussed in the past sounded intimidating anymore. "Actually, I'd like that. It would be really nice to go on a trip with you."

"Wow. Is this a prank call? Are you really my daughter?"

She laughed.

"Anyway, I'll let you go, since this is probably costing you a fortune," he said. "But I'm glad you called. Let's take a rain check on Christmas this time, okay?"

"Okay, Dad. Thanks. Merry Christmas."

"Merry Christmas, honey. And I'll still see you on New Year's, right? You're not skipping my place entirely, are you?"

"No." Grace laughed. "I'm leaving here on the first, and flying over the date line, so I'll see you the same day."

"I'll be looking forward to it."

On the last day of the year, she sent two long apologies—one to Simon, one to Jean. It would be the first time she'd replied to either of them.

Her inbox was brimming with unread messages. Grace felt bad when she read through them, especially the apology from Jean that had been sitting untouched for over a week.

I can't blame you for ignoring my texts. If I were you, I would be mad at me, too. I decided to write you an email instead.

The first thing to say is that I'm sorry, because you were right. One of the girls took me aside and told me about Christian's girlfriend. I don't know why I didn't believe it when you told me.

Even if it wasn't true, I'm still to blame. I wanted so badly to have this that I totally glossed over all the red flags. I should have trusted your judgment. I guess, I was looking out for you all the time. It never occurred to me I'd end up in a situation where I needed you to look out for me.

I'm not going back to the Drama Club next semester. I think I have more than enough drama going on in my life without having to be around Christian all the time. Maybe I can get back to the stage life next year when we're in uni.

I hope this isn't going to affect our friendship. You're still my BFF, always.

xoxo

J

Simon's messages were shorter, almost like news bites, and numerous. He'd written her every day since the beginning of Christmas break. Grace wasn't sure she could say what she needed to say when she saw him again...what she *was* sure about was that things couldn't go on like they had been. Maybe it would be better for them to return to being friends until she figured out what she wanted. Deep down, Grace already knew it had nothing to do with Simon and everything to do with her, but knowing that didn't really make her sad. Her social life would be turbulent for the next little while, whether Simon ended the relationship or not.

She wanted to make up with Jean, but Grace stopped short at asking her to come to the airport. Maybe it would be better if Jean proposed her own time and place for them to see each other.

When she had sent the two messages, Grace took a bath, lingering for a while in the big metal tub. As a guest in the house she bathed first, and so the water was a little hotter than she preferred, but she stoically endured it, distracted by her thoughts. What would happen to her first relationship? Was it going to be her last? Were they over, now?

Maybe *they* hadn't been what she'd thought they were. She wondered what he was feeling now.

Simon weighed heavily on her mind until late into the evening, when she sat with her suitcase in Kana's room, repacking all the clothes Himeko had washed. They still had a few hours to do away with, and then they would be going to a shrine to do a traditional New Year's visit, *hatsumoude*. Grace had never heard of this custom, but Kana said the shrines would be packed with people doing their annual visit at midnight. It was the only day of the year that trains continued to run through the early morning.

It seemed to Grace to be a fitting way to spend her last night in Japan.

Normally, Kana told her, the Momokawa family would all go

together to a local shrine in Saitama on one of the first few days of January. This year, though, since Grace was leaving the next day, Kana wanted to make a special visit to a Tokyo shrine she particularly liked. That suited Grace fine, as she wasn't sure she would be able to sleep that night anyway.

In truth, she didn't feel ready to leave Japan anymore, not in the way she had before Christmas. Time since then had flown by at top speed; the days blurred into each other so much that she couldn't remember what she had done with them all. Tomorrow, though, whether she liked it or not, Grace would be going home.

She didn't have material souvenirs to remember it all by, but Grace didn't care. What mattered most was that she and Kana had grown closer, and each had seen firsthand what kind of person her pen pal was. The imaginary version of Kana that Grace had come up with based on their text exchanges had been replaced with a real girl.

Kana herself stood at the bureau, putting on a baby blue sweater over her one-piece dress. Right now she didn't look like the young fashionista with the closed mouth smile who had caught Grace's eye in that issue of *SwEET*, nor the Shibuya schoolgirl posing in a photo booth. Grace felt extremely grateful to know this Kana, too; the Kana who talked in her sleep and grabbed most of the tofu out of the *sukiyaki* pot and hummed American pop songs as she read. A girl who could spend hundreds of hours studying for an exam and blow it all for the sake of fifteen minutes' extra sleep, but get right back up and keep going. Grace admired her even more than the Kana she had imagined before she came to Japan. It felt good to have such a friend in her corner.

"Are you ready?" Kana had sensed Grace watching her.

Hurriedly Grace closed the suitcase and zipped it up. "Yeah. Ready."

"Okay." She checked her watch. "We can go to the train now."

The two of them put on coats and scarves, and Kana led the way down the stairs, calling out to her parents. "We're leaving."

The rest of the Momokawa family stayed in the living room. Himeko came to the doorway to see them out. "See you later. Be careful coming home."

"Okay."

Kana and Grace walked the short distance to the station, crossed the tracks and waited for the train. Some of the other travellers were dressed in *kimono* for their shrine visits.

"They look so beautiful." Grace looked on wistfully.

"Let's try wearing *kimono*, next time you come to Japan," Kana said.

"I'd love to."

On the train, both girls fell silent. Grace had noticed early on that trains in Japan were designated as quiet spaces. That was all right with her; she still thought about the message she had sent to Simon, and was unsure how to bring it up with her friend. She wanted counsel, but she felt afraid Kana's advice would mirror what her own instincts were telling her. Instead, she looked out the window at the dark countryside giving way to urban sprawl.

It was nice having someone else there to navigate. Even Shinjuku Station was a minor thing with Kana leading the way. Grace only had to follow her friend until they reached a station called Tokyo Teleport (this, she thought, had to go down in the books for "best train station name ever") and disembarked. She was shocked to see all the other passengers on their train car get off here as well. They walked as part of a little mob, up the escalator and out onto the darkened plaza.

"We're not going to Harajuku, are we?"

"No. The Meiji Shrine there is the busiest one on New Year's," Kana replied. "I want to go on New Year's sometime, but this shrine is important to me right now. I thought it would be less crowded. I hope there aren't too many people."

Something about the area seemed familiar, but Grace

couldn't quite put her finger on it. They crossed the road and entered a shopping centre, half-open. Vendors were selling lunch boxes inside the doors. Grace looked around, taken aback. It was so late for lunch boxes! Like the train schedules, New Year's Eve seemed to call for its own rules.

Kana led them to an escalator bedecked with *torii* gates. Grace had never visited a Shinto shrine, but she recognized these from her short stint hanging around the bridge outside Harajuku Station. "It's up *here?* In the mall?"

"It's on the roof of the mall."

"Ah, Japan." Grace chuckled.

The next floor was jam-packed with people buying charms, arrows and amulets from vendors set up at tables, and even more were outside the glass doors on the terrace. Grace could hear someone revving up the crowd with a microphone. She took a party favour and followed Kana out into the wind.

This wasn't what she had expected when Kana said they were going to a shrine. She had pictured something like on TV, or like Meiji, a venerable old structure with huge ancient *torii* and long-haired priestesses in red and white robes. Women in *kimono* ringing the bells as they prayed, and so on. Here, though, Grace could barely see the tiny shrine for all the people surrounding it, lorded over by the giant shadow of the TV station building looming behind. The patrons were mostly young, and laughing at the men on the microphones, who were doing some sort of stand-up comedy. It seemed somewhat un-Japanese, but decidedly *Tokyo*.

When she turned away from the crowd Grace realized why she had felt this place to be so familiar. Beyond the railing she saw Tokyo Bay, and on the other side of it, Tokyo Tower. This was the same view she had looked out on during her first days in the city. It seemed like a long time ago, though it had been only a couple of weeks; the sight of it made her nostalgic. Kana clearly felt the same, gazing out at the city with a contemplative look on her face.

"Nice view."

"It is. Daisuke-kun likes this place."

So that was why they had come all the way here, Grace thought. She wanted to ask about him, but the roar of the crowd built as midnight drew closer. The emcees were preparing everyone for a countdown. Instead, she and Kana looked on silently, distancing themselves from the festivities until the enthusiastic group began to shout. *"Ten!"*

"Nine! Eight! Seven!"

"Six, five, four..." Kana continued, in English.

"Three! Two! One! *Happy new year!*"

The revellers raised party favours to the air, and shining streamers burst out overhead. Somewhere, someone was ringing a bell. Kana and Grace cheered too, huge smiles on their faces. Everyone rushed to form a line to toss coins into the donation box. Grace stood behind Kana so she could watch, and when Kana threw in the money, they bowed together twice, and clapped their hands twice, then stepped out to make way for the people behind them.

"So is this like New Year's in your country at all?" Kana asked, once they had left the building and wandered out onto the boardwalk, clutching amulets and protective arrows in their hands.

Grace laughed. "*Nothing* at all like it. Back home, there would have been a band doing a countdown on TV and fireworks being set off in the park."

"Fireworks? In winter?"

Grace shrugged.

"Having New Year's abroad sounds interesting."

"I'd say so." How to even start explaining that the entire atmosphere of the holiday was different here? "Some things are like at home—the countdown, the party favours, the people all gathering at midnight. But the feeling is totally different. Nobody gets that excited for New Year's the *holiday*, only for the party." Christmas in Japan had been a bit of a disappointment, but New Year's had real potential, Grace thought. She wished she could try some of the other customs, like sending New Year's postcards. She wanted to eat the special lunch boxes, too. "Honestly, I like here better for New Year's. But it's fun at home too, of course."

"Maybe someday I could come visit you for it. In Canada."

"I'd like that." Grace smiled. They walked down the promenade stairs and out onto the street, through the tree line. When they emerged, the bridge, with its red, yellow and blue lights loomed up ahead. Concrete under Grace's feet gave way to soft sand. "Oh, it's the beach."

"The water is very beautiful at night. I love this place; the sea and the Rainbow Bridge." Kana paused. "It's called Rainbow Bridge, but actually, this is a special illumination. You can only see this rainbow colour on special days."

"That's weird," said Grace. "If it's called Rainbow Bridge, it should be a rainbow all the time, right?"

"I think that would be nice, don't you? Maybe, instead of Rainbow, we should have called it White Bridge." She paused. "A joke."

Grace laughed. Kana cracking jokes was so rare, it didn't really matter to Grace if they were funny or not. "Well, I'm glad I could see it while it was a rainbow."

The two of them sat down on the boardwalk with their boots in the sand. They weren't the only ones who had the idea of sitting out on the water; even though the hour had drawn so late, there were many groups and couples on the beach, and plenty of brightly-coloured boats floating in Tokyo Bay. Grace was glad they'd gone somewhere quiet—she felt awkward trying to bring up the topic on her mind. "I wanted to ask you something."

"Sure."

"I sent a message to my boyfriend today." Grace stared hard at the water's edge. "I realized that I didn't miss him very much while I was here. In fact, I was happy being on my own for the first time."

"Oh."

"I feel bad about it." She felt strange bringing up this topic with Kana, as though Grace had toed some line they hadn't broached before. She hoped it wouldn't make Kana uncomfortable. "Like I haven't been a very good girlfriend or even a friend. I didn't even tell him I was coming to Japan."

"How long are you going out with him?"

"Since June. But we were friends since Grade Ten. After Jean, he was my *best* friend."

"And then you started to like him?"

"Well...no." That would be the problem, she thought, right there. "*He* liked *me*, and so he asked me out."

"You *didn't* like him?"

"I...liked that he asked me out. And I liked him as my friend. I thought it would be great if I had a boyfriend that was such a good friend, and I'd start to like him like that, too." Grace's face burned with shame. She felt thankful for the darkness of the beach. "Maybe I accepted for the wrong reasons."

Kana seemed to consider this. "How did he feel when you left?"

"He missed me. A lot, it seems like." Both of them were quiet for a long few moments, and then Grace spoke again. "I guess I could tell him that going to Japan changed me, and that would be true, but I don't think it changed how I felt about him. I think I always felt this way, that maybe dating isn't for me, but I didn't want to admit it. I wanted to be like everybody else and have a romance. I still kind of want that, the romance part, that is. It was nice."

"But nothing else?"

"I don't know," she replied softly. "Maybe someday it could be love. But I don't feel the kind of physical attraction I read about in books. The spark. I don't think I've ever felt that for anyone at all."

"Ah."

"I *know* he's good-looking, so I don't understand why. And he's a nice guy, too. The best."

Kana's voice had taken on a wistful quality. "It's more shameful to stay if you know it won't change. If he loves you."

"Yeah." Her friend only confirmed what Grace had been thinking all evening. "I know he does. So I guess when I get home, we'll talk about it, and maybe he'll want to break up. If anyone could understand me, it'd be him."

"*Naruhodo.*"

Grace recognized an opening for the question she'd wanted to ask for a while. "What will you do about Daisuke?"

Kana looked out at the skyline. "I wonder."

"He pretty much asked you out. If you like him, you should accept. You *do* like him."

"I like him." Kana frowned. "And I wished before that he would notice me. But what if something goes wrong? With his new job, or Europe..."

"You can't worry about those things yet. You don't know what's going to happen."

Kana chuckled. "That's just like you, Megucchi. You're so brave."

"Brave? *Me?*" The idea seemed so ludicrous that Grace laughed out loud.

"Why not?" Kana looked at her, eyes shining with the reflections on the water. "You just said something so bold. What if *I* turned out not to like Daisuke-kun so much? I couldn't tell him so. And you came all the way here alone."

"That wasn't bravery. That was stupidity, and a little luck."

"'Stupidity'? Like...stupid?" Kana almost reached for the dictionary she hadn't thought to bring.

"It means, I didn't think about it." Grace sighed.

"You would not have come, if you had thought?" Her friend seemed to mull this over. "Oh. In that case, thinking *too* much could be bad."

"There you go. That's your answer, right?"

The Japanese girl looked confused. "My answer to what?"

Grace felt sure of it now, certain the answer both of them were seeking was the same. "About what to do. If you feel it's right, you have to act—because if you think too much about something, you might never find the courage to follow through."

The next morning was the first day of the new year.

Grace woke up in her *futon* for the last time, ate a breakfast of special New Year's soup with rice cakes, brushed her hair and put on her favourite black jumper over green tartan tights. It was hard to believe she was truly leaving this time, not going to Narita Airport to sit for the day.

Kana had offered to come see her off, but Grace didn't feel like she ought to let her friend endure four hours on the train or bus for that. They compromised; Kana would come as far as Shibuya for an early lunch. It took Grace out of her way, since she could have taken an airport bus from Omiya, but Shibuya seemed like the perfect place to end her visit. They strolled together in Hachiko Square, fenced in by the statue, the JR station, the police box and the crosswalk. It was a chilly morning, but crisp, with a bright sun untouched by clouds. Grace loosened her scarf and put her gloves in her bag. Kana's bare knees peeking out between her boots and skirt seemed far less out of place on a nice day like today.

They used the extra time to revisit familiar places. Grace took Kana on her own tour, this time. They walked up Center Street and Spain Hill, back down Park Street and along Meiji Street. They ate curry rice for lunch and admired department store displays. Eventually, they returned to the square and lingered by Hachiko awhile.

Kana spoke first, as they sat side-by-side on the railing. "I think I'll ask him to meet me today, after I've properly seen you off."

Grace clapped her hands together. "Daisuke?"

Kana nodded, looking pensive. "What you said yesterday made sense. I don't know what will happen in a few months, but this is happening now...so..."

"I bet he's been waiting for you to message him."

"Maybe. I hope so. Should I?"

"Yes! You definitely should!" At least one of them didn't have to strike out in the romance department, Grace thought to herself. Daisuke was obviously a different sort of guy than Kana had envisioned herself with, but that didn't mean it wasn't going to work. Grace thought Daisuke was actually a lot like Rumi, and she and Kana had been best friends for a long time, so why *couldn't* it work?

While Kana wrote her message, Grace stood up and moved closer to Hachiko. She patted the dog's bronze leg affectionately. "I'm gonna miss this guy."

Kana looked up, smiling. "He'll still be here next time you visit. That's what's so great about Hachi, even if everything else around him is different by the time you come again."

"I'll probably be forty by then."

"What's another twenty years?" Kana stood as well, patting the dog's head. Then they both stepped back to allow someone to take a photo with Hachiko. "Shibuya changes, but he never does, even in a hundred years or so. That's kind of nice."

Grace nodded. She hoped it wouldn't be *that* long before she made it back to Japan.

They were quiet for a moment, watching tourists taking pictures with the statue. She wasn't wearing her watch, but Grace sensed the hour was growing late. "I guess it's about time, huh?"

Even though she said it, she didn't want to go yet. Kana stared off toward the intersection. Around them, Shibuya continued to flow and pause and laugh and strut.

Kana's cell phone trilled, barely audible over the crowd noise. She nodded an apology as she took it out. "Oh, it's

Otsuka-kun. Daisuke-kun. He wants to meet this afternoon, at Aqua City again."

Grace smiled. "Good. I think you should go for it. Whatever happens, happens."

Her friend smiled back. "I hope it's something good."

"I'm sure it will be."

"In that case, I'll take you to Shinagawa, since it looks like I'm going that way now." Kana slid the phone into her pocket. "But we should go soon. It's already one-thirty."

Grace patted the statue one last time, and together they collected her backpack and suitcase from the station lockers. They had to wait on the platform for a few moments, holding the bags. A heavy silence seemed to hang in the air until a Yamanote train finally rolled in. "*Shibuya. Shibuya.*"

They stood together, Grace leaning on the suitcase, watching out the window while Kana fretted over her response to Daisuke. By the time she finished writing, they were halfway to their destination. Kana caught sight of a sign outside as it flashed by. "Gotanda. Just a bit more until we change trains. The airport train is fast; probably less than an hour."

"Good." Grace sighed. It was bad enough she was about to spend over twelve hours sitting down.

Kana played with the charms on her phone. She looked nervous, and the way she fidgeted made Grace even more anxious. "Hey, are you okay?"

"I'm okay, but maybe I should get off here too. You might need help reserving the seat."

Grace got the impression that Kana still felt bad about not taking her all the way to the airport. She hardly needed help buying a ticket; Grace had already been back to the airport so many times on her own. The next day or so was sure to be lonely, though, and Grace wanted Kana to stay as long as possible. She accepted the offer of companionship without complaint. "Be my guest."

They stepped out of the car together, and after buying

Grace's ticket, took an escalator to the platform. The airport train was due to arrive a few moments later.

Grace felt as apprehensive then as she had been the first time they had said goodbye, a week before. This would be as far as Kana could go, and her last chance to say anything face to face. She wanted to say a lot, but wasn't sure where to start. Kana herself looked a little sad.

"I guess this is it," Grace offered, though it seemed like a trite thing to say compared to all the things she was feeling; how glad she was to have come, how grateful to have gotten to know Kana better. How much she wished Kana would be able to strike up something with Daisuke after all these months of holding back.

Kana, too, looked like she had something else on her mind. She held her tongue, though, until the train approached, and then she frowned slightly. "I hope you..." she struggled to find the right English phrase, "...fix everything. With your parents, and with Jean and Simon, too."

"Thanks. I hope you and Daisuke...well, I know it'll work out."

Kana cracked a smile. "We'll see."

"Anyway, I might be grounded for the next ten years, but I'll be in touch."

"Grounded?" Her friend tilted her head.

"It's like jail, but in your house. It's okay. I deserve it." Grace smiled back. "I'll still talk to you soon."

"Thank you for coming, Megucchi. I was glad to meet you. Here—I got this. For you." She pressed a brown paper bag into Grace's arms. "Open it later, okay? There's something you'll like on page seventeen."

"Kana-chan..." The doors opened, and the train paused on the platform to load passengers and their luggage. The electronic sign over their heads signalled less than a minute for her to say a proper goodbye. Somehow, Grace thought, it had been harder the first time, when she was leaving Japan without truly *knowing* Kana. She didn't have to imagine anymore whether it would be okay to hug her as they parted or avoid looking her in the eye. She already knew that she would talk to Kana again, if not the next day, then the next. She could listen to the stories about Kana's family and friends and better understand them. And she knew, too, that she would come back to Tokyo someday.

Maybe Kana felt the same way, because she threw her arms around Grace without hesitation. "I will miss you."

Grace hugged back. "I'll miss you, too." Then she stepped inside the doors, dropping her suitcase beside her. Kana stayed outside, an arm's length away. The conductor announced the names of stops en route to the airport.

Kana laughed. "It's not like Japanese."

"What isn't?"

"This kind of long goodbye. If we were both Japanese, maybe we would smile and wave through the windows. But not hug and block the door."

"Is it okay?"

"It's okay." Kana smiled sincerely. "Though the employees might get worried for me soon."

Overhead, a musical tone began to play to signal the train's departure. The two girls dropped their hands and Kana took a step back to stand behind the yellow line.

"*Sayonara,*" Grace said, scrambling for the right word with her limited vocabulary.

"*Sayonara* is for long goodbyes. Don't be gone so long." Kana raised her hand in a stilled wave. "Let's say '*see you later*' instead. *Mata ne.*"

There was a lump in Grace's throat that prevented her from saying anything more. Instead, she raised her hand to mirror her friend's, and the door slid shut between them. The train pulled away at a slow pace, leaving Kana alone there for a moment; then she stepped back into the gathering crowd of travellers with tickets for the next departure and vanished from

Grace's line of sight. The train picked up speed and left all of them behind.

She continued to stand at the door for a long time, not sure what she was waiting for, still clutching the brown paper bag. Inside, Grace found a cellophane-wrapped magazine—the newest issue of *SwEET*. Kana must have stopped somewhere and bought it in secret.

Behind Grace, in the train carriage, the recorded voice carried on announcing the list of stops en route to the airport. The luggage had all been stowed. The seats were half-full, and travellers murmured among themselves, sipping canned coffee while they eagerly peered out the windows. Except for Grace, they were all ready to go wherever they were going. The whole car buzzed with a sense of anticipation.

Well, why not? She put her luggage on the rack and sat down. The voice soothingly recited their itinerary in English, while Grace prepared to ease her changed self back into the world she'd left behind. It wasn't a perfect place, her small town, and her small role in it. She knew she wouldn't be there forever; might not even be there that much longer, not with this fluttering in her heart that drew her curiosity outward. Away from her family and that town that never changed. For now, though, she looked forward to seeing home, and everyone there, again. Looked forward to hugging her dad, and later, her mom. To fixing things between her and Simon and Jean. Everyone was waiting for her.

The computerized voice came at last to the end of its monologue. "Our final destination is Narita Airport Station."

It wasn't Grace's true destination, nor would it be her final. But she settled into her seat anyway, finally ready to arrive.

－おわり－

Hi, Megucchi!

I hope you had a nice flight to Newfoundland. I thought I would send a long message so that I can update after a very busy yesterday and today, but I understand if you can't reply me!! | *⎺ ∇⎺ | I'll wait for you!

I finished my application paperwork (again...) for Nishidai and today I put it in the mailbox. The exam will be on January 26. It's Tuesday, so there's no way anyone won't check me that morning. Ha ha ha. Just kidding, I think it'll be OK. Now I'm feeling good about this test, and my English teacher wrote me a very good recommendation letter, too.

Yesterday, I met with Daisuke-kun again. It's the third time in one week. Calling him by first name sounds so strange to me but I'm getting used to it bit by bit. Was it a date!? I think it was a date. We took a train to Kamakura and visited some sightseeing places. The Buddha, and the sea, and an old-fashioned village. I'd never been there before. It's so nice to have a long break from school.

I'm waiting to hear about what will happen for you, too. What did your mother say?? And I want to know about your boyfriend, too. Please tell me as soon as you can!

♡ Kana

Thanks for waiting while I couldn't reply! I knew this would happen, but of course, there was big trouble when I got home. >_>; Mom confiscated my phone AND my keyboard. I could see your message, but I couldn't write back! I have to use a public computer at school, for now.

It wasn't as bad as I expected, though, to be totally honest. Dad really went to bat for me and tried to talk Mom out of the grounding. I couldn't believe the two of them actually TALKED to each other, civilly, for more than an hour. A+ parenting all of a sudden, huh?

Mom also let me go out to see Simon yesterday. I think she knows something's not right and so she gave me one hour (while she sat in the parking lot waiting, lol. Talk about stress). I'm glad, though, because I didn't want today at school to be the first time seeing him since telling him how I felt. I did see Jean today and I think things are finally back to normal between us. That makes me really, really happy. I missed her a lot.

Simon and I aren't breaking up. Not yet, anyway. I don't know what might be in the future for us, maybe he won't want to be with someone who isn't really in 100%. But he said there's a scale for these things. It's not all black and white. Until one of us is *unhappy*, we'll stick together. And we made a pact that if it ends, we'll try to be friends. I hope that's enough. Maybe now that the pressure's off, I can enjoy having a friend who's also a partner.

I'm super happy to hear about you and Daisuke, though. I knew you two were a good match! If anyone can work out long distance from Europe to Japan someday, it's definitely going to be you guys.

By the way—I photocopied my picture from the issue of *SwEET* you gave me. It's going up in my redecorated room. ♡♡♡

I'll be waiting for your next message!

~Megucchi

Afterword

Meet You By Hachiko was penned over winter 2008–2009, and finally made its way to print in 2020 after an exceptionally long time in the editing stage.

A lot has changed in Tokyo and around the world since the day Kana and Grace met. Some of the locations referenced in the story are gone; others have been drastically altered. With the advent of public Wi-Fi in Japan, translation apps, smartphones and social media, it takes quite a bit more suspension of disbelief to imagine Grace's struggles.

The fashion trends described in this story were rooted in those of the mid-2000s, while the technology was the height of pre-smartphone Japan.

Maybe, with smartphones in their hands, Grace and Kana would never have met.

While I removed some of the obvious dating for the sake of a 21st-century audience, this story is still a love letter to the sights, sounds, styles and tech of Shibuya, circa 2008, as Tokyo evolved past a difficult post-bubble time and into a new digital era. If you were there, you'll remember. And if you weren't, I hope *Hachiko* gave you a glimpse into what things were like during this short but unique window of time.

If you enjoyed *Meet You By Hachiko*, I would love for you to drop by on Goodreads, Amazon, Indigo or wherever you fancy and tell me what you thought.

Until next time, *mata ne!*

Acknowledgements

This novel has been in development for so long and throughout so many stages of my life that I had a hard time reaching back into my memory for everyone who needed to be thanked. I hope I can cover all the names of everyone who contributed directly to *Hachiko*, because there are quite a few of them.

My earliest supporters and beta-readers stepped up long before there was an actual book for them to read. My thanks to Pata, Genevieve, Erin, Jen, Win King, Shaun and Eric M. for all the work they did in the early days, the late aughts, reading those first drafts. Marisa, who brought Owada Station to life. Alyssa, for the beautiful cover illustration. Zippo, who typeset the cover and encouraged me to get the first version out there even when I wasn't sure what I was doing. Kelly, my steadfast supporter through the query process (and reader of so many past writings of dubious quality), and the first one to have a final product in her hands.

I couldn't have done any of it without Emily, my cheerleader every day during the process of writing while we were living in Japan. I'm sure she heard more about this project than anyone else. My co-teachers and students in Osaka may not ever have a chance to read this, but their daily presence and advice helped me bring a story about a Japanese high school to life, and for that I will always be grateful for my wonderful experience there.

To the friends back on the North American side of the pond who supported me virtually during the final days of writing in Japan, we may not be in touch as often as we'd like, but I won't forget your support. I miss you guys.

Fast forward to 2020: My editor Angela, who bolstered my confidence when I most needed it, and Geri, who was so enthusiastic about bringing her illustration of Hachiko to life. My family, who have always been by my side. My friends back home on the Rock as well as the ones in Toronto.

Last but never least, Daniel, who supported me through this after encouraging me to stop waiting for a perfect time to publish. The perfect time turned out to be 2020, and it certainly has been a memorable one.

About the Author

Loren grew up hoping to be the next Gordon Korman, except she wasn't particularly funny, which was a bit problematic. Later, she wanted to become an exchange student in Japan, and use her newfound fluency to consume Japanese comic books by the boatload. That didn't work out as planned, either.

She earned an English degree in her hometown of St. John's, Newfoundland and went off to teach English abroad, where she's been writing about Japan since the day she arrived at Narita Airport. *Meet You By Hachiko* is her first novel.

Loren is currently working on her next projects; another Japan-set friendship story titled *Edokko,* a Newfoundland-set teen drama titled *Small Ball*, and an as-yet-untitled adventure trilogy co-written with a partner. A serialized web fiction series is due to begin in early 2021.

Find her online at www.lorengreene.com, and follow @shibuyaloren to hear about what's coming next!

CPSIA information can be obtained
at www.ICGtesting.com
Printed in the USA
LVHW111606110221
679070LV00005B/1124